SAFETY in Small Craft

SAFETY in Small Craft

Mike Scanlan

Royal New Zealand Coastguard Federation

First published in 1962
This edition first published in 1989
Revised edition 1994
by the Education Committee
of the Royal New Zealand Coastguard Federation
P.O. Box 51-163, Pakuranga, Auckland.

ISBN 0 473 00751 7

Production by Edsetera, Auckland
Typeset by Typocrafters Ltd, Auckland
Printed in Hong Kong

CONTENTS

FOREWORD

I am not quite sure how many people ever read the foreword to a book, but as an encouragement I shall err on the side of brevity.

Sea sense is like horse sense, which is attributed to horses precisely because they have the intellect not to gamble on people. This book is similarly intended to assist in removing the guesswork from basic seamanship.

I pay tribute to the Education Committee of the Royal New Zealand Coastguard Federation in general, and to Mike Scanlan in particular, for providing an outstanding contribution to a fundamental building block of safe boating — knowledge — which is an essential prerequisite to practice.

I commend this book to all aspiring boaties, which in New Zealand means just about everybody.

K. Michael Saull
Rear Admiral Rtd
Vice-Patron Royal New Zealand Coastguard Federation

PREFACE

Hurrah! the seaward breezes
sweep down the bay again:
Heave up, my lads, the anchor!
Run up the sail again!
Leave to the lubber landsmen
the railroad and the steed,
the stars of heaven shall guide us,
the breath of heaven shall speed.

— J. G. Whittier

A number of important changes have recently taken place within New Zealand's boating scene. In many cases these changes significantly affect the safety of boats, the changes ranging from the introduction of satellite-coherent EPIRBs to the demise of the B.C.F. fire extinguisher. There have also been major advances in the field of boating education, with the introduction of several new boating courses and certificates, in particular the New Zealand Day Skipper.

In preparing this new edition of *Safety in Small Craft* I am greatly indebted to the assistance given by Alan Haddock, Chairman of the RNZCGF Education Committee; to committee members David Pitham and Basil Irwin; to Bill Skelton, former president of the Federation; and to Tony Date of the Maritime Safety Authority.

That changes are taking place in the boating scene is a healthy sign. That we keep abreast of these changes is a challenge for all seafarers.

Mike Scanlan
May, 1994

1

THE BOAT

I must down to the seas again, to the lonely sea and the sky,
And all I ask is a tall ship . . .

— John Masefield

A boat has often been described as a hole in the water into which all the owner's money is poured. There is more than a modicum of truth in this, and your boat must certainly fit your pocket, but it must also be tailored to suit the purpose and waters in which it is to be used.

Boat types

A fishing boat must provide a stable platform on which one can work and move round freely. Its stability must not be impaired by the loading and over-side lifting to be expected. Therefore, a wide-beamed boat with high sides and plenty of unobstructed deck space is needed, together with substantial deck machinery and fittings.

A diving boat will also need to be beamy, but it must provide easier access into and out of the water. Lower sides are needed. Deck fittings and machinery are designed for other purposes and will not need to be as rugged as on a fishing boat.

A pleasure boat is built more for comfort and will require a greater proportion of accommodation than a working boat. The size of the boat will determine the amount of enclosed living space available. To give sufficient headroom in a cabin, the boat's profile is raised from the squatter form of the work boat. This invariably means less stability and a greater susceptibility to the wind.

A racing boat may have to be built to class specifications, and unless these are strictly adhered to, disqualification may result. Generally, the faster the boat, the less comfortable it will be in the way it rides and in its accommodation.

Boating areas

Some New Zealand waters are sheltered, some are semi-sheltered, and some are unsheltered. Specific areas are not designated as such, but these classifications give us an idea of the shape and size of boat most suited to an area.

Sheltered waters are those protected by surrounding land, such as the smaller lakes, rivers, and inlets or sounds of less than two miles across. Most small open boats would be satisfactory in these waters; punts or flat-bottomed boats are ideal for use in shallower water. Hull form is not critical.

Semi-sheltered waters are those where less protection from the land is available — the medium-sized lakes, bays and sounds, or the wider stretches of rivers. An open boat is not recommended, for here the wind may raise a sizeable chop to the surface. The boat's sides must be higher, and some decking provided to prevent water lapping over the side. A more rounded hull form, with some flare to the bow, is preferable. Permanent internal buoyancy should be fitted.

Unsheltered waters include the larger, more exposed lakes, harbours, sounds and rivers, and the open sea. A boat to match the conditions to be expected in these waters must be well built and equipped. It must be totally decked over, and the decks shaped to allow water to be quickly shed. All openings in the hull must be capable of being secured against the sea, and the cockpit or cabin must be well protected with breakwaters and strong windows. If an open cockpit is fitted, it should be self-draining and access to the boat's interior well protected. To allow the boat to rise to the waves, the hull must be suitably shaped with a large, well-flared bow and a similarly shaped stern.

The boat's capacity

Overloading is a major cause of boating fatalities. Although a boat may appear to have sufficient freeboard, excessive loading could prevent it from lifting to the waves, resulting in water being shipped. The boat's hull shape and size, its speed and the manner in which it is being handled, together with the weather and the state of the sea, will all affect the maximum load that can be carried before the boat will founder.

The distribution of the weight is equally important. Weight in the bow or stern will reduce the boat's reaction to the waves, and weights placed too high or too far from the boat's centre could affect its stability (discussed in Chapter 9).

With so many variables, determination of a boat's loading limit should be left to the experts. But only you can judge how these variables are affecting that limit from day to day. The feel of the boat will often indicate excessive loading. It will often be felt as a sluggishness amongst the waves, or as a poor response to the helm.

If in doubt, consult a marine surveyor, the boatbuilder or manufacturer. As a very rough guide, the following quick calculations may provide an estimate of the boat's theoretical capacity:

- To find (in kilograms) the approximate safe load of passengers, gear and engine a hull should carry, multiply the boat's length (in metres), by maximum breadth, by minimum effective depth by 120.
- To find a safe maximum number of passengers, multiply the boat's length in metres, by beam, by 0.6.

The shape of a boat

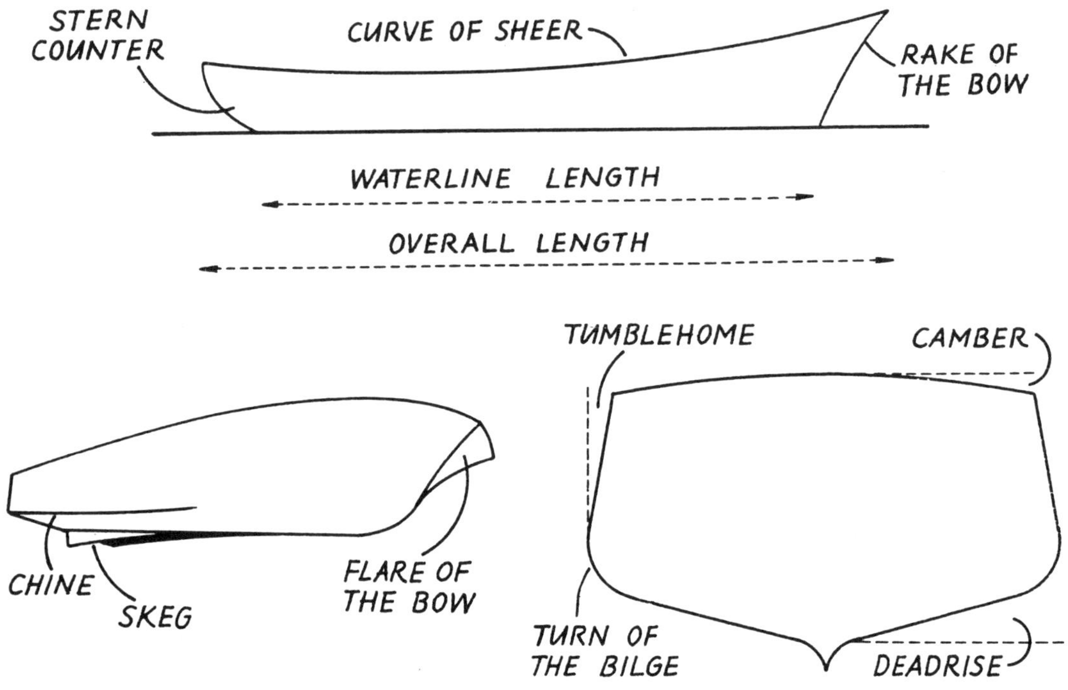

The parts of a boat

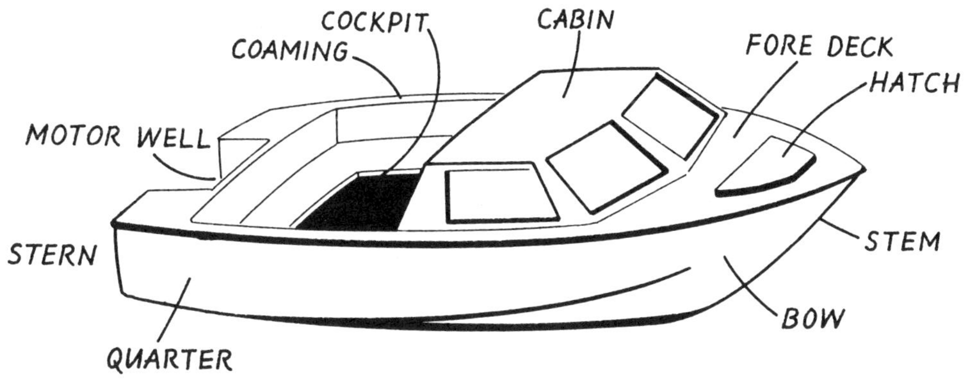

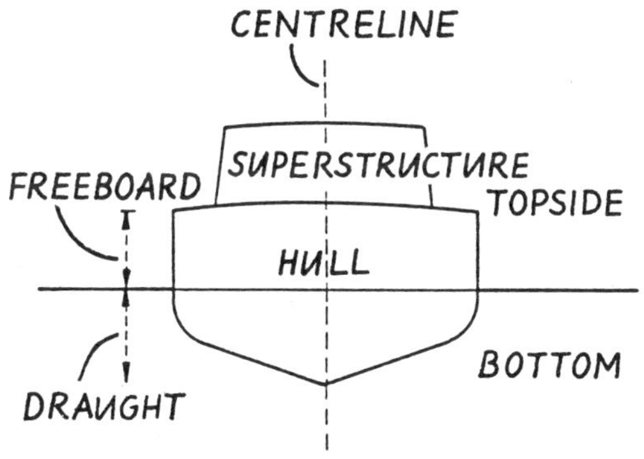

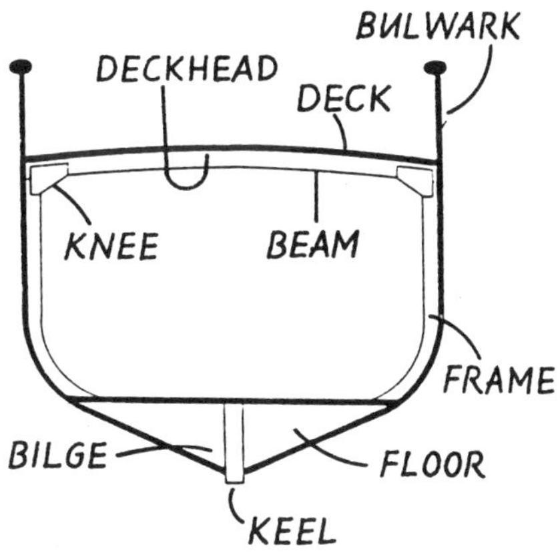

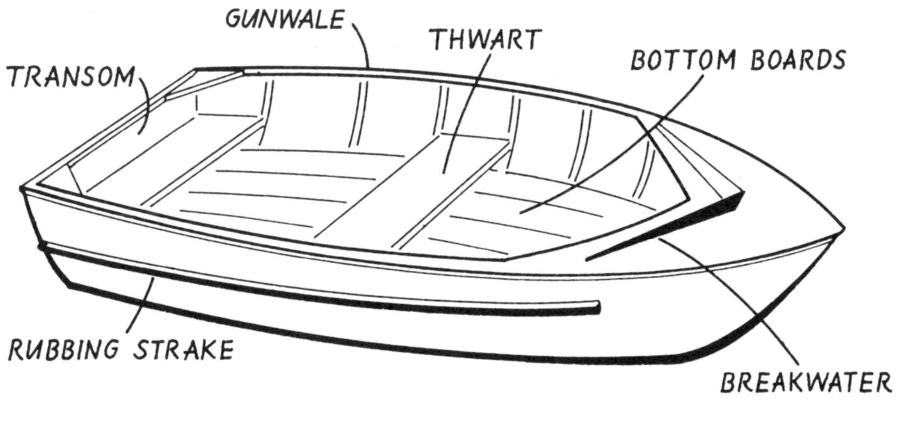

The parts of a sailing dinghy

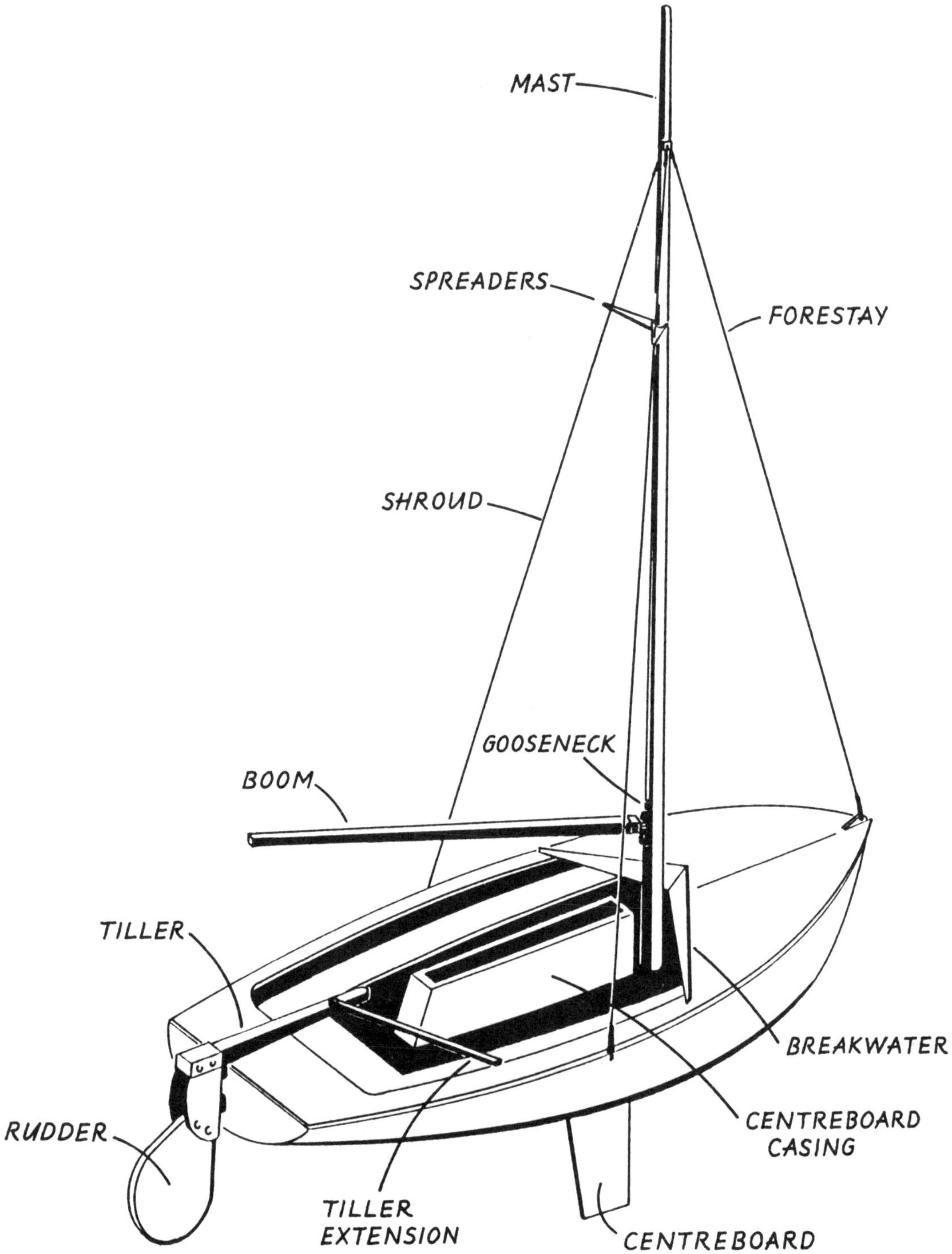

A yacht's rigging

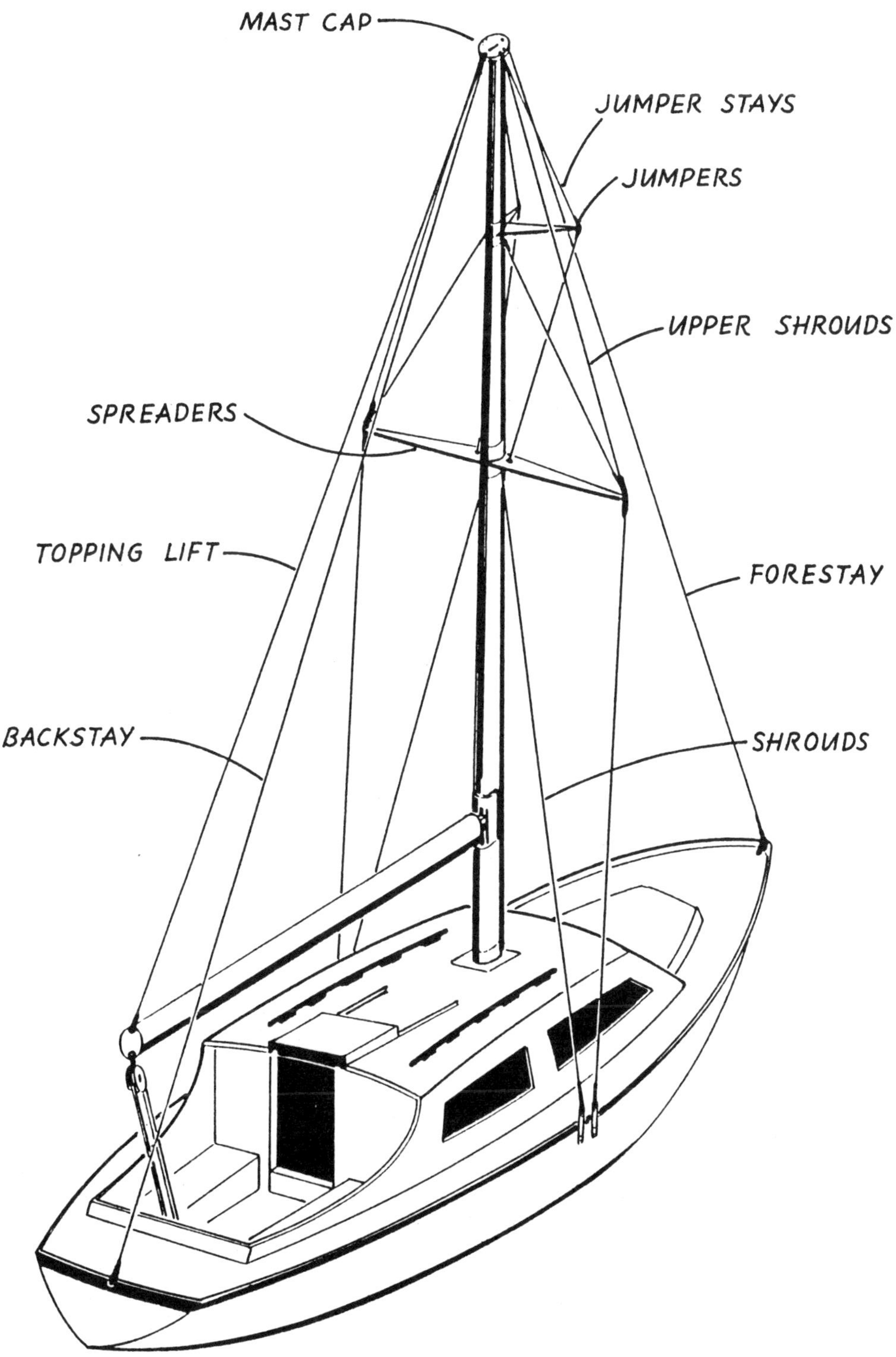

Directions beyond the boat

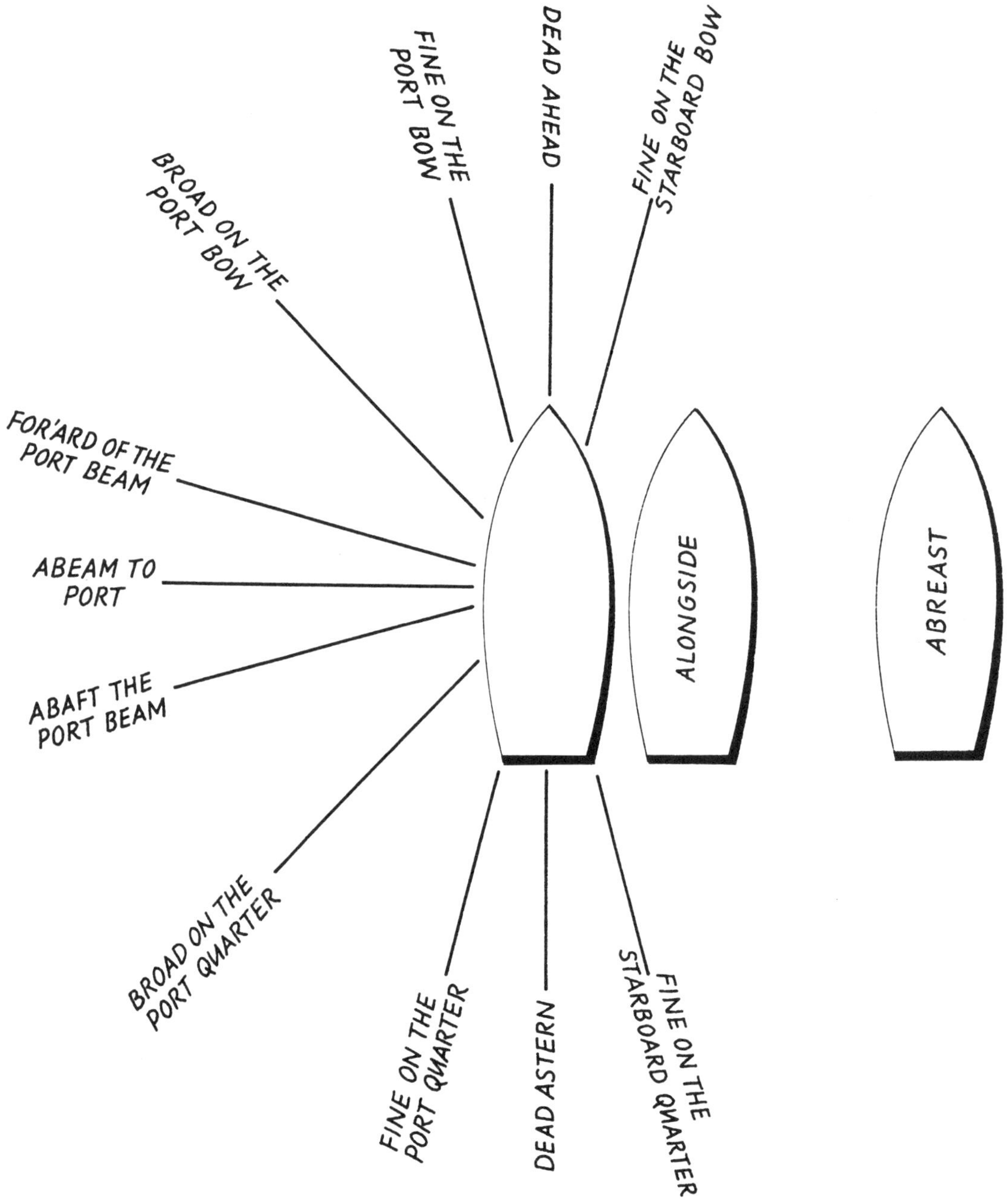

Directions within the boat

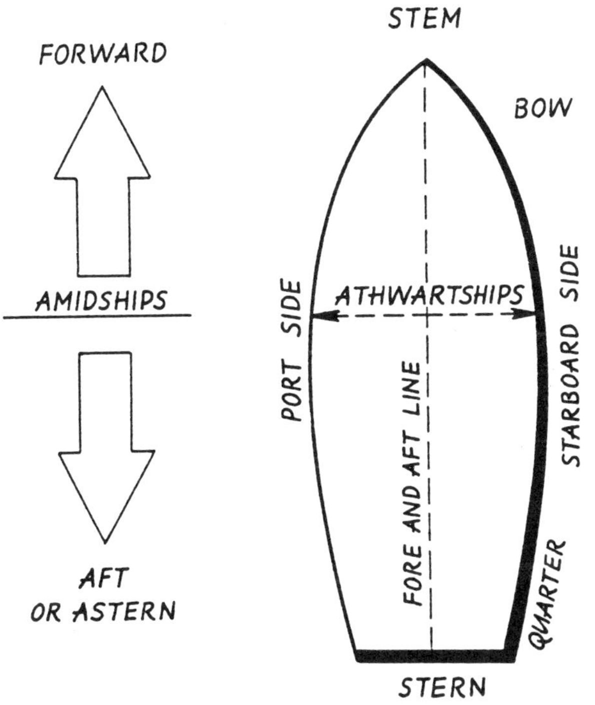

The boat's hull

The shape of the boat ultimately affects the way it handles and how it will react to the weather and sea. The hull form is also the major factor in determining the boat's speed. Although a larger engine or more sail area will provide more power, it is the shape of the hull that will govern how the power is translated into boat speed.

There are two basic hull types: the displacement hull, which travels *through* the water, and the planing hull, which travels *over* the water.

Displacement hulls

When a stationary boat sits in the water its hull makes a depression, the water being displaced to make room for the immersed portion of the hull. The weight of the displaced water is equal to the weight of the boat and everything aboard, hence tonnage of boats and ships is referred to as displacement tonnage.

If the boat is now made to move through the water, movement is restricted by skin resistance and wave action.

Skin resistance is the effect of friction between the water and the immersed portion of the hull. The greater the amount of immersed hull, the greater the friction. A smooth, polished hull will reduce skin friction, but any unstreamlined projection beneath the water will increase resistance and reduce the boat's speed.

The water pushed away from the bow creates a bow wave, angling outwards and astern as the boat moves ahead. Wave action is also produced by the water flowing astern to fill in the space left by the moving boat, creating another wave near the boat's stern. This wave travels with the boat, its length approximately equal to the boat's length at the waterline.

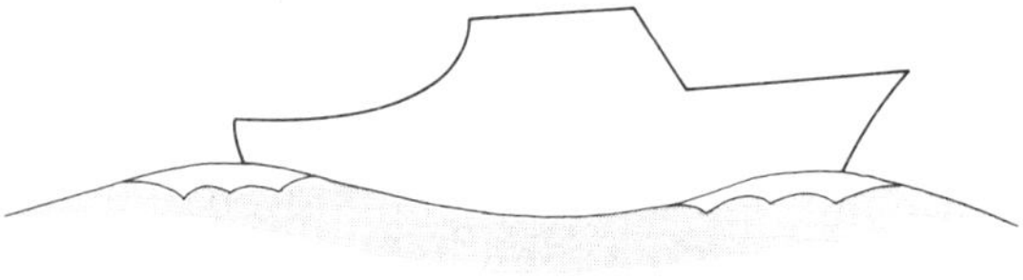

There is a close relationship between the length of a wave and the speed at which it travels:

$$\text{Speed of wave (knots)} = 2.5 \times \sqrt{\text{wave length (m)}}$$

Hence, the longer the wave, the faster it can travel. Because of this relationship, the boat, which is travelling at the same speed as this wave, cannot theoretically exceed its maximum displacement speed.

$$\text{Displacement speed} = 2.5 \times \sqrt{\text{waterline length}}$$

If the boat attempts to exceed this speed by applying more power, the wave travelling with the boat must increase its length, and the wave crest at the stern will fall back further behind the boat. The boat's stern will now squat into the trough. In this attitude much of the extra power is being used to drive the boat up and over its own bow wave, out of the trough.

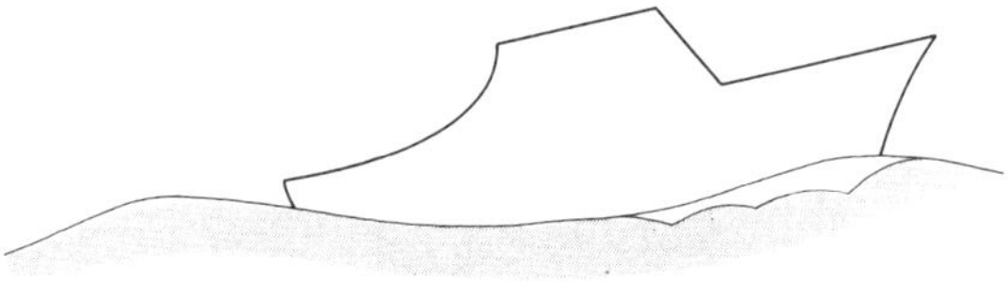

Any further increase in power will only make the bow wave larger and the wave length longer, putting the stern deeper into the trough and giving the boat an even larger 'hill' to climb. This provides no appreciable increase in speed, and frequently creates dangerous boathandling deficiencies.

A displacement hull may have a flat, rounded or vee-shaped bottom. The bow is ideally fine at the waterline to cut cleanly through the water, but flared above the waterline to provide lift in heavier seas and to prevent water coming aboard. A tapered stern will add speed by assisting the smooth flow of water along the hull. A boat with a longer waterline length will achieve a faster speed than a similarly shaped boat of shorter length.

The displacement hull

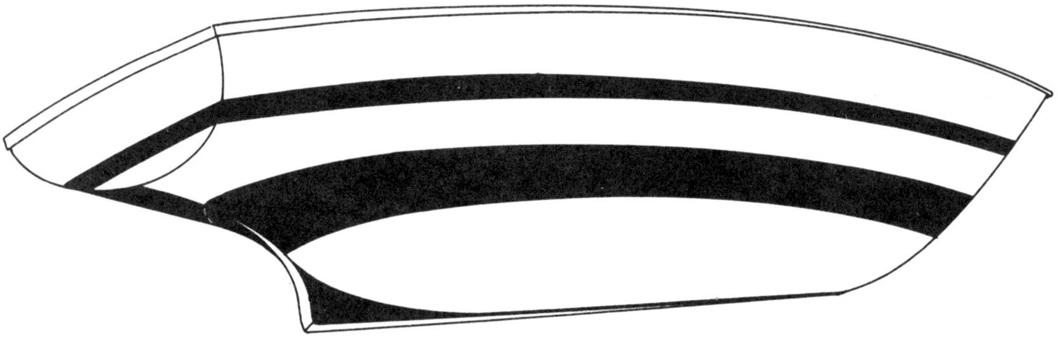

Planing hulls

At slow speeds a planing hull displaces water and creates waves in the same way as a displacement boat.

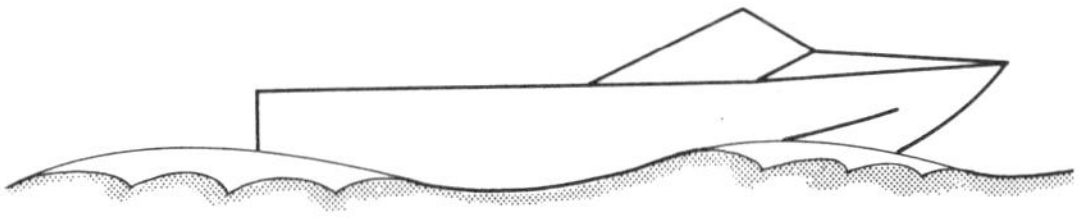

As speed is increased, water pressure increases on the broader underside of the hull, lifting it onto the water surface. The boat is now planing — skimming along the water surface. With only a very small portion of the hull in the water, skin resistance and wave resistance are substantially reduced.

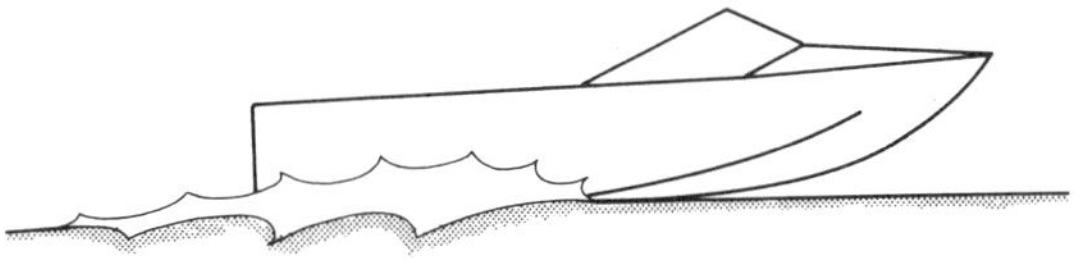

Less power, and therefore less fuel, is required when travelling on the plane than when at slower, displacement speeds. Considerable spray and foam are produced, but this helps to reduce friction and also cushions the boat.

The planing hull is essentially flat-bottomed. To lift the back of the boat out of the squat, the stern is much broader than a displacement hull, with little or no taper.

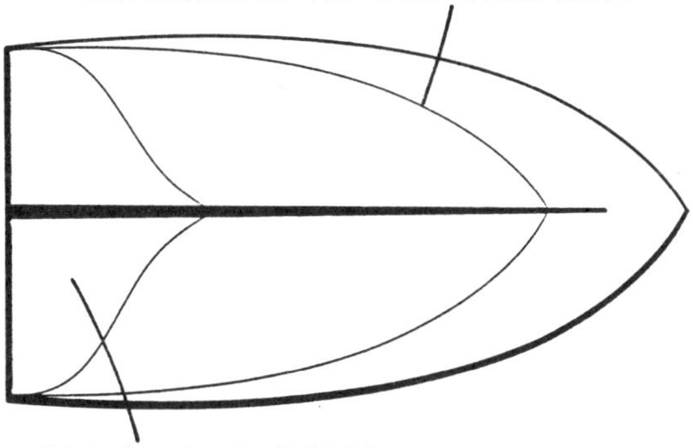

Although a flat-bottomed boat would be fast and skim the water well, it would lack directional stability, with nothing to prevent the boat slipping sideways. Such a boat would be difficult to manoeuvre and vulnerable to spinning out of a fast turn. To increase directional stability, fins or skegs may be fitted, or the hull bottom is vee-shaped.

Typical planing hulls have a flared bow, deeply veed at the waterline, the hull then flattening to a broader and flatter vee stern section. Generally, the deeper the vee of a hull, the slower the boat, but the better the handling characteristics. The flatter the vee, the greater the speed, but boat control and seaworthiness will be reduced.

The planing hull

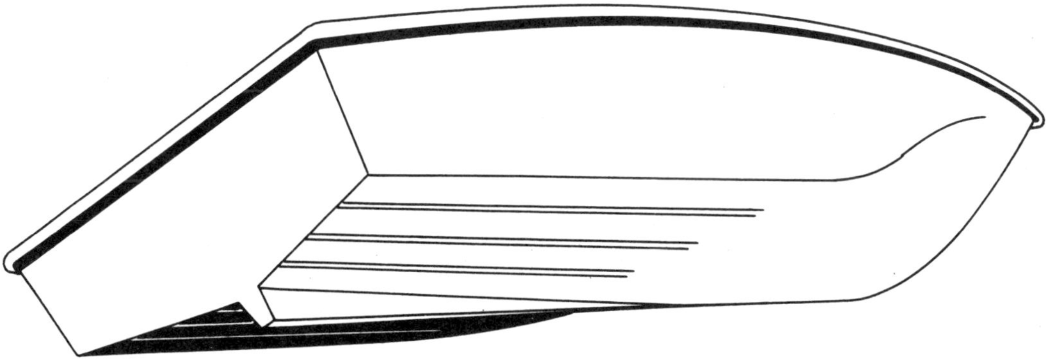

Powered boats

The power required to propel a displacement boat is lower than that required for an equivalent-sized planing boat. There is little benefit in overpowering a displacement boat, for once the theoretical maximum displacement speed is reached the power-to-speed ratio changes drastically.

The power requirements of a planing boat are somewhat different. Initially a large amount of power is required to lift the boat onto the plane, but once planing, with the effects of wave and skin resistance very much reduced, the throttle can be eased to keep the boat just on the plane. Further increase in power will produce faster planing speeds, but the power-to-speed ratio will not be the same.

Although there may not be a theoretical limit to the power used on a planing boat, safety limits must be considered. The hull is designed to cope with certain limits of vibration, pressure and thrust, and to exceed these limits is both uneconomic and dangerous.

Petrol or diesel?

Power for power, diesel engines are larger, heavier and more expensive than petrol engines. Noise and vibration levels are also higher. However, a diesel's running cost is less than that of a petrol engine; it is more rugged and is not as vulnerable to problems with dampness. Diesel fuel does not have the same fire and explosion hazard as petrol. Consequently, the diesel is more suited to the larger, sea-going displacement boat. The petrol engine, with its better power-to-weight ratio, is preferable for the smaller, faster boat.

Powered drive systems

The outboard engine is generally more economical than other powered systems, and is well suited to planing boats in sheltered waters. It may be mounted on the transom, or in a self-draining motor well. The engine can be tilted for retrieval on a trailer and for transportation on the road, and its angle can be finely adjusted to improve the riding attitude of the boat in the water.

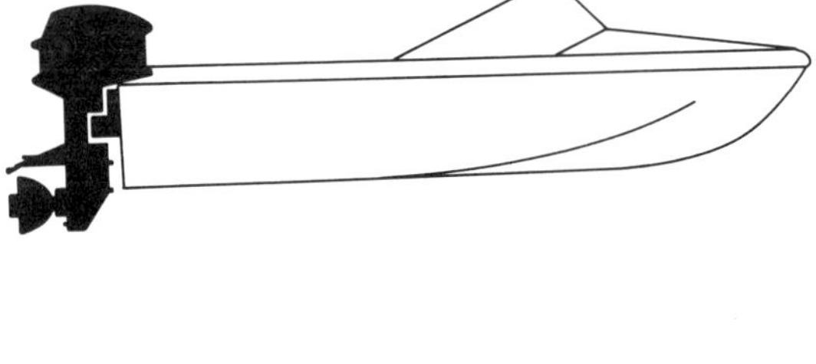

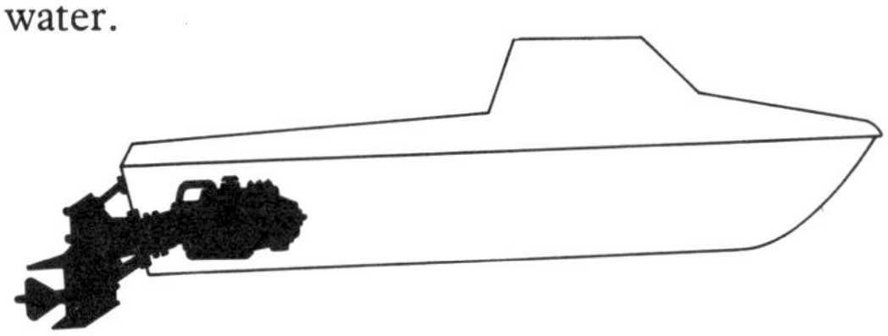

An inboard-outboard engine is situated within the boat, and thus achieves more protection than the outboard. The drive unit, called the stern-drive or outdrive, is mounted on the transom and, like the outboard, may be tilted. This unit has the ruggedness required for medium-sized boats operating in open waters.

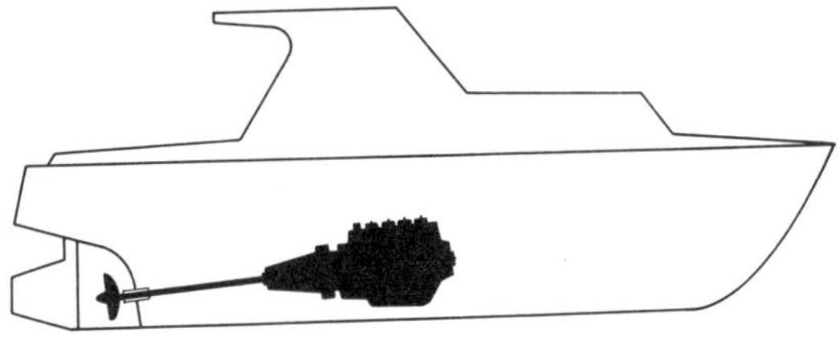

Inboard engines have the ruggedness and protection required in a boat for less sheltered conditions. An inboard may be diesel or a marinised petrol engine. The propeller shaft passes through the boat's hull through the stern gland, which must be frequently checked for watertightness. It should not be so tight as to overheat.

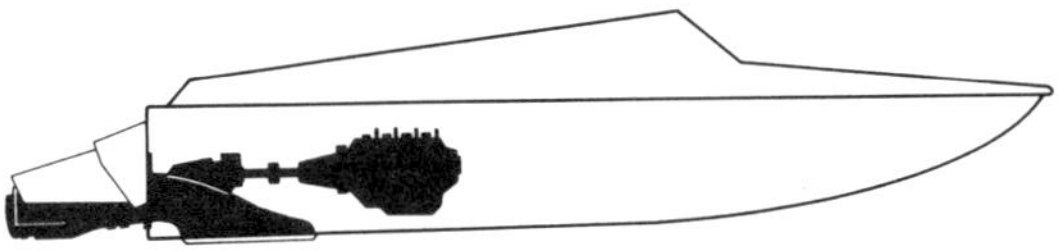

A jet unit is essentially a pump, drawing water in through a screen beneath the hull and pumping it out through a jet nozzle on the transom. It is important to check that the screen is clear before starting the unit. Steering is achieved with deflector plates mounted on each side of the nozzle, and a deflection 'bucket' drops over the nozzle to give astern power.

Sailing boats

Sails

The sail carried abaft the mast is the mainsail. Any sail carried forward of the mast is a headsail, but if carried on the forestay, it is termed a jib. If more than one headsail is carried, the inner is the staysail. The genoa is a larger headsail, which extends to the masthead and overlaps the mainsail. The spinnaker, used when the boat is running before the wind, is a large, bulbous and often brightly decorated headsail.

Sailing rigs

The wind provides the motive power for a sailing boat, and the sails and mast transmit this power to the hull. The arrangement of sails and masts on a sailing boat is its rig.

A Bermudian mainsail is triangular, with its entire area lying aft of the mast, which forms the sail's leading edge. It is the most efficient form of mainsail. A mainsail with its upper edge supported by a yard, or gaff, is a gaff sail. If the gaff is vertical the boat is gunter rigged. If the gaff extends forward of the mast, the sail is a lugsail.

The addition of a single headsail creates the sloop rig. Probably the most popular among smaller sailing vessels, it is found on most cruising and racing dinghies, and on larger keel yachts. If the foresail extends to the masthead the boat is a masthead sloop, otherwise it is a fractional sloop. If more than one headsail is carried, the vessel is a cutter. She may be Bermudian or gaff rigged.

To achieve a larger sail area while keeping individual sails down to a manageable size, larger yachts may be two-masted. If the after mast is smaller, it is called a mizzen mast. If the mizzen is stepped aft of the rudder, or where the stern meets the waterline, the yacht is a yawl. If the mizzen is stepped forward of the rudder, it is a ketch. If the after mast is taller than the forward mast, the yacht is schooner rigged.

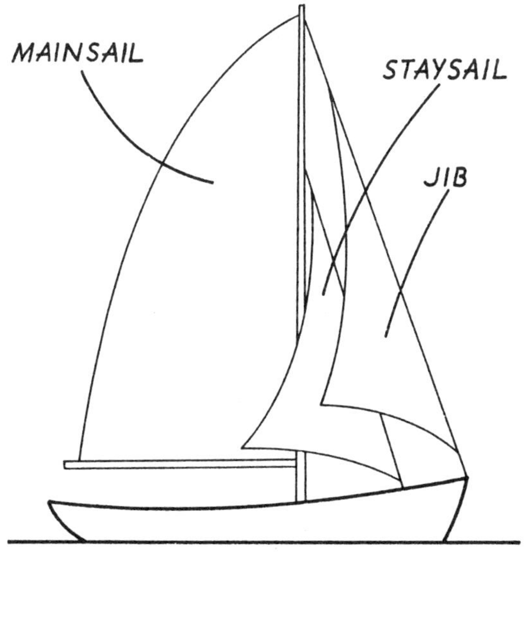

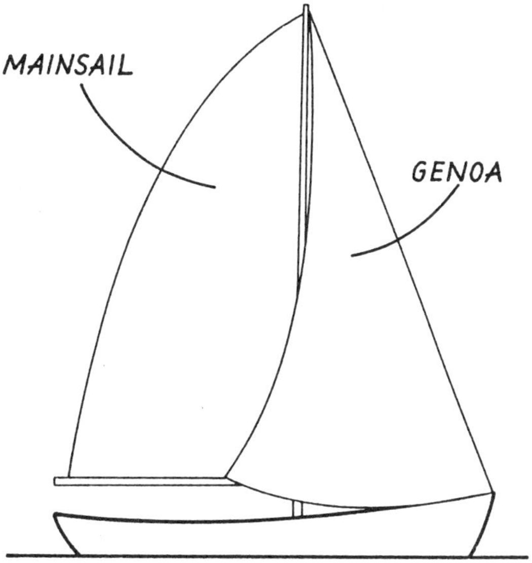

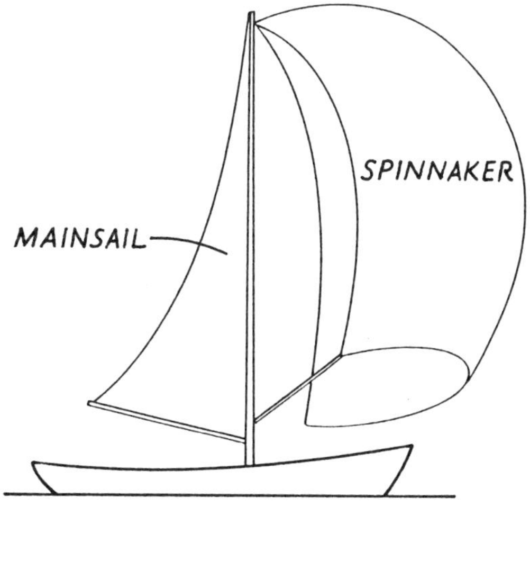

The parts of a sail

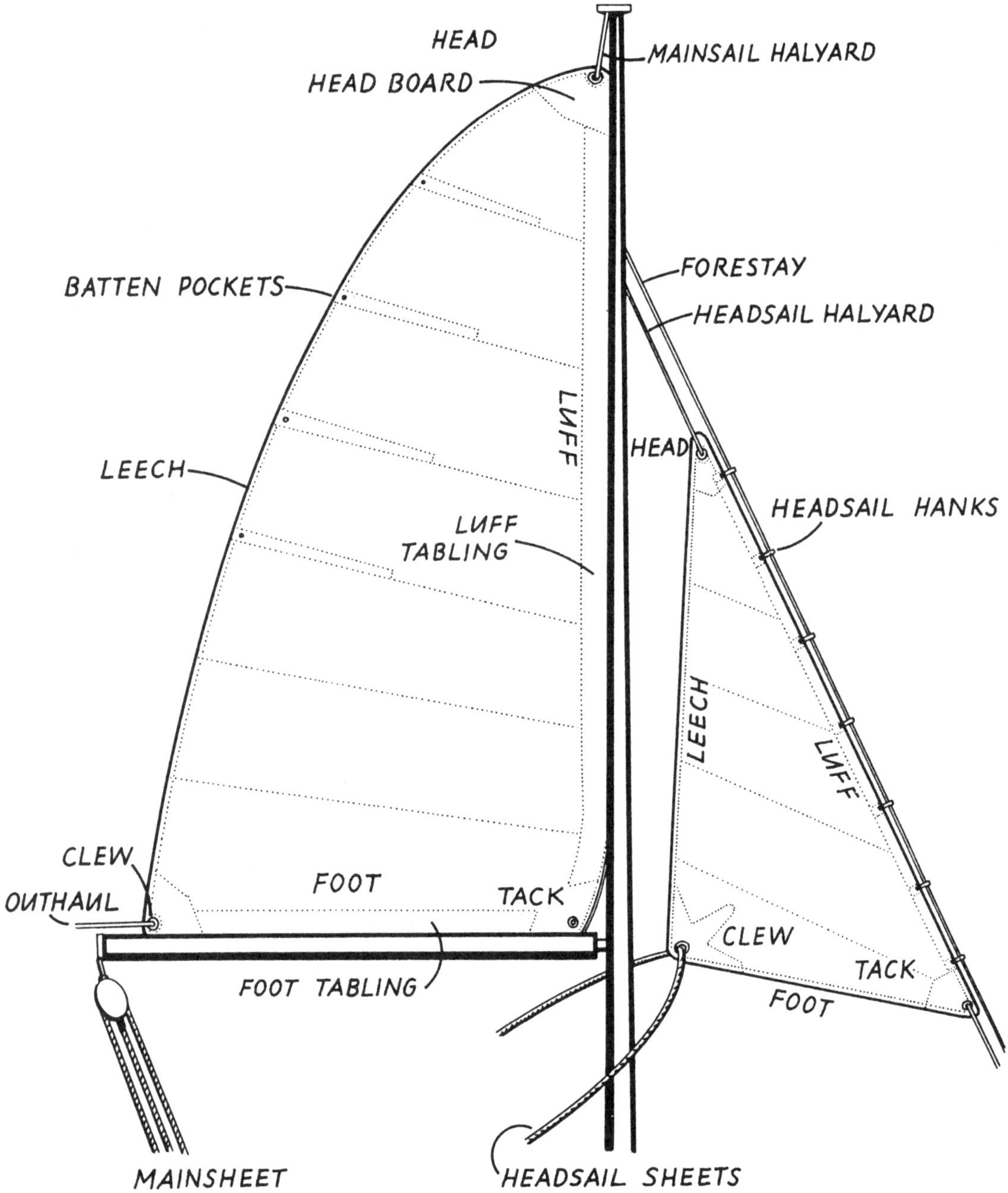

Sailing rigs

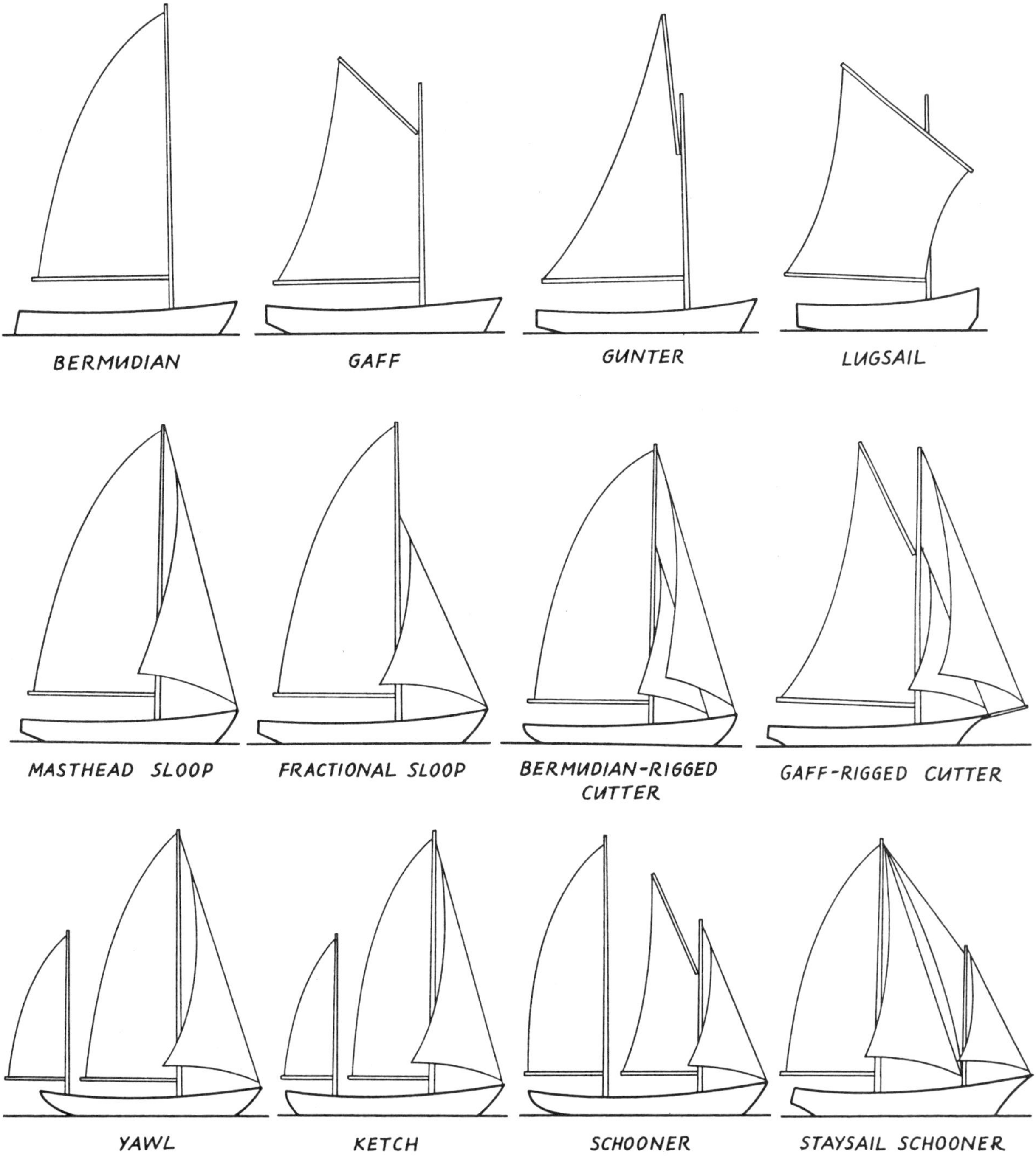

How a boat sails

It is easy to see how a boat sails with the wind from behind, but to understand how it sails against the wind requires some explanation of the wind's action upon a sail.

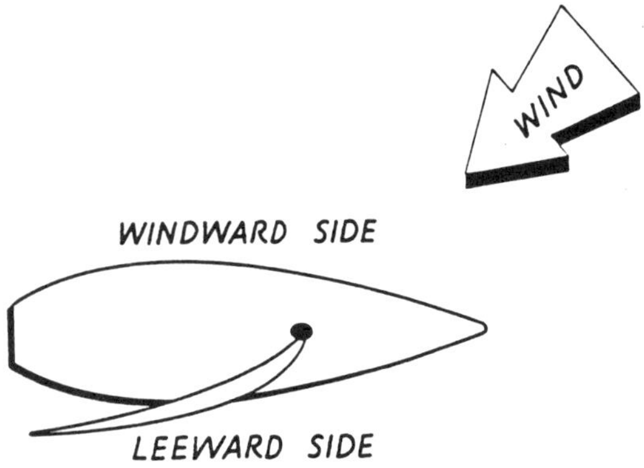

A good sail, which has been properly trimmed, has a curve resembling an aircraft wing; indeed the same principle is involved. As the wind passes over the sail its flow is deflected by the sail's curve, with air passing on both sides of the curve. Because of this curve, the air flowing to leeward must travel a greater distance, and thus it speeds up. An increase in speed of an airflow creates a reduction in pressure, and a pressure difference now exists across the sail. This pressure difference creates a force that 'lifts' the sail to leeward; the same force that provides lift to an aircraft wing.

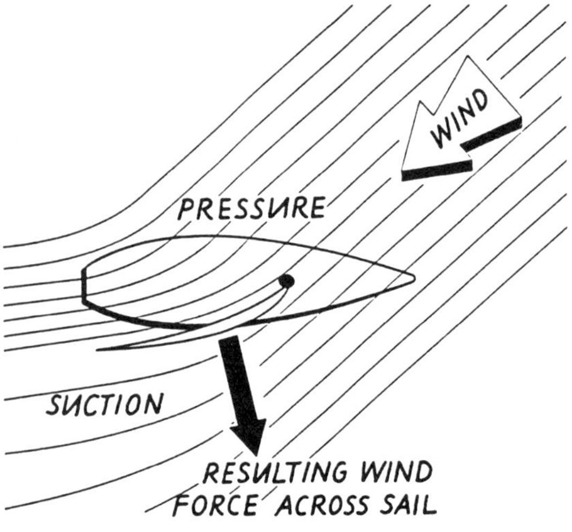

This force across the sail can be considered as acting in two directions: side force, attempting to move the boat sideways, and a forward thrust, attempting to drive the boat forwards. Beneath the water the boat's keel resists the side force, leaving the forward thrust to drive the boat forwards.

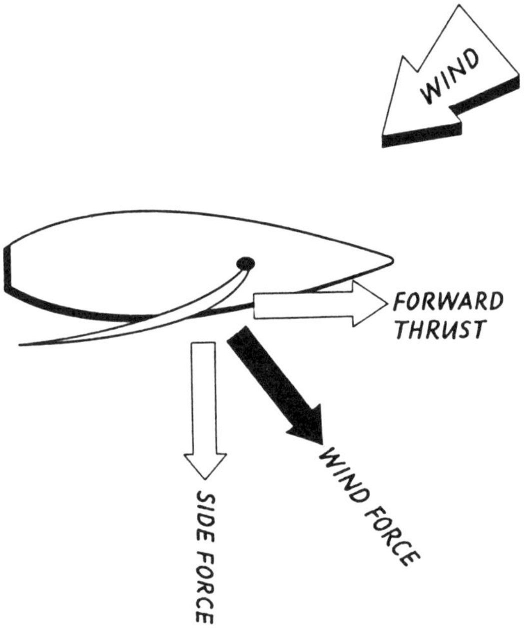

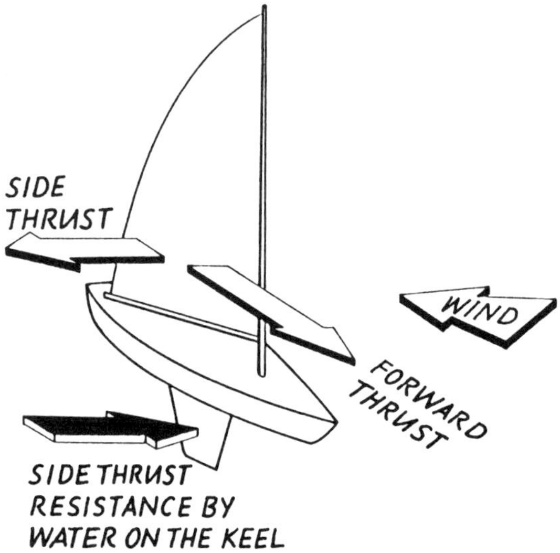

A properly set headsail will channel air through the slot between the headsail and the mainsail. This will increase the speed of the air-flow over the mainsail's leeward side, and thus increase its lift.

If the headsail is poorly set, eddies may develop in the flow of air through the slot. Loss of the slot effect will appear as a deformation in the aerofoil shape of the mainsail, or as a fluttering of the headsail.

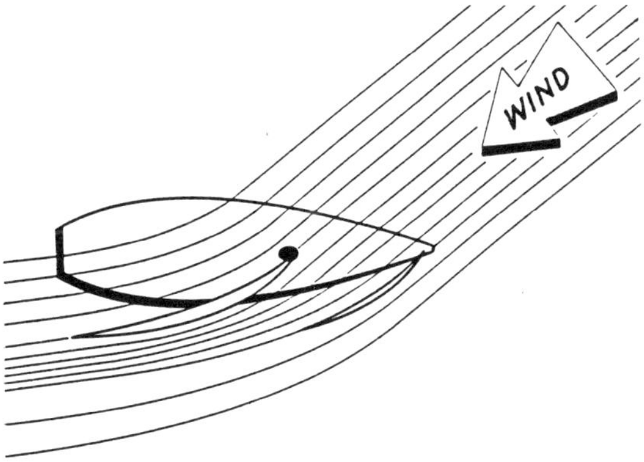

The points of sailing

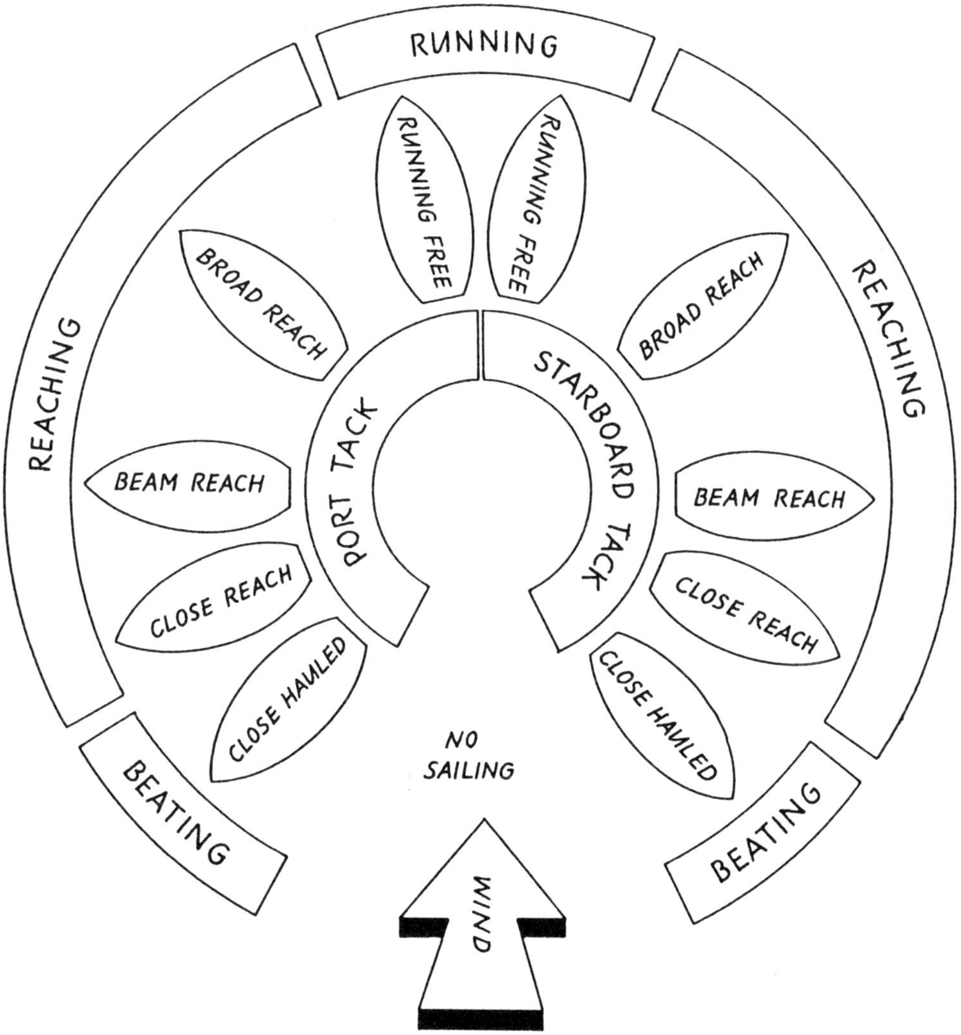

The trailer

The mobility of a trailered boat enables a very versatile approach to boating. Although there is the extra initial cost of the trailer and a towbar, the advantages usually make this the cheapest form of boating. A large number of launching ramps now exist throughout the country, and many river banks and beaches provide a sufficiently firm surface from which to launch and recover smaller boats. You can boat from wherever there is access for your car, and this will be considerably cheaper and less time-consuming than getting there by sea.

If the boat is trailered and towed on the roads, a number of traffic regulations must be taken into account. Details of trailer and coupling requirements are contained in the New Zealand Standard 5467.

■ If the boat, mast or outboard extends more than 1 metre behind the trailer it must be marked at its end by a flag of at least 40 by 30 centimetres. No part of the boat must extend more than 4 metres behind the rear axle of the trailer. If the boat and trailer exceed 2.5 metres in width, or 4.25 metres above the ground, a special permit must be obtained before they can be taken on the road.

■ The trailer must have a current warrant of fitness on display. These are valid for six months, but the trailer must be up to standard at all times. The warrant must be less than one month old if a trailer is sold. A numberplate and a current road licence sticker must also be displayed.

■ A white numberplate illumination light must be fitted, and two red reflectors. The trailer must also have at least one red rear light or, if first registered after 1 February 1977 and more than 1.5 metres wide, two red rear lights to clearly indicate the trailer's width. If more than 2 metres wide, or if the boat extends more than 1 metre to the side of the trailer's centreline, there must also be two forward-facing white lights to indicate width.

■ If the car's signals and stop lights will be obscured from behind by the boat, direction indicators and stop lights must also be fitted to the trailer. Boat trailers often present difficulties in mounting these lights. There is no objection to mounting the lights on a board, which can then be attached to the boat while it is carried on the trailer.

■ The tyres on the trailer must be in good condition. If the combined weight of boat and trailer exceed 1000 kg, there must be a minimum of 1.5 mm tread over three-quarters of the width of the tyre and around its entire circumference.

■ Trailer tyres are generally at a higher air pressure than car tyres. Check the pressure frequently. Low pressure on one or both sides will cause the trailer and boat to sway when under tow, particularly with radial tyres.

■ If the combined weight of the boat and trailer exceeds 2000 kg, the trailer must have a proper braking system, operated from the driver's foot brake, and also a mechanical parking brake. These brakes must apply automatically if the trailer comes adrift while under tow.

■ Rust is something all car and boat owners have to contend with, but it is particularly important with a boat trailer to ensure that rust and other forms of corrosion are not allowed to take hold and render the trailer unsafe.

■ The trailer must have mudguards, a proper coupling and a safety chain. As an extra precaution, anchor the safety chain to a separate point on the drawbar rather than to the coupling, in case the coupling breaks.

■ If you cannot see beyond the boat through your car's rear-view mirror, a larger, side-mounted mirror should be fitted.

■ The speed limit while towing on the open road in New Zealand is 70 km/h.

Apart from these regulatory requirements, common sense also dictates a few further requirements.

Submerging the trailer in the water while loading and unloading the boat will wash out grease very quickly. If the wheel bearings are hot, water immersion will cause quick contrac-

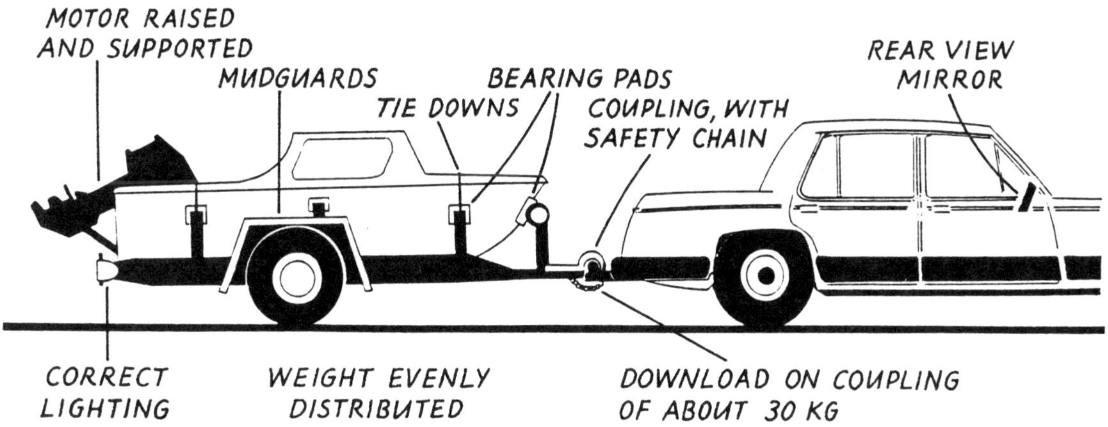

tion and water ingress, which can quickly lead to bearing failure. Check the bearings frequently and repack with grease as necessary.

For similar reasons, frequently check and lubricate the trailer winch, the winch cable, and the roller bearings.

The weight distribution on the trailer will affect the road handling of the towing vehicle. A well-balanced trailer should have a down-load on the coupling of about 30 kg; in other words, you should be able to lift the drawbar of the trailer comfortably by hand. Some of your extra gear can be stowed in the boat to improve trailer balance while on the road.

The boat should sit firmly on the trailer, the bearing pads giving equal and evenly spaced support to the hull. To prevent movement, secure the boat to the trailer with strong tie-downs. These must not only prevent lateral movement of the boat on the trailer, but must also prevent the boat from moving forwards or backwards. You do not want the bow of the boat or the mast coming in through the back window of the car if you have to stop suddenly. The outboard must be supported in the raised position with a suitably placed strut.

High-tensile chain through the coupling or through the wheels may deter tow-away thefts, but consider removing the coupling altogether when boat and trailer are parked unattended. Mark the trailer with welding, or some similar permanent method, with a means of identification — either the boat's name or your own name and address. This may well speed your rescue at sea if the trailer is found abandoned on the shore.

Driving with a trailed boat requires particular care. Apart from getting to know how your vehicle and trailer handle, how they corner, how much extra distance you need for stopping, and how to reverse without jack-knifing the trailer, you should make regular stops to check that the boat is still secure.

Remember to carry a spare trailer wheel and a jack. Without a spare you will have to leave the trailer and boat on the roadside. It is also wise to carry a set of wheel chocks for the trailer, and a stout towline for retrieving the trailer from the water.

Always disconnect the electric wiring from the car before immersing the trailer in the water, and after immersion remember to reconnect and check the electrics and your brakes.

Boat insurance

Insurance is necessary, and you will find that the insurance covers offered by different companies vary considerably. Some will base their rates on the boat's speed, the premiums increasing as the boat's speed increases; others base their rates on the boat's size or type. Some companies will only insure a boat within certain areas, perhaps a limit of 12 miles off the coast. Others impose a surcharge if the boat is taken across Cook Strait, and some will not consider river boating.

There are often variations on the premiums if the boat is at moorings or on a trailer. If you intend racing your boat, you will find that some companies will insure sailing boats but not power boats.

If you belong to a club that specialises in a particular form of boating, ask around to find out how they are insured, or go to a marine insurance broker. In any event, don't sign up until you know exactly what is covered, and when it is covered. Make sure you know:

- What period is covered by the policy. Is it annual, or only the boating season?
- Is the trailer covered as well as the boat? Is the trailer covered for theft from the beach while you are out sailing?
- Does the policy cover the boat while being towed on its trailer on the roads?
- Will your car insurance policy be rendered invalid by towing the boat?
- Does the policy cover the cost of repairing mechanical breakdowns, and damage to the boat's rudder and propeller?
- Does the policy include damage to or replacement of sails?
- Does the policy include use of the boat for water-skiing?
- What boat's equipment is included in the policy?
- What excesses are offered by the insurer?

Registration of your boat

A pleasure boat may be registered with its class association, and it may be registered under the Shipping and Seamen Act as a New Zealand ship.

Class registration is entirely voluntary but certainly well worth considering. Among the advantages offered are the speedy location of the owner of the boat if the boat is found to be in danger, and efficient indentification in a search and rescue operation or in cases of theft. It is also a form of protection for boat buyers and sellers.

To register a keeler, there is a nominal fee and a registration form can be obtained from the New Zealand Yachting Federation. For classed boats other than keelers, the boat is registered with the class owner's association. The yacht register is published annually by the New Zealand Yachting Federation.

A pleasure boat is required to be registered as a New Zealand ship only if it exceeds 15 register tons. A smaller boat is not obliged to be registered unless it proceeds overseas, but may be if the owner so desires. (A register ton is not a measurement of weight but of volume; one register ton is 100 cubic feet.)

A boat can be registered in New Zealand only if it is wholly owned by a British subject or by a corporate body established under, and subject to, the law of a Commonwealth country and having its principal place of business in a Commonwealth country.

The advantages of registration are many. The boat is entitled to fly the New Zealand red ensign, entry in the register provides evidence of the boat's ownership and nationality, and the owner's status is established in any legal matter involving the boat.

Buying a boat

Choose your boat carefully, and buy it only if you are completely satisfied that it is the type of boat you require, that it will suit your pocket, and that the boat is thoroughly sound. Rotten wood and other defects can be hidden by an unscrupulous dealer. Your life may depend upon decisions made when buying a boat.

Whether buying privately or from a dealer:

- Before purchase, have the boat checked by an independent surveyor or boatbuilder.
- Do not hesitate to seek a second opinion.
- If buying a second-hand boat, it is especially important to know something of the boat's history.
- Always ask for a sea trial.
- Be sure to find out exactly what you are getting with the boat, and get a written agreement that lists all the items to be included in the sale.

2

THE BOAT'S EQUIPMENT

Then fearing lest we should have fallen upon rocks, they cast four anchors out of the stern, and wished for the day.
— St Paul, The Act of the Apostles

All boats should carry sufficient equipment to ensure that minimum safety standards are met. A wise boat-owner will see that his craft is equipped to meet the maximum safety standards (see page 30). In any waters a boat must at least have these items aboard:

— a secondary method of propulsion;
— firefighting equipment;
— signalling equipment;
— a method of getting water out of the boat;
— a lifejacket for each person on the boat;
— an anchor and spare line; and
— someone who knows how to use these items properly.

Anchors

An anchor can provide:

■ A means of mooring the boat temporarily, such as for leisure stops, fishing, picnicking or hunting ashore.

■ A method of holding the boat in an emergency, such as during a breakdown, dismasting, or inclement weather.

■ A useful manoeuvring aid (for arresting the boat's bow movement as the stern is manipulated with the rudder and propeller).

The parts of an anchor

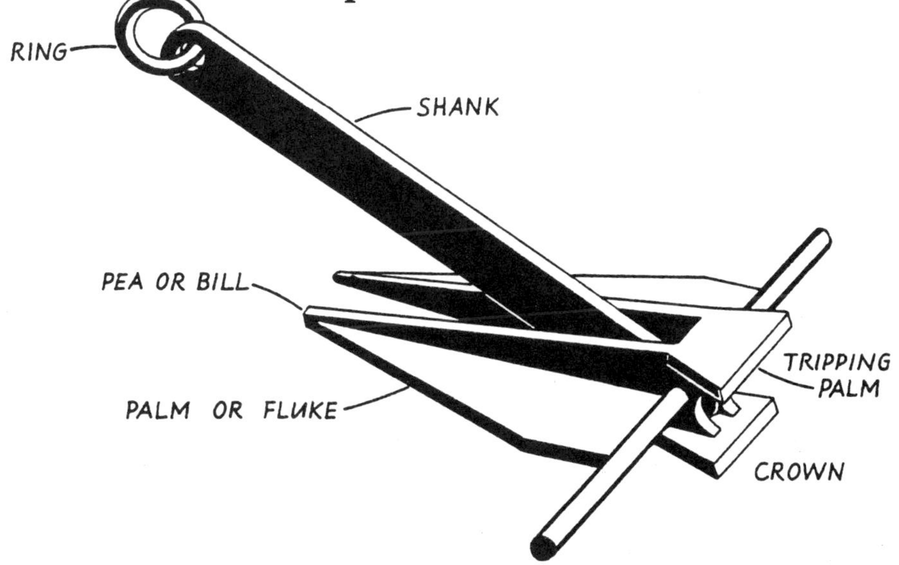

Safety equipment check list

Boat length	*Up to 5 metres*			*5–8 metres*			*8–12 metres*		
Boating area	*Offshore*	*Coastal*	*Inshore*	*Offshore*	*Coastal*	*Inshore*	*Offshore*	*Coastal*	*Inshore*
Anchor	N	N	N	N	N	N	N	N	N
Anchor (spare)	N	R	D	N	R	D	N	R	D
Bailer	N	N	N	N	N	N	N	N	N
Bilge pump	N	R	D	N	R	R	N	N	N
Boat hook	R	R	R	R	R	R	N	N	N
Bucket	N	N	N	N	N	N	N	N	N
Buoyant cushions	R	R	R	R	R	R	R	R	R
Charts	N	N	D	N	N	D	N	N	R
Compass	N	N	D	N	N	D	N	N	R
Depth finder	D	D	D	R	R	D	N	N	R
Distress sheet	R	R	R	R	R	R	R	R	R
Fire extinguisher	N	N	N	N	N	N	N	N	N
First-aid kit	N	N	N	N	N	N	N	N	N
Flares — parachute	N	N	D	N	N	D	N	N	D
— handflare	N	N	N	N	N	N	N	N	N
— orange smoke	N	N	D	N	N	D	N	N	D
Foghorn	R	R	D	N	R	D	N	N	R
Heliograph	R	R	D	R	R	D	R	R	D
Knife	N	N	N	N	N	N	N	N	N
Lifebuoy	D	D	D	N	N	R	N	N	N
Lifejacket (1 per person)	N	N	N	N	N	N	N	N	N
Liferaft (inflatable)	D	–	–	R	D	–	N	R	D
Locator beacon (EPIRB)	N	R	–	N	R	–	N	R	–
Paddles, oars, spare motor	N	N	N	N	N	N	N	N	N
Radar reflector	N	R	D	N	R	D	N	R	D
Radio telephone	R	R	–	N	R	D	N	R	D
Rations and water	N	N	N	N	N	N	N	N	N
Safety harness	N	R	D	N	R	D	N	R	D
Sea anchor (drogue)	N	N	D	N	N	D	N	N	D
Side ladder	–	–	–	R	R	R	N	N	N
Spare bungs	N	N	N	N	N	N	N	N	N
Spare engine parts	N	N	N	N	N	N	N	N	N
Spare fuel	N	N	R	N	N	R	N	N	R
Spare rope	N	N	R	N	N	N	N	N	N
Throwing quoit & line	N	N	N	N	N	N	N	N	N
Tools	N	N	N	N	N	N	N	N	N
Torch	N	N	N	N	N	N	N	N	N
Warm & waterproof clothing	N	N	N	N	N	N	N	N	N

Offshore = Open waters and beyond seven miles from land.
Coastal = Up to seven miles from land; lakes; harbours and large bays.
Inshore = Small lakes (less than two miles across); rivers; small enclosed bays; sounds; and harbours where the shore is never more than one mile away.

N = Necessary for safety.
R = Recommended for extra safety.
D = Desirable for efficiency.

The efficiency of an anchor will depend on its shape, its weight and how well it has been laid upon the seabed. Anchor shapes are many and varied. They all serve the same purpose, to hold the boat to the seabed, but can be broadly divided into two classes. There are those designed to hold on soft bottoms, such as sand, mud or gravel; and there are those designed for use on hard bottoms, such as rock and coral.

A soft-bottom anchor must have flat palms that are angled or pivoted to the anchor's shank. The crown is shaped to elevate this end of the anchor and allow the palms to dig in. Typical soft-bottom anchors are the Danforth, Bruce and the CQR, or plough.

The principle of a hard-bottom anchor is quite different to that of a soft-bottom anchor. Typical anchors of this type are the grapnel and fisherman's anchor; their long prongs are shaped to hook and snare any rocky outcrop or obstacle lying on the seabed.

A simple form of grapnel can be made at home. Four 12 mm iron bars are inserted into a hollow pipe and bent to the shape of a grapnel. If these prongs now catch on an obstruction and become jammed, a strong steady pull will bend the iron bars straight, allowing the grapnel to pull free and be recovered. The bars can later be bent back into shape for use again. Never leave the boat unattended while lying to this form of anchor.

It is obviously not possible always to match the seabed to the anchor you are carrying, and some compromise may be necessary. However, some anchors serve both purposes and are good general purpose anchors. The plough and Bruce, for example, have sufficient projections to enable them to work well on a hard bottom; and the fisherman's anchor frequently has flat enough palms to serve as a soft-bottom anchor.

The optimum weight of an anchor depends primarily on the boat's size, but other factors

Common types of anchor

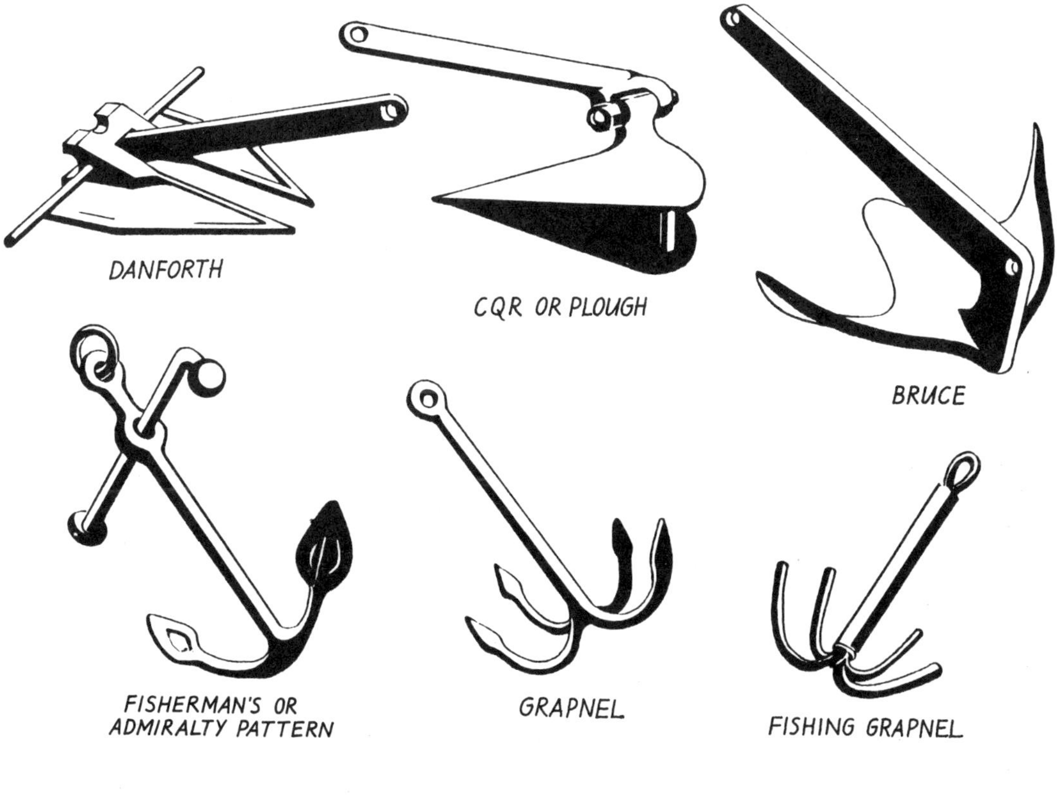

must also be taken into account. For example, a boat that sits high out of the water, offering higher windage, will exert a greater pull on the anchor than one of low windage.

Consider also how the anchor is to be handled. Unless a mechanical windlass is used, a large anchor will require much time and energy in heaving it up.

As a very rough guide, on boats up to 15 metres in length, anchor weight in kilograms should be equal to about one and a half times the length of the boat. If a good general purpose anchor is used, it may not need to be as heavy, but anchor weight should never be less than the boat's length. For boats longer than 15 metres, the anchor's weight should be about double the boat's length.

Anchor lines

An anchor will dig itself into the seabed as long as the pull on the anchor line is kept as close to the horizontal as possible. Any vertical pull may lift the shank and break the anchor out. For this reason a length of chain is essential. It will act as a shock absorber or spring, absorbing any sudden upward pull exerted by the boat as it lifts to the waves. The boat will lie to the chain, leaving the anchor undisturbed.

The action of a soft-bottom anchor

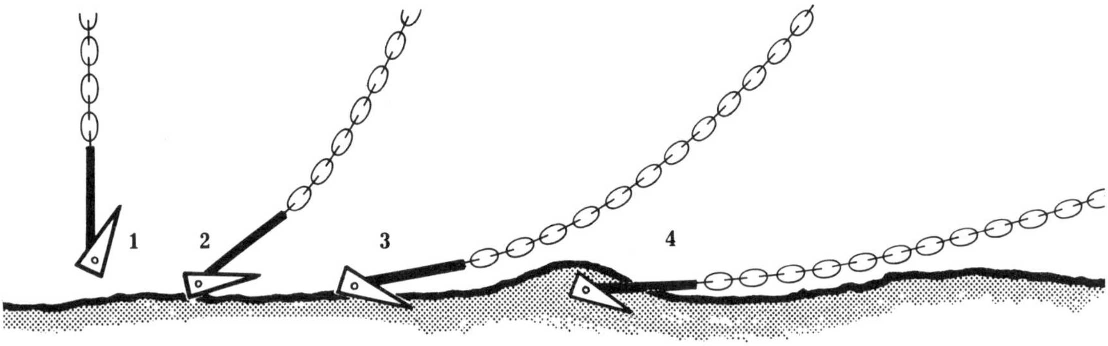

1
The anchor is lowered to the seabed. (It must not be dropped in such a way that may allow the anchor line to foul the anchor.)

2
The flukes rotate downwards as the anchor and line are laid out along the seabed.

3
A horizontal strain is applied to the line, to dig in the flukes of the anchor.

4
The anchor is buried; the anchor's shank being kept horizontal by the weight of the chain.

The action of a hard-bottom anchor

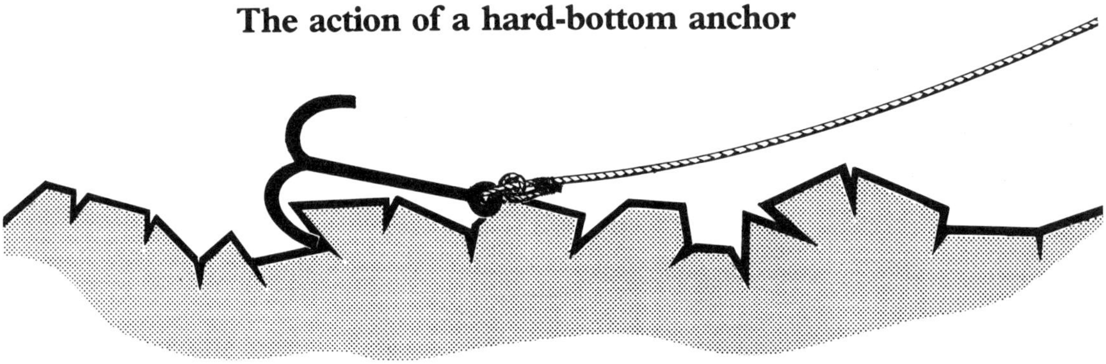

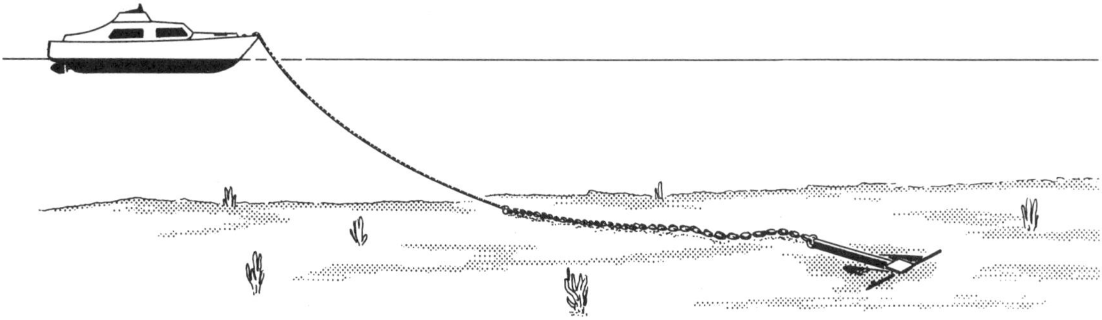

The chain will also reduce chafe of the anchor line as it moves over the seabed.

On many smaller boats it is not practical to have an anchor line entirely of chain, but you should endeavour to have a chain pennant of at least a boat length attached to your anchor. The weight of the chain should equal or exceed the weight of the anchor.

The rope used for the remaining line may be nylon or polyester. Polypropylene or polythene lines will float and are not suitable; they may foul your propeller, or someone else's. The table below is for boats proposing to venture into coastal waters and beyond, not necessarily inland waters. However, never have less than 20 metres of anchor line.

So that you will know how much anchor line you have paid out, mark your chain or line at regular intervals. Chain may be divided into equal lengths, separated by a brightly painted shackle. The shackles also permit easy removal of any part of the line, perhaps if the anchor becomes fouled. The anchor rope can be marked with small tails of cloth or line woven between the rope's strands.

Anchors have an unfortunate habit of getting fouled and lost. A spare anchor, chain and line will never be wasted. It can also be used as a second anchor when anchored in heavy weather or in restricted space. A spare should be carried on any boat over seven metres in length.

No matter how good an anchor you have, it will only hold your boat if it is correctly laid out upon the seabed. Anchoring techniques are explained on page 92.

The sea anchor (drogue)

Whereas an anchor will hold the boat to the seabed, the sea anchor is intended to anchor the boat to the sea.

In cases of emergency, perhaps in heavy weather or through breakdown or dismasting, you may have to lie stopped in water too deep in which to anchor. Most boats, when lying stopped in a seaway, have a natural tendency to turn themselves beam on to the sea and roll with the waves. This is both uncomfortable and dangerous, and so it is essential you keep the boat's head to the sea.

A sea anchor resembles a wind-sock or a parachute. It is streamed on a hawser from the bow of the boat, or perhaps from the stern of a yacht

Boat length	*Chain pennant*		*Anchor rope*	
	Size	*Length*	*Size**	*Length*
Up to 5 metres	6 mm	3 m	8 mm	50– 75 m
5–8 metres	6 mm	6 m	10 mm	75–100 m
8–14 metres	9 mm	10 m	12 mm	100–125 m
Over 14 metres	12 mm	Equal to boat's length	16 mm	100–125 m

*Rope sizes are for nylon line

The sea anchor

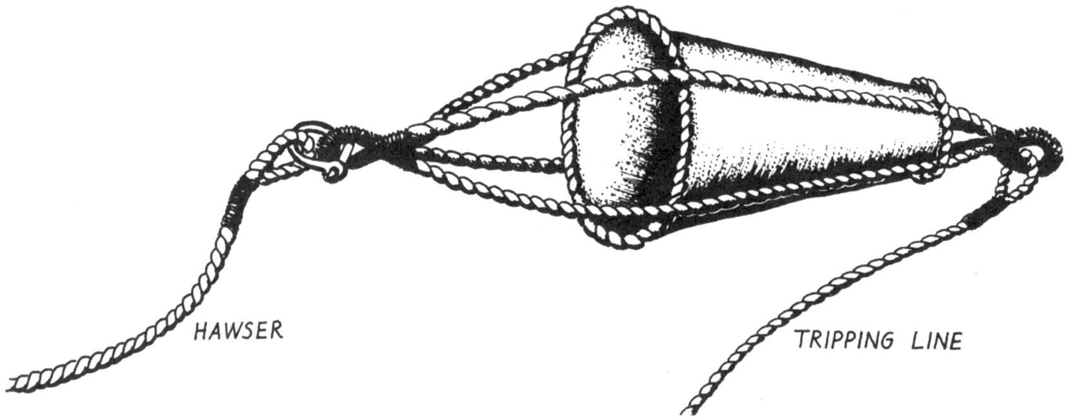

if the rudder cannot be unshipped.

A tripping line may be fitted to ease recovery of the drogue after use. The boat will be blown downwind from the drogue, the hawser pulling the boat's bow up into the wind.

Should a proper sea anchor not be available, one can be quickly improvised. Anything trailed in the water will act as a drogue — a mattress, sail, sail-bag or even a long length of rope. A simple bucket will be effective, although the attached line should be fastened around the rim of a plastic bucket rather than to the handle. A hole knocked in the bottom of the bucket may improve its efficiency.

Whether using a proper sea anchor or an improvised one, its line should be as long as possible. Too short a line will either lift the sea anchor out of the water, or prevent the bow from lifting to the waves.

Boathook

Used either for retrieval of ropes or other objects from the water, a boathook is also a useful tool for pushing or pulling your boat off another boat or a jetty. Stow the boathook on deck where it can quickly be reached, perhaps along the cabin top or side, in quick-release spring clips. Its long handle can be graduated and marked for use as a seabed probe and depth finder around the boat in shallow water.

Knife

A sharp knife is often termed a seaman's best friend. It will find a multitude of uses, from gutting fish to clearing fouled rigging and lines. Like the boathook, it will only be of use if stowed in a readily accessible position. Keep it in a sheath or pocket near the cabin door.

Use of a bucket as a sea anchor

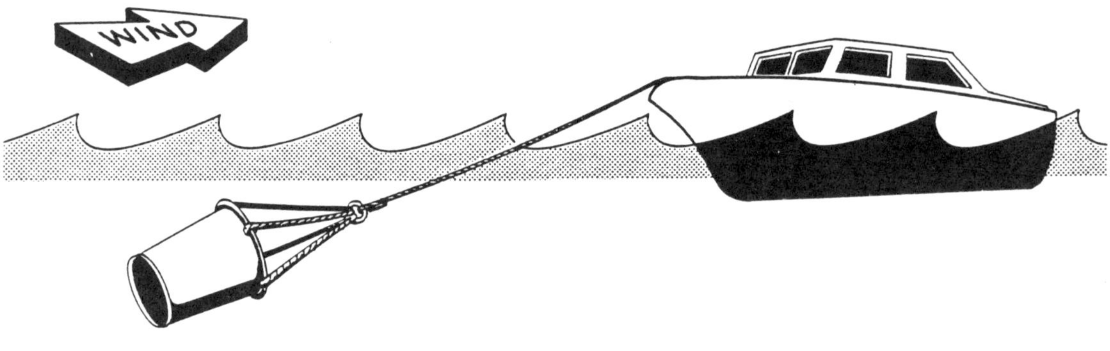

Bucket

A bucket is handy for bailing, firefighting, washing down, as a makeshift sea anchor, a storage receptacle, and a host of other uses. Upturned, it may provide a means of flotation in water. Attach a line to the bucket so that it can be dropped over the side to bring water aboard.

Bailer

A bailer is essential for removing water quickly from the boat, or, in cases of fire, for scooping water into the boat. A simple plastic detergent container with its end cut off makes an ideal water scoop for the smaller dinghy. Attach a line for securing it to the boat and so that it can be slipped over your wrist when bailing.

Foghorn

The Collision Regulations require any boat over 12 metres to have a foghorn, but it is an important safety and signalling device on any boat. It may be sounded by compressed air or by electrical or mechanical means, or may simply be a portable aerosol unit with replaceable cylinders. Fog signals are described on page 127, and foghorn specifications are prescribed in Annex III of the Collision Regulations.

Heliograph

A signalling mirror may be used to attract attention when in difficulty or distress. Proper heliographs are available with sighting devices for aiming at distant targets, but a simple mirror may suffice.

Bungs

Don't overlook the possibility that your boat's regular bung may get lost or broken. Carry spares; they may also be useful as temporary leak stoppers. Even self-draining devices can fail, so carry something that will block the hole.

Torch

Carry a reliable torch, preferably one that is strong, waterproof and buoyant. A signalling button will enable it to be used for communication as well as illumination. Attach a lanyard to the handle, so that it can be carried around your wrist or your neck to leave your hands free. Do not use a torch with a magnetic handle; it will interfere with your compass. And don't forget to carry spare batteries and bulbs.

Compass

At night or in poor visibility, when there is no horizon to give you an indication of direction, a compass will be your most important navigational aid.

Early marine compasses were divided into 32 points, because that was about the accuracy with which these compasses could be read. Modern navigation uses the 360-degree notation, allowing a more precise and simpler method of indicating direction. Boat compasses may use either or both methods of notation.

The hand-bearing compass is a portable hand-held compass, fitted with a prism or similar sighting device for reading bearings. For use at night it may be fitted with a radiant strip, luminous markings or a light powered by batteries within the handle.

The steering compass is a permanently fitted compass, sited at the boat's steering position. Some are designed to be mounted vertically on a bulkhead, and others onto a horizontal surface. The compass is slung in gimbals so that it remains upright whatever the boat's attitude. Larger steering compasses are placed in a binnacle, a casing that protects the compass, supports it in gimbals, and houses the compass's correctors.

A lubber line is marked on the compass bowl, or on the binnacle, to indicate to the helmsman the direction in which the boat is heading. The lubber line must be parallel to the boat's fore-and-aft line. To steer a course, the helmsman must keep the appropriate direction on the compass card aligned with the lubber line.

The liquid compass

Pivot assembly: A sapphire bearing upon an iridium point, for maximum freedom from friction. Placed so that the card remains balanced horizontally, and so that it will not disengage if the compass is inverted.

Liquid: A low freezing temperature liquid, which dampens unnecessary movement of the card, oil or a water/alcohol mixture being most common.

Compass needle: Bar or ring shaped magnets which rotate the card for alignment with the earth's horizontal magnetic field. Coated for protection against corrosion in the liquid.

Compass bowl: Constructed from brass or a similar non-magnetic material.

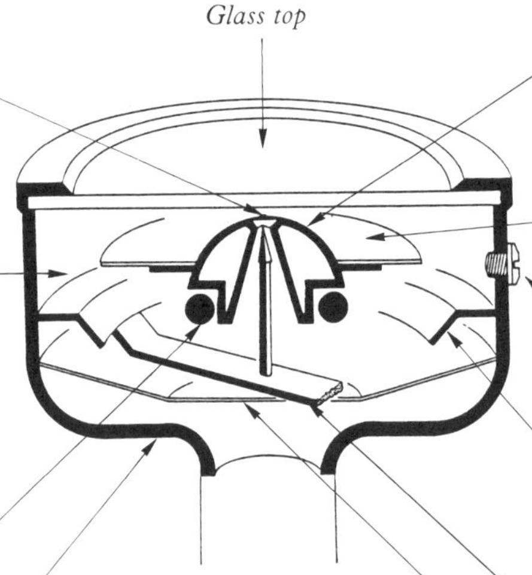

Float: Filled with buoyant material, bringing the card to almost neutral buoyancy, reducing the weight on the pivot.

Card: Constructed in mica or a similar material that is unaffected by the liquid.

Filling plug: Through which more liquid can be injected to remove air bubbles.

Bubble trap: Inversion of the compass will trap any air bubbles here, preventing them from appearing beneath the glass top.

Bridge: To support the pivot.

Flexible bottom: To allow the liquid to expand and contract with changes in temperature.

The compass card

Wherever the compass is placed on a boat there is always the possibility of magnetic interference by nearby electrical or metallic objects. This is deviation and is explained on page 54.

■ If used as a steering compass, the compass must be within easy view of the helmsman, wherever he needs to be to steer the boat.

■ The compass must not be placed in a position where it could be screened from the earth's magnetic field. Do not enclose it in a steel cabin or wheelhouse, and don't place it too low in the boat.

■ Mount the compass as far as possible from any ferro-magnetic fittings. Even if unmagnetised, these fittings will still affect the compass.

■ Electrical and electronic equipment, engine gauges, etc., must be mounted as far as possible from your compass to prevent interference. This equipment will affect the compass even if switched off.

■ Do not place portable transistor radios, calculators, cameras, tools, chart instruments, etc., anywhere near a compass.

■ Site the compass so that it cannot be affected or damaged by sail-handling gear, or by crew working with this gear.

■ Mount the compass on the boat's centreline, or as close to the centreline as possible.

■ Make sure that the lubber line is correctly aligned with the boat's fore-and-aft line.

■ Protect the compass from the weather, particularly direct sunlight.

■ Protect the compass from vandalism, perhaps by unshipping it while the boat is unattended at her moorings.

■ Ensure that any electrical wiring near the compass is kept to a minimum. DC wiring near the compass must be twin, so that the magnetic field around each wire cancels the other.

■ Screws, bolts, mounting brackets and other fittings in the vicinity of the compass must be non-ferrous.

■ When using the hand-bearing compass, stand well away from any part of the boat or its equipment that could cause magnetic interference. Bear in mind that articles of clothing such as metal buttons or buckles, or metal-framed glasses, may also affect the compass.

■ If two compasses are to be placed on the boat, keep them away from each other; they will interfere with each other. This includes the compass in an autopilot.

The use of the compass for navigation is explained in Chapter 4.

Depth finders

The echo sounder projects supersonic pulses down to the seabed, which reflect and return as echoes. By measuring the time interval between transmission and reception of each pulse, depth is computed. Depth may be displayed digitally or by meter, or recorded on a sensitised-paper graph.

A transducer, for transmitting and receiving the pulses, is fitted inside or into the underside of the hull. The transducer must be carefully sited, and kept clean of paint, oil deposits and sea growth.

Various factors can cause false readings, or perhaps no reading at all, and so depth indication in shallow water must not be implicitly relied upon. Verify the depth beneath the boat with other methods.

By attaching a weight to a length of line, one can plumb the shallower depths. Mark the sounding line with knots or tails of twine at regular intervals.

For very shallow water a pole, such as the boathook, can be graduated and used as a depth probe.

Personal flotation devices

Play safe. Never assume that your boating will always be done on top of the water. You may have to take to the water at any time; perhaps everyone at the same time. Carry at least one flotation device for each person aboard the boat.

Select your flotation devices according to the area in which you will be boating and the style of boating or watersport you will be pursuing.

Lifejacket or buoyancy vest?

A lifejacket carried on a commercial vessel must comply with the specifications of the Shipping Lifesaving Appliances Rules, administered by the Maritime Safety Authority. It must turn the wearer, conscious or otherwise, to a safe floating attitude and keep the person in that position with the mouth supported at least 15 cm from the water. A lifejacket providing this degree of buoyancy is, however, too bulky to be worn easily in small boats, and something more convenient has been devised by New Zealand Standard 5823.

COASTAL LIFEJACKET

NZS 5823 defines any device designed to assist a person to remain afloat in water until rescue is effected as a buoyancy aid. It includes personal flotation devices designed to be worn on the body, and float-off aids such as buoyant cushions and rescue buoys. The term lifejacket is therefore loosely used to include any personal flotation device that is worn on the body.

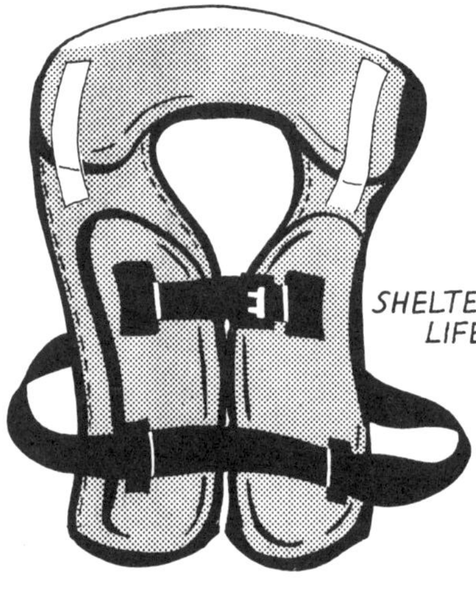

SHELTERED-WATER LIFEJACKET

A boating lifejacket that complies with NZS 5823 may be classed as a coastal lifejacket or a sheltered-water lifejacket. Neither has the degree of buoyancy provided by the commercial-vessel lifejacket. The coastal lifejacket is suitable for continuous wear. It is designed to turn the wearer so that the mouth is brought clear of the water within five seconds and stabilise the wearer in a backward-inclined position. It is for use in rougher waters than the sheltered-water lifejacket. It may be used for coastal and offshore sailing, cruising, fishing and racing.

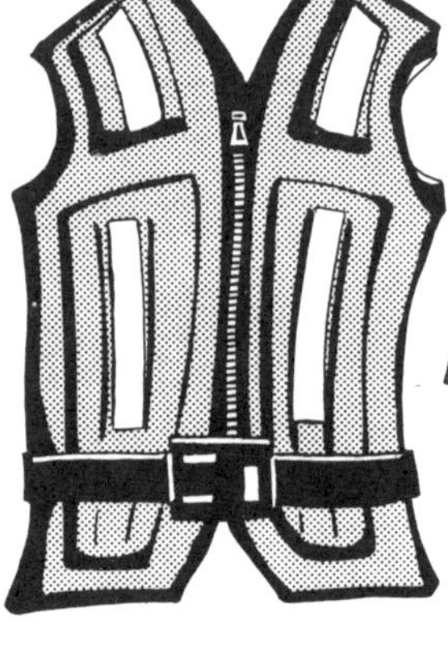

BUOYANCY VEST

The sheltered-water lifejacket has no roll-over requirement, but must not tilt the wearer forward from the vertical when in the water. It is for use in sheltered waters where early rescue may be anticipated. It may be used for cruising and general boating in enclosed waters, close to the shore, on rivers and lakes; all within areas of high boating activity.

The buoyancy vest is intended for use in aquatic sports where more freedom of movement is needed. It will assist in flotation during short-term immersion in smooth waters, but is not designed to turn the wearer to a safe floating position. Special purpose vests are available for water-skiing, jet skiing, jet boating, board sailing and other activities.

The effectiveness of any personal flotation device is considerably reduced in rough or breaking seas. Where speedy rescue could be unlikely, the maximum protection of a lifejacket should be used.

The buoyancy garment is a buoyancy aid, other than a lifejacket or buoyancy vest, worn on the body and intended for use when the wearer is at risk of immersion in the water. Special purpose garments are available for use in fast-flowing waters, for canoeists, jet boaters and rafters, where design could provide protection from injury around the chest and kidneys if swept into rocks and obstacles. It is also suitable for angling, rock fishing and paragliding.

Special buoyancy vests and garments are designed for particular forms of water sports. Canoeing, for example, requires a vest with a short waist. A lifejacket with too much buoyancy may be a hindrance when you are caught under the sails of a capsized yacht; the lower buoyancy rating of a buoyant vest or buoyancy garment will allow you to swim down and out from under a sail or a capsized boat.

A wetsuit with added buoyancy is intended for use in aquatic sports where hypothermia and frequent immersion in the water may place the wearer at risk. It is not designed to turn the wearer into a safe floating position. Because a proportion of buoyancy is in the legs, these suits could cause some instability, which could cause concern to the inexperienced wearer. It is ideal for water-skiers, board sailors and small-dinghy sailors, and may be used in conjunction with another buoyancy aid.

BUOYANCY GARMENT

BUOYANCY-AID WETSUIT

Using your personal flotation device

Your lifejacket must always be immediately available. Children, non-swimmers and those on small boats liable to capsize, should wear them all the time.

■ Ensure that children wear a lifejacket designed specifically for children. It must fit the child securely and comfortably.

■ Consult a local club specialising in the sport you intend pursuing. Seek their views on the type of personal flotation device suited to that sport. For example, coming off water-skis at high speed while wearing a large lifejacket can be very dangerous; the jacket may be driven up suddenly under your chin.

■ When purchasing a lifejacket, look for the New Zealand Standards Institute stamp. Study the label and note its capabilities and suggested maintenance.

■ Avoid snagging the fabric, and do not puncture the inner buoyancy compartments. Inspect the lifejacket frequently, and give it a thorough check after a season's use. Check all stitching, zips, belts, buckles and attachments.

■ To check the buoyancy compartments, squeeze each one firmly. If it feels unusually hard, or if you hear escaping air, it may be punctured. Have it checked and repaired.

■ Waterlogged buoyancy compartments will make the lifejacket heavier than normal. Weigh the lifejacket after use as a quick check.

■ Do not use your lifejacket as a cushion or as a fender. Apart from the risk of permanent damage, prolonged compression of the buoyancy chambers may affect their efficiency.

■ If a lifejacket is left in a damp space, the buoyancy material may eventually lose its flotation qualities and become unsafe. Dry the jacket before stowing it away. Most jackets can be sponged clean with warm soapy water, but not dry-cleaned. Check with the manufacturer.

■ More people die in the water from hypothermia than from drowning. If your activity takes place in cold conditions, select a lifejacket that gives added protection against the cold, and wear a wetsuit.

■ When jumping into the water while wearing a lifejacket, cross your arms and grasp the collar to prevent it from riding up over your body.

■ All lifejackets should be conspicuously coloured in yellow, orange, or red. If the colour has faded, it is time to renew the jacket.

Inflatable lifejackets require particular care in their handling and maintenance, and the manufacturer's recommendations must be closely followed. At least two independent buoyancy compartments should be incorporated in the lifejacket as a safety precaution against failure. One compartment may be of inherent buoyancy, and the other an air compartment; or both may be inflatable. Automatic inflation is by a small gas cylinder, but oral inflation must be possible in case of malfunction of the automatic system.

Always wear an inflatable lifejacket at least partially inflated. In this way it will immediately give some support if you are accidentally knocked over the side, perhaps in a semi-stunned condition, before being able to inflate it fully. This will also provide a constant check on its condition, showing up any small leaks.

Attachments

The wearing of any lifejacket does not guarantee your safety, nor your ultimate rescue, but there are a few extras that could improve your chances if attached to your lifejacket:

■ Retro-reflective tape is usually fitted as a standard, but ask for it if it is not. It will greatly assist in detection at night.

■ A whistle, attached to the lifejacket with a lanyard, will help attract attention to yourself.

■ A light, either a sea-activated cell or a Cyalume light will aid detection at night.

Lifebuoys (rescue buoys)

These may be circular or horseshoe in shape, and are for throwing or otherwise delivering to a person in the water. They are buoyancy aids, and will assist in flotation until rescue is effected. A lifeline becketed around the buoy provides hand-holds for the person to hang onto,

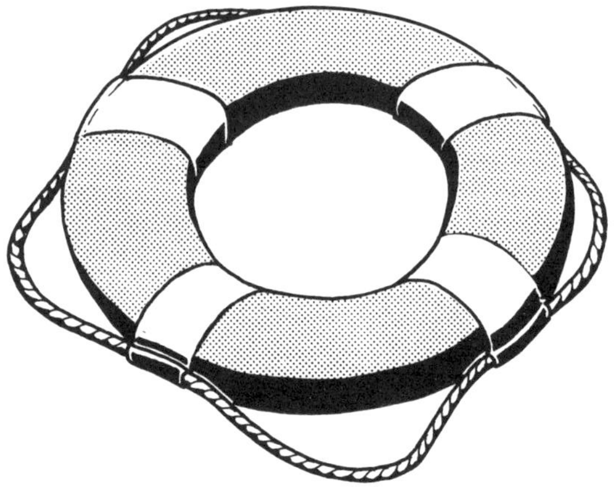

or the buoy can be slipped over the body. A length of line attached to the buoy will enable the person to be pulled back to the boat.

Stow the lifebuoy on deck within easy reach of the helmsman and provide quick-release arrangements so that it can be quickly launched in the event of man overboard. To aid visibility, the buoy should be a bright red, orange or yellow; and retro-reflective tape or paint can be applied for detection at night. A self-igniting light or smoke marker, a whistle, a drogue or a dan buoy could also be attached.

Throwing quoit

In addition to the lifebuoy, or as an alternative on a small boat, a small buoyant rubber quoit with a long length of buoyant (polypropylene) line will make an excellent rescue aid in the event of man overboard. The quoit can be tossed, or can be slipped over the arm and taken by a swimmer to the victim. The other end of the line is attached to the boat and provides constant contact between the boat and those in the water.

The quoit also provides an excellent means of passing a line to another boat for towing or rescue purposes, or for tossing to someone ashore to pass a mooring line. The quoit's line can then be used as a heaving line to enable a stronger line to be passed.

Buoyant cushions

These are float-off buoyancy aids that are carried as loose cushions on the boat, but in the event of the boat sinking they will float free and provide additional buoyancy for those in the water.

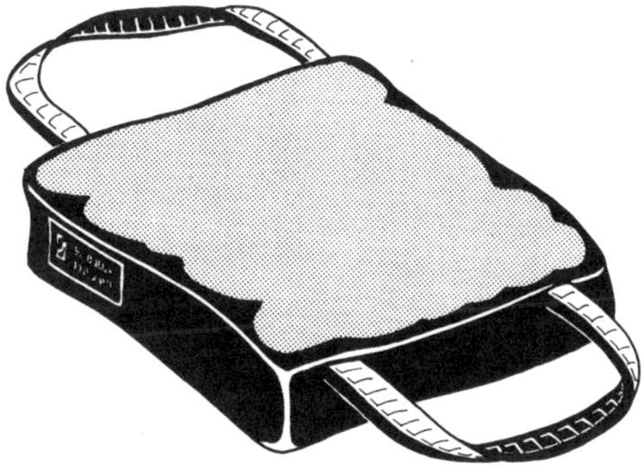

The large handles allow the cushion to be tossed to anyone in the water. For extra buoyancy in the water, the cushion may be worn across the chest by slipping the arms through the handles — but never wear the cushion upon your back, it may tip your face forwards into the water.

Liferaft

An inflatable liferaft is an important lifesaving appliance on any boat venturing offshore. There is a technique for using these rafts, both in their launching and in using them for survival. Owners, and those contemplating purchase of a raft, should attend liferaft demonstrations held regularly at boat clubs, training schools and liferaft service stations.

Inflatable liferafts must be serviced annually, and can be packed and equipped to suit your own requirements.

Secondary means of propulsion

A secondary means of propulsion is essential, no matter what the type or size of boat. A small boat, whether under sail or power, should carry paddles. A larger boat should carry an auxiliary engine, or even a small low-powered outboard carried as a spare on the transom.

Spare rope

Carry on board at least 20 metres of spare rope. You will find many uses for it: as a painter, for lengthening mooring lines or anchor lines, for towing or for being towed, for rigging a sea anchor and for rescue work.

Side ladder

Boarding a boat from the water is not easy, particularly if the boat is high-sided, if the hull has a smooth polished surface, and if the person trying to board is clothed, tired, cold or injured. On boats with a high freeboard a boarding ladder should always be available. It may be permanently fitted at the stern, or portable so that it can be placed over the side at the point of lowest freeboard.

Radar reflector

Radar is an electronic navigational aid used by larger ships and many boats to detect other objects around them. Pulses of high-frequency radio energy are transmitted from a radar scanner, which reflect from any target within range and return to the scanner as echoes.

Fibreglass, plastic and wood are particularly poor reflectors of radar energy, and a boat constructed in these materials will consequently make a very poor radar target. This is especially so in rough seas, where waves may provide better radar reflections than the boat, and the boat's image on the radar screen could be totally masked by the sea clutter. If the boat is rising and falling among the waves, its radar image may only appear intermittently on the screen.

To help the small-boat owner make his boat a better radar target, a radar reflector should be carried. When carried aloft, the radar detection range of a boat can be increased from a typical two miles, to about five or six miles. The advantages are obvious, for everyday safety and in search and rescue operations.

Any metal object (bucket, fuel can, kitchen foil, etc.), hoisted as high as possible, will increase radar detection range, but a properly constructed radar reflector is cheap and simple to rig. It consists of three metal plates, each at right angles to the other so that eight corner apertures are created. It can be permanently attached at the masthead, or collapsible reflectors are available for simple stowage when not in use. When rigged, the reflector should ideally be in the 'catch-rain' attitude shown here, with one of its apertures pointing skywards.

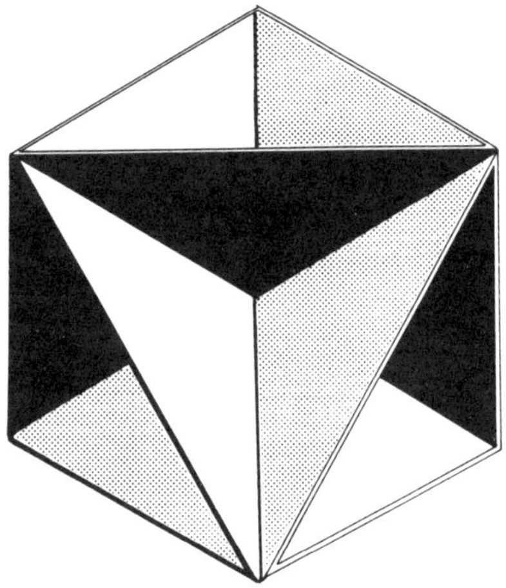

Safety harness

'One hand for the boat and one for yourself' is sound advice, but when working around the boat it is often necessary to get both hands to the job. The safety harness is a webbing body harness, with a length of line terminating in a strong spring clip that can quickly be fastened to a strong point on the boat. If you slip, fall or are washed by a wave, you are still attached to the boat.

Do not make the line fast to a side rail that is not substantial. A stout fore-and-aft safety line should be rigged for the purpose in heavy weather.

Toddlers should wear an attached harness constantly while on the boat, and everyone should wear a harness when on deck at night and in rough weather.

3

FIRE

Ships fear fire more than water.
— Proverb

A fire at sea can be a most terrifying experience. Your surroundings are burning, and you are trapped. You can either stay and fight the fire, or go into the water. The fire brigade is beyond reach; you must be your own fire brigade.

Even in the most efficient boats fires are always a possibility. In a small boat your fire-fighting gear may be limited to one fire extinguisher and a bailer, but their handiness and their condition, together with a rudimentary knowledge of firefighting techniques, could make the vital difference between safety and disaster.

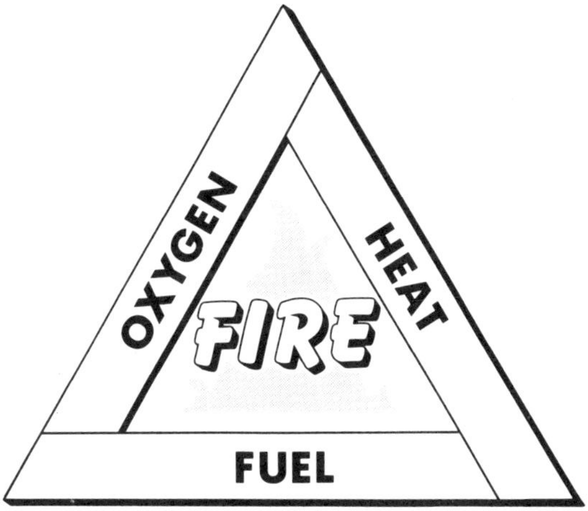

What is a fire?

A fire is a reaction. For this reaction to take place, three elements are necessary: fuel, heat and oxygen. These are often expressed as a fire triangle. Each element forms a side to the triangle, and a fire will only continue to burn as long as the triangle is intact.

There are many materials aboard a boat that constitute a suitable fuel for a fire: petrol, diesel, wood, paintwork, clothing, upholstery, etc. Each of these materials is not necessarily a fire risk on its own, but with the application of heat they will each emit a gas as part of the chemical process of oxidation. In a boat there are several sources of heat, such as the engine, the exhaust system and cooking installations.

At a certain temperature the gas emitted from the fuel, when combined in the right proportions with oxygen from the air, will form a combustible mixture. At this temperature, the flashpoint, the mixture will catch fire if exposed to a naked flame or spark. It is worth remembering that the flashpoint of some petrols is as low as −43°C; in other words, petrol vapours will readily ignite at any temperature above −43° as soon as a flame or spark is introduced. Diesel does not possess this danger; its flashpoint is considerably higher, at between 43 and 88°C.

At a higher temperature is the ignition point, when the mixture of gas and oxygen will ignite on its own without the introduction of a naked light.

The causes of fire

The common causes of fires on small craft are:
— engine backfiring in vapour-laden air;
— electrical short circuit in vapour-laden air;

— naked flames in vapour-laden air;
— hot exhaust pipes igniting surrounding materials;
— cooking stoves igniting surrounding materials;
— spontaneous combustion of oily rags in badly ventilated compartments;
— static electricity discharges during refuelling;
— fuel lines leaking onto hot areas.

There are many other causes. Each can be attributed to some form of oversight or carelessness. In fact, it is probably fair to say that all boat fires are due to three principal causes: men, women and children.

The classes of fire

To make the choice of fire extinguishant and method of extinguishing easier, fires are classified according to the nature of the burning material.

Portable fire extinguishers generally carry a label indicating the class of fire on which they should be used. But be careful, until recently a fire in live electrical equipment was termed a class C fire. If you have an old extinguisher bearing a C label, this may be referring to its suitability on electrical fires, and not necessarily its suitability for gas fires.

Fire extinguishers

Water

May be applied by bucket or bailer from over the side, or by portable extinguisher.

To operate a portable extinguisher, follow the instructions on the extinguisher. Apply as a spray.

Fights the fire by its cooling action.
Suitable for class A fires (burning solids).
Not suitable on class B fires (burning liquids).
Not suitable for use in the presence of electricity.

Foam

To operate, follow the instructions on the extinguisher. Aim the foam at a vertical surface and allow it to slide over the fire without disturbing the liquid; or arch the stream onto the fire.
Fights the fire by smothering with a foam blanket to exclude oxygen.
Suitable for class B fires (burning liquids).
Not suitable for use in the presence of electricity.

Carbon dioxide (CO_2)

To operate, remove the safety pin. Aim at the base of the fire and squeeze the trigger.
Fights the fire by smothering with a blanket of heavier-than-air gas to exclude oxygen.
Suitable for all classes of fire.

Class	*Type of fire*	*Typical sources of such a fire aboard boat*	*Action necessary to fight the fire*	*Suitable extinguishers*
A	A fire involving combustible solid materials of organic nature, normally occurring with the formation of glowing embers.	Wood, fibreglass, paper, clothing, bedding, upholstery, rubber, rope, sails, etc.	Cool by saturation with water, and/or smother to exclude oxygen.	Water CO_2 Multi-purpose dry powder
B	A fire involving burning liquids or liquifiable solids.	Petrol, diesel, engine oils, grease, kerosene, cooking oils and fats, spirits, paints, solvents, etc.	Isolate the fuel supply. Contain the liquid to prevent its spread. Smother to exclude oxygen.	Foam CO_2 Dry powder
C	A fire involving burning gases or liquified gases.	Various liquified petroleum gas systems used to fuel cooking stoves.	Isolate the fuel supply, and then cool and smother the fire.	CO_2
	An electrical fire.	Overloading, or a fault in any wiring or electrical equipment.	Isolate the electrical supply, and then treat as a class 'A' or 'B' fire.	CO_2 Dry powder

Burning material	*Water*	*Foam*	*CO_2*	*Dry powder**
Wood, paper and textiles	Y	N	Y	Y
Upholstery	Y	Y	Y	Y
Oils, fats, petrol, kerosene	N	Y	Y	Y
Engine	N	N	Y	Y
Live electrical equipment	N	N	Y	Y

*Multi-purpose powders only

Dry powder
To operate, remove the safety pin and free the nozzle. Shake the extinguisher. Aim directly at the fire and squeeze the trigger.
Fights the fire by smothering, to exclude oxygen.
Suitable for most classes of fire, depending on the type of powder.

B.C.F.
Although used for many years as an efficient fire extinguishant, the high fluorocarbon content of B.C.F. (bromochlorodifluoromethane) has now made this extinguisher unacceptable under the 1990 Ozone Layer Protection Act. Manufacture of these extinguishers has now ceased and, although existing extinguishers may still be used, they will no longer be serviced or recharged.

Firefighting

To fight a fire, the fire triangle must be broken by eliminating one or more of its three elements; fuel, oxygen and heat.

Starvation of the fire is achieved by removal of the fuel. With burning liquids and gases, prevent any further fuel from reaching the fire by operating the isolating valve.

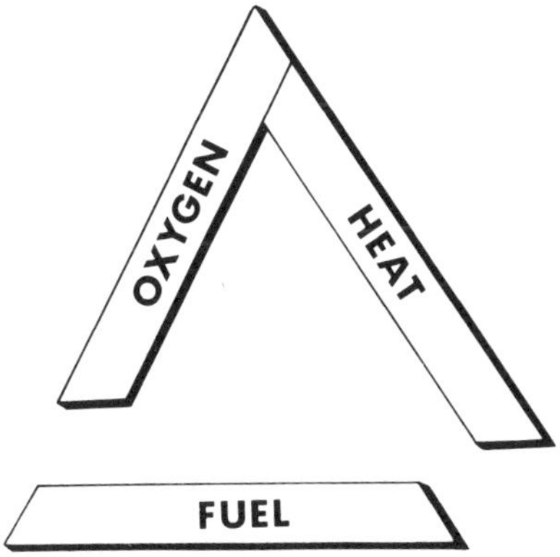

Cooling of the fire will remove its heat. This is best achieved by the application of water, dry powder will also help, to a lesser extent, in reducing temperature.

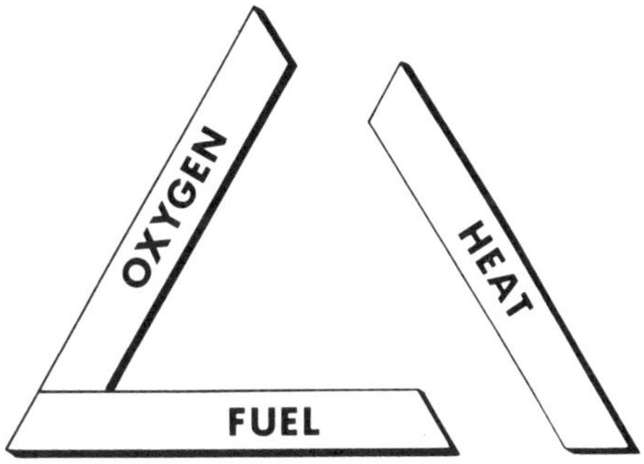

Smothering the fire will prevent the access of oxygen. A foam extinguisher provides a blanket of foam over the fire, and CO_2 extinguishers create a blanket of heavier-than-air CO_2 gas.

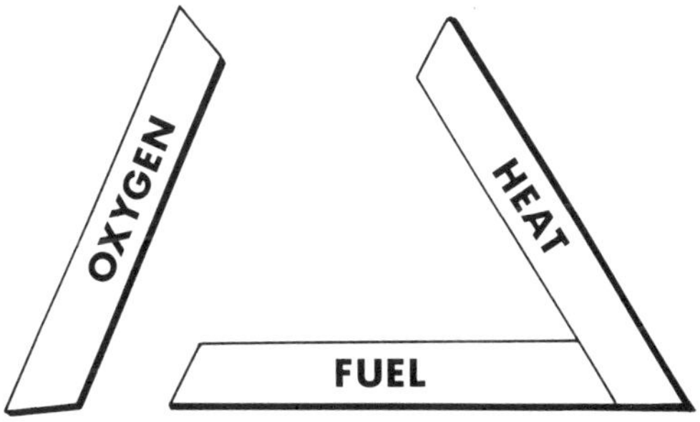

■ Water is plentiful and free. Apply it to the fire with a bucket or bailer, or take the fire to the water by throwing burning cushions and suchlike over the side. (Water brought into the boat for firefighting must also be removed, to prevent loss of the boat's stability.)

■ Water applied to burning liquids will spread the fire rather than extinguish it.

■ Water and foam conduct electricity. Remember to isolate the electrical supply before tackling the fire.

■ CO_2, being a gas, is liable to be blown away by a wind, thus allowing the oxygen back to the fire. Beware of re-ignition. After the fire is extinguished, stand back and be ready to use the extinguisher again.

■ Dry powder may settle in the extinguisher with prolonged stowage. Shake the extinguisher regularly, and before use.

■ Carbon tetrachloride (C.T.C.) extinguishers give off a poisonous gas and are not recommended for use on boats.

■ Attack a fire quickly. The more time you waste, the more hold it will gain.

■ Think before using your extinguisher. Is it suitable for the type of fire? Is the electricity turned off? Is the fuel isolated?

■ Turn the boat so that the fire is downwind from the rest of the boat, and will not spread.

■ Suffocate fires in lockers and ovens by closing the door.

■ Enclosed fires need air. Do not open the door to see how the fire is getting on; it will leap out towards the fresh air.

■ Gas fires should be attacked only after the gas supply has been turned off. If the fire is extinguished and gas is still escaping, an explosion may occur.

■ Fat fires on the cooking stove must not be fought with water. Smother, or use CO_2 or dry powder — but do not let the blast of the extinguisher spill the fat.

■ Upholstery and cushions may emit dangerous fumes when burning, and may smoulder for hours after the fire has apparently been extinguished. Thoroughly soak them, perhaps by putting them overboard.

■ Engine fires should be dealt with after the fuel supply has been isolated.

■ A back-up fire extinguishant should always be available, even if it is only water.

■ Every fire is dangerous, no matter how small. A small fire is only a large fire getting started.

■ Place your extinguishers where they can be seen by all on the boat, and where they can be quickly reached. Do not place an extinguisher on or in an engine compartment, place it nearby. Place an extinguisher near the door to a compartment, not on the side of the compartment opposite to the door.

■ The extinguisher must be stowed where it is visible, and everyone aboard must know its whereabouts. Make sure everyone knows how to release the extinguisher from its bracket, knows how to operate it, and its limitations.

■ In the open air, stand upwind of the fire to use the extinguisher. Beware of re-ignition problems, particularly when using CO_2.

■ An escape route must always be available when fighting a fire. Do not advance into a space through its only entrance, only to find the fire re-igniting behind you.

■ Panic will mask your ability to think clearly. Panic can only be overcome with practice in the use of the boat's firefighting appliances, and practice in firefighting techniques. Hold practice fire drills.

Maintenance

All equipment on a boat requires regular maintenance, none more so than fire extinguishers. Frequently examine the operating head for signs of rust, corrosion, or tampering. If in doubt, return the extinguisher to a servicing centre.

All extinguishers must be refilled immediately after use. This also applies to any extinguisher that has only partially been used, such as a trigger-operated CO_2 or dry powder extinguisher, for they may slowly leak once the gas seal has been broken.

Gas detectors

A common cause of fire and explosion aboard boats is the ignition of fuel vapours. These vapours are heavier than air and accumulate in bilges and other low, unventilated spaces. Some of these gases can be detected by smell, but their presence can also be detected by an electronic gas detector. Detector heads are placed in dangerous accumulation spaces in the boat, and are connected to a central alarm unit, which will warn of dangerous levels of gas. The unit can also be wired to the engine ignition system to prevent starting of the engine if gas is detected. Regular maintenance is required of the detector heads to see that they remain clean.

Gas cooking installations

Cooking-stove installations on boats are usually powered by cylinders of gas. These gases are heavier than air, and any leakage would cause the gas to accumulate in the lower parts of the boat. Naked lights, or a spark from a motor or generator, can cause an explosion if the gas concentration is within certain limits. To reduce this danger:

■ Gas cylinders, including spare and empty cylinders, regulating and relief valves, should be properly secured above deck outside the superstructure and not within the hull.

■ The complete system should be protected from the sun's rays and heat, and be accessible for inspection and maintenance.

■ Cooking systems with continuous-burning pilot lights should not be used.

■ When not in use, the gas should be turned off at the stove and at the cylinder.

■ Adequate bilge ventilation is essential in any compartment where a gas installation is fitted. A small exhaust fan is desirable, providing it is of an approved spark-free type, and should be used before the stove is lit.

Refuelling

Petrol vapours are heavier than air and will find their way to the lower parts of a boat, where a naked light or spark could cause an explosion.

A cupful of petrol that has vaporised in a closed space has the same explosive force as 2.5 kg of dynamite.

When refuelling:

■ Have your boat properly secured fore and aft at the jetty to reduce unnecessary movement.

■ Outboard motors may be refuelled at sea, but the motor must be shut off.

■ Allow no smoking and no naked lights or flames of any kind.

■ Switch off and isolate the stove. There must be no red-hot stove elements.

■ Close all portholes, hatches and doors that could allow access of vapours to the lower parts of the boat.

■ Switch off all electrical equipment at the main isolating switch. Do not throw any switches whilst refuelling.

■ Have a suitable fire extinguisher at hand.

■ If any spillage occurs, wipe it up immediately.

■ Except in emergencies, always refuel in daylight.

■ Maintain metal-to-metal contact between the filling pipe and the filling hose or can, to prevent static electricity sparks.

■ Do not overfill tanks. Allow space for expansion of the fuel.

■ Do not allow children (or adults) to run around the boat. They may rock the boat or trip over the hose and cause a spillage. Send them ashore.

■ Never leave the filling hose unattended. If you have to temporarily stop, return the hose ashore.

When refuelling is completed, close all filling pipes tightly. Wipe up any spillages, and then open up the hatches again. Ventilate the bilges thoroughly for at least five minutes before returning the electrical power and restarting the engine. Use a good through-draught of fresh air and, if fitted, use a proper bilge blower. Before pressing the start button, check the bilge for any smell of petrol.

Enclosed smothering systems

CO_2 cylinders may be fitted permanently within the boat, and connected by a piping system to nozzles placed inside the boat's engine compartment.

The advantage of this firefighting system over portable extinguishers is that the engine compartment can now be flooded with fire-extinguishing gas without the necessity of having to open the compartment and allow the ingress of air.

The system can be remotely operated from the cylinders, which should be installed away from the engine and fuel tanks. Automatic discharge can be achieved by fitting a heat-sensitive trigger device in the engine compartment.

Fire prevention

Good housekeeping is the key to fire prevention. Clean, tidy and well-ventilated spaces are less likely to harbour dangerous vapours, oily rags and fire-hungry rubbish; and if a fire should occur, access to it will be easier.

The engine, its associated fuel arrangements, and the exhaust system are principal fire danger areas. Chapter 7 lists those steps that can be taken to maintain an efficient machinery space, and thereby reduce the risk of fire in these areas.

Fire is your number one enemy. He is both clever and cunning; clever because he will always strike at your weakest point, and cunning because he can strike back just when you think you have him licked. He is an enemy that uses fear as his main tactic, and has a brute force that has no regard for life or property. Your defences against him must be impeccable, and these defences must never be relaxed. You must have the weapons to use against him, always ready for use and where you can reach them.

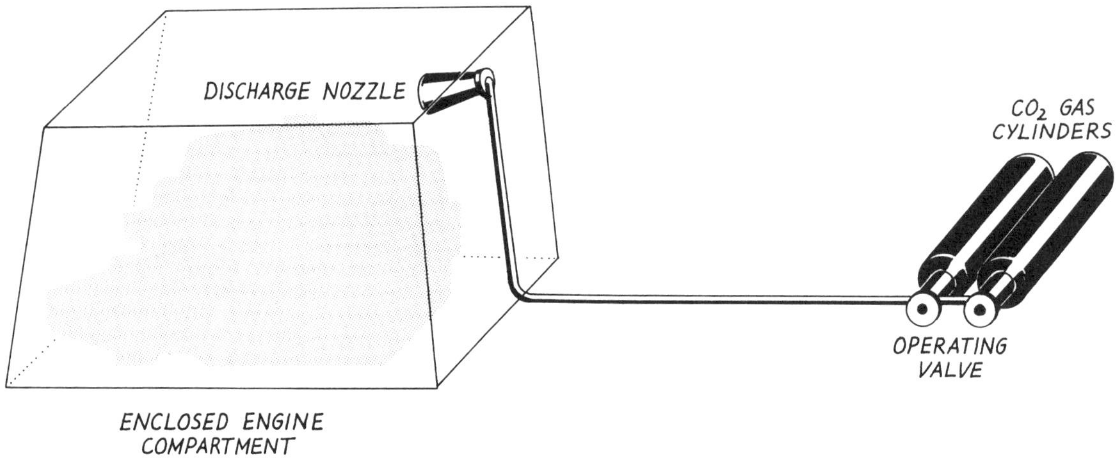

4

NAVIGATION

Where lies the land to which the ship would go!
Far, far ahead, is all her seamen know.
And where the land she travels from? Away,
Far, far behind, is all that they can say.
— Arthur Clough

Navigation is the art of finding the vessel's position at sea, and conducting her safely from place to place. Positions are found by relating to other fixed objects of known position. In coastal navigation these objects are landmarks around the coast, the positions of which are located on charts.

The chart

New Zealand charts are published by the Hydrographic Office of the Royal New Zealand Navy. The *New Zealand Chart Catalogue* contains a complete list of all charts in the New Zealand area.

Latitude

To allow position to be determined as a grid reference, the earth is inscribed with imaginary circles of latitude and longitude. A circle of latitude will always cross a circle of longitude at right angles.

The circles of latitude are parallel to the Equator. Each parallel is named as an angle, the angle being measured at the earth's centre between the Equator and that parallel. Latitude is named north or south depending upon hemisphere. Thus the latitude of the Equator is 0° and the North and South Poles are 90°N and 90°S respectively. New Zealand is in south latitude.

To enable more accuracy in measurement, each degree is divided into 60 minutes, and into decimals of a minute. On a chart the parallels of latitude run horizontally across the chart, with the scale of latitude running down the left- and right-hand borders.

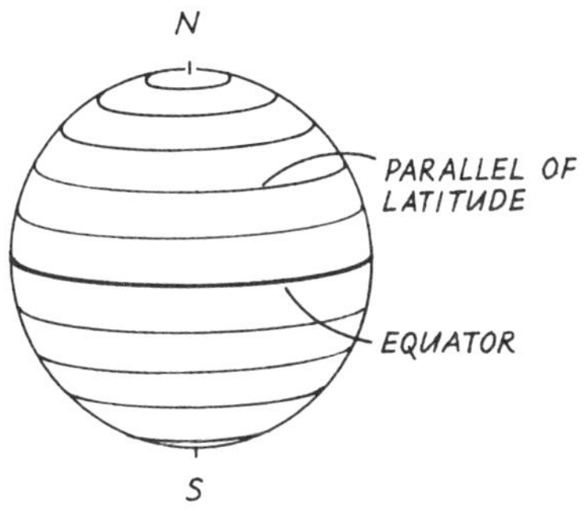

Longitude

The meridians of longitude run north/south, each passing through the earth's North and South Poles. Longitude is measured as an angle at the earth's centre between the meridian

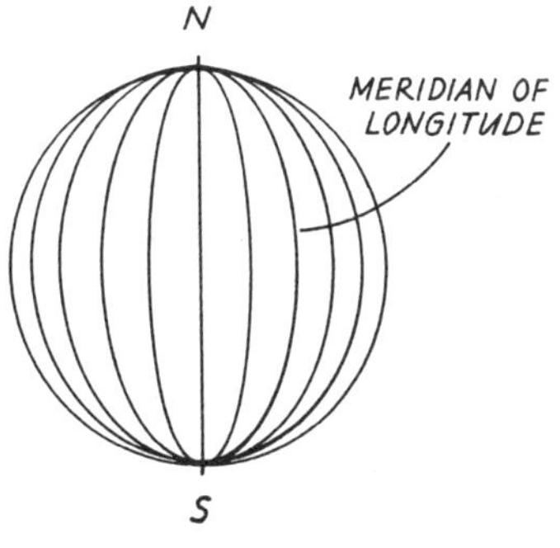

Chart symbols

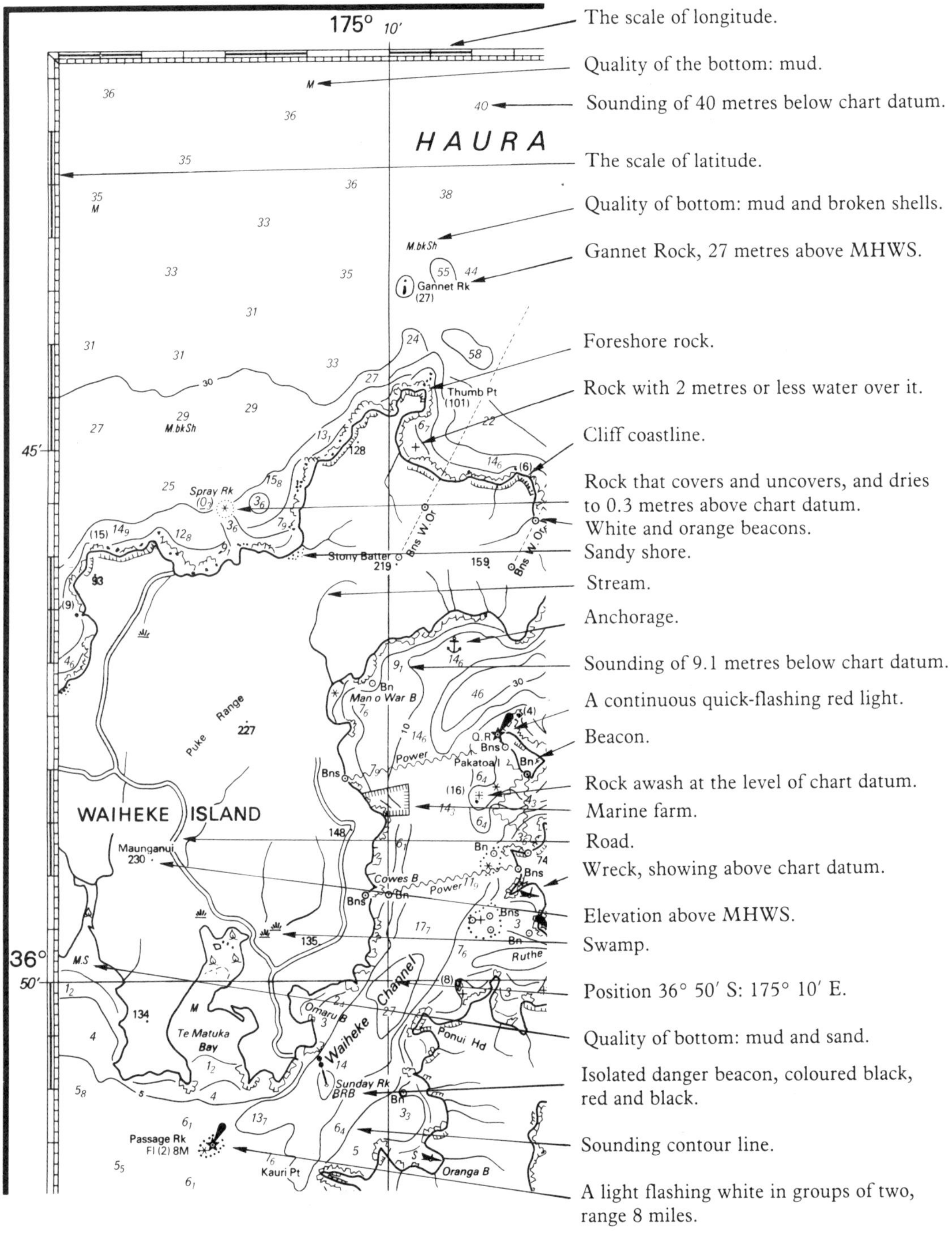

passing through Greenwich and the meridian passing through the particular place. Longitude is named east or west according to which side of Greenwich the meridian lies. New Zealand is in longitude east.

As with latitude, longitude can be expressed more accurately in degrees, minutes, and decimals of a minute. The meridians of longitude run vertically down a chart, with the longitude scale across the top and bottom borders of the chart.

Projection

To represent a curved portion of the earth on a flat chart, the Mercator projection is generally used for coastal charts. On a Mercator chart the lines of latitude and longitude cross at right angles, as they do on the earth's surface, so that direction can be correctly displayed.

Scale

The scale of a chart is the ratio between a length measured on the chart and a corresponding length measured on the earth's surface. A small-scale chart is one that covers a large area, like the Tasman Sea. On such a chart, fine detail cannot be shown. A large-scale chart is one covering a small area and on which a large amount of detail can be shown. When close inshore, a good navigator will always navigate on the largest scale chart available.

Correcting the chart

Changes are constantly taking place along our coastlines. To enable us to keep our charts up to date, any chart ammendment is issued by the Hydrographic Office as a *Notice to Mariners*. These notices are numbered consecutively through the year, and published weekly in booklet form. After correcting your chart as directed by the notice, a record of that correction should be made at the bottom left-hand corner of the chart by noting the year and the notice number.

Datums of measurement

Since the level of the sea is constantly changing, a fixed datum from which to measure depths is chosen. This is known as chart datum. For safety reasons, chart datum is chosen to be so low that the tide seldom, if ever, falls below it. It is frequently Lowest Astronomical Tide. The heights of tides in the tide tables are given above chart datum (except if the tabulated height is preceded by a minus sign), while the depths of water, or soundings, are given on the chart below chart datum. Total depth of water is found by summing the tide table height of tide to the charted depth.

Banks and shoals that dry at chart datum but are covered at high water have their drying heights underlined on the chart and are measured above chart datum.

For similar safety reasons, heights of land features are given above a high-water level, Mean High Water Springs (MHWS).

Lights

The lights and beacons around our coasts provide the navigational landmarks we need for position fixing at night. Each light displays a distinctive pattern, which is indicated on the chart. To identify a light at night, carefully watch its light pattern, and time this pattern to identify its period (see page 52).

To avoid cluttering the coastal chart with too much detail, only the most important features of a light may be given. A larger scale chart must then be consulted. Complete details of all lights around the New Zealand coasts are listed in the *New Zealand Nautical Almanac.*

Light sectors

Coloured sectors are sometimes used in port approaches to inform a navigator whether he is in the centre of a channel. A change of colour of a light may inform that he has strayed too far off the centre of the channel. Many coastal lights also have coloured sectors to indicate dangerous areas. Light sectors are always indicated on a chart, together with information about the light.

Datums of measurement

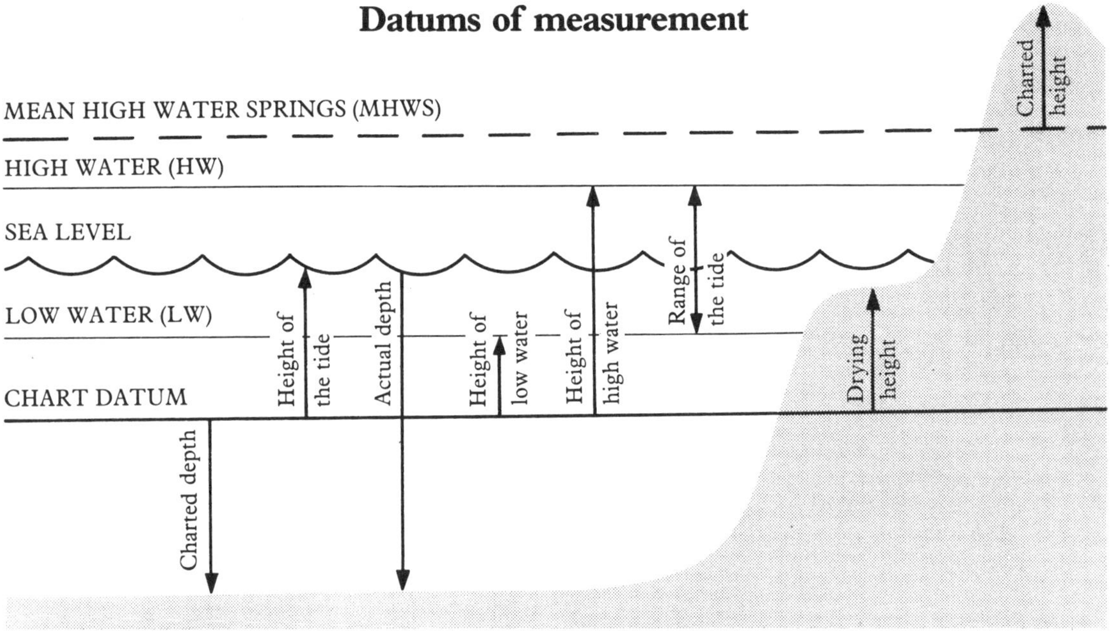

Light characteristics

Class of Light	*Charted abbreviation*
Fixed	F
Flashing	Fl
Group-flashing	Fl(2)
Group-flashing	Fl(3)
Composite group-flashing	Fl(2+1)
Long-flashing	L Fl
Occulting	Oc
Group-occulting	Oc(2)
Morse code	Mo (A)
Isophase	Iso
Quick-flashing	Q
Group quick-flashing	Q(3)
Quick- and long-flashing	Q(6)+L Fl
Alternating	Al. WR

Note: All charted lights are white unless stated otherwise.

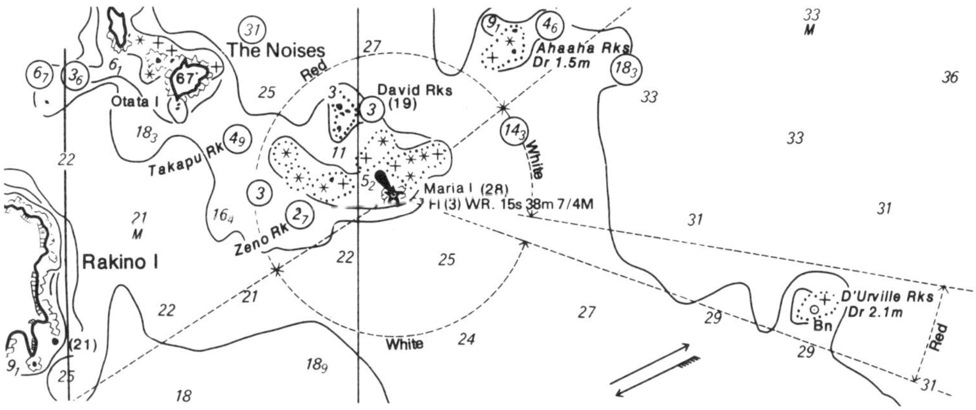

A sectored light

Maria Island light flashes in groups of threes every 15 seconds. The light will appear white or red according to the sector in which the boat lies. The light is 38 metres above Mean High Water Springs. The white light has a nominal range of 7 miles, and the red light a nominal range of 4 miles.

Measurement of distance and speed

The standard distance measurement used for navigation is the distance represented on the earth's surface by one minute of latitude. This is known as the nautical mile. Because of the irregular shape of the earth, a mean value of 1852 metres has been adopted as the international nautical mile.

1 nautical mile = 1 minute of latitude
= 1852 metres
= 1.852 kilometres
= 6076 feet
= 1.15 land miles

Distance is measured on the chart along the latitude scale (down the left- or right-hand border), or from the special distance scales drawn on some large-scale charts. Never measure distance along the longitude scale.

The unit for measurement of speed is the knot. One knot is one nautical mile per hour. (It is incorrect to say 'knots per hour'.)

Measurement of direction

A course is the direction in which the boat is heading, as indicated by the compass lubber line.

A bearing is the direction of anything from the boat.

If directions are related to True North, the course is a true course and bearings are true bearings. If related to Magnetic North, the course is a magnetic course and bearings are magnetic bearings. If related to Compass North, the course is a compass course and bearings are compass bearings.

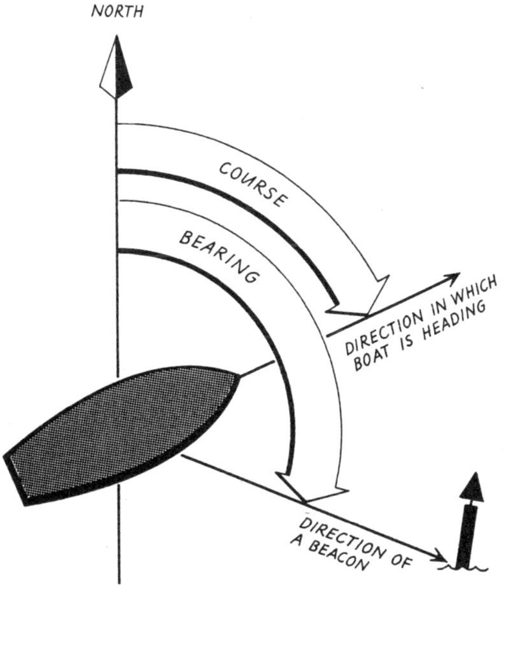

Variation

The magnetic compass relies on the earth's magnetic field for its directional properties, but the poles of this field do not coincide with the earth's true (geographic) poles.

At present the North Magnetic Pole is situated in the vicinity of Hudson Bay, in Canada. In New Zealand waters a magnetic compass will therefore point to a direction to the right of True North.

The angle between the direction of True North and Magnetic North is called variation. It will vary from place to place and may be named east or west. In New Zealand variation is always easterly, because the direction of Magnetic North is to the east of True North.

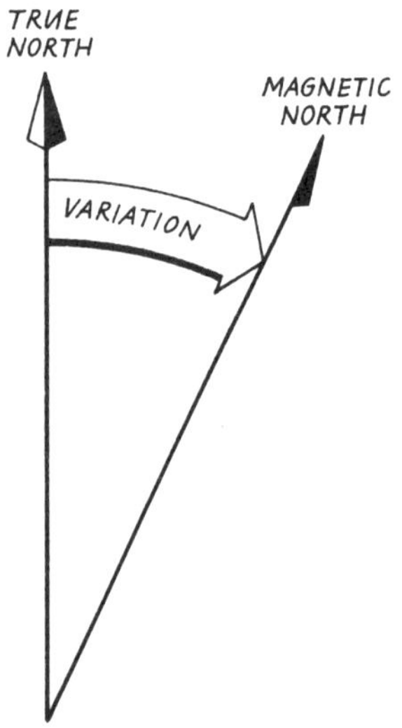

Due to the wandering of the North Magnetic Pole, the angle of variation changes. The value of the variation for a particular place, and its annual change, is noted across the compass rose on the chart.

Deviation

In addition to responding to the earth's magnetic field, the compass will also respond to other magnetic fields in its vicinity. Aboard a boat there are many stray magnetic fields, caused by equipment and fittings, any of which may affect the compass. Deflections of the compass caused by the boat and its equipment is called deviation.

If the compass is deflected to the right of Magnetic North, deviation is named east and must be added to any compass reading to obtain a magnetic direction; or subtracted from a magnetic direction to obtain a compass reading.

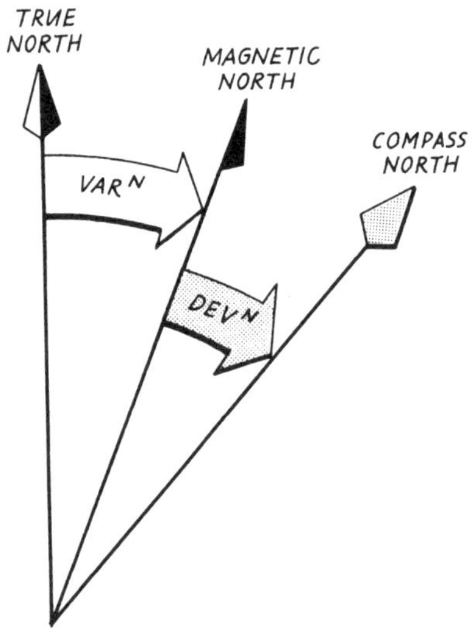

If the compass is deflected to the left of Magnetic North, deviation is named west and must be subtracted from any compass reading to obtain a magnetic direction, or added to a magnetic direction to obtain a compass reading.

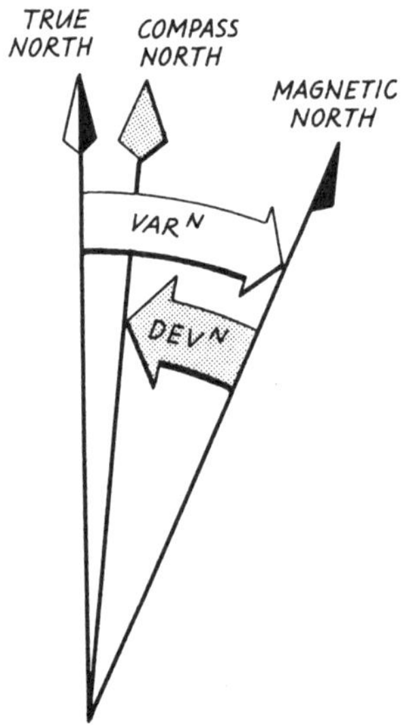

The effects of deviation will vary from boat to boat, and will also vary with the direction in which the boat is heading.

The value of deviation may be found by a compass adjuster, and recorded on a deviation card on which the deviations are tabulated against compass courses.

If deviations are known, they can be allowed for. If unknown, you must bear in mind that they always exist and compass readings must be treated with appropriate caution.

The combined effect of variation and deviation is the compass error, the total deflection of the compass from True North. A method of checking the compass error is by transits, explained on page 58.

Fixing position

Many methods are available for determining position, including electronic position-fixing equipment. The most practical method aboard a small boat is by plotting bearings taken with a hand-bearing compass.

If two or more simultaneous bearings are taken of known landmarks and plotted on the chart, the boat's position is at the intersection of the bearings. Always note the time of the fix.

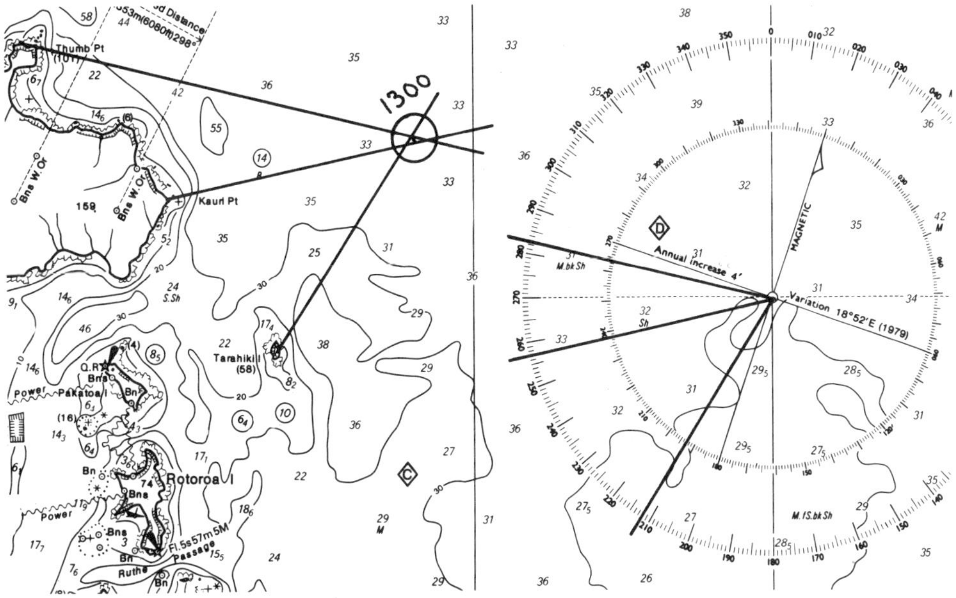

Fixing position by bearings

At 1300, using a hand-bearing compass, the bearing of Thumb Point is found to be 264° magnetic; the bearing of Kauri Point is found to be 238° magnetic; and the bearing of Tarahiki Island is found to be 193° magnetic.

Variation for 1979 = 18° 52′ E (from compass rose)
Increase in 8 years 8 × 4′ = + 32′
Variation for 1987 = 19° 24′ E (19° E to the nearest degree)

	Thumb Pt.	*Kauri Pt.*	*Tarahiki Is.*	
Magnetic bearings	264°	238°	193°	(Inner compass rose)
Variation	19° E	19° E	19° E	
True bearings	283°	257°	212°	(Outer compass rose)

These directions are plotted on the compass rose and transferred to their respective landmarks with parallel rules. The boat's position is at the intersection of the three bearings.

Recording position

Whenever it is necessary to record your position or to indicate your position to someone else, there are two accepted methods.

Bearing and distance is the preferred method when you are inshore or close to the coast. Position is given as a true or magnetic bearing and distance from a landmark. Choose a conspicuous, well-known landmark for your reference position, and state whether the bearing is true or magnetic and whether the bearing is *to* the landmark or *from* the landmark. The latter is preferable.

You should practise estimating distances at sea, so that you can state your distance as accurately as possible.

The latitude and longitude method is used when you are offshore and no convenient landmarks are available. Position is given as a latitude and longitude grid reference.

Plotting a course

A line marking the intended route to be taken is drawn on the chart from the boat's position to her destination. The chart must be carefully checked for any dangers and for sufficient depth of water on or in the vicinity of the course line. If considered safe, the course is then transferred to the compass rose with parallel rulers, and the course is read from the rose. Allowance for variation, and deviation if known, is made and the course noted on the chart alongside the course line. Distance along the track is measured from the latitude scale (at the side of the chart) in nautical miles.

Tidal streams

Most charts carry detailed information about currents and tidal streams in the area. One or more tidal stream positions may be located on the chart, and by using tide tables and the reference table on the chart, the direction and rate of the stream can be calculated for any given time.

Remember that tidal stream information is approximate only. Directions and rates of the streams may be seriously affected by weather conditions existing at the time.

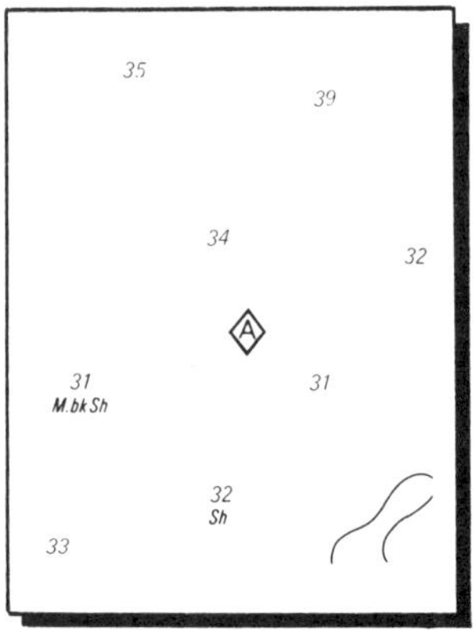

Tidal Streams referred to HW at AUCKLAND

Hours		Ⓐ Lat 36°46′S Long 175 18 E		
		Directn	Rate (Knots) Sp	Np
Before HW	6	142°	0.2	0.1
	5	191	0.3	0.2
	4	185	0.5	0.3
	3	180	0.6	0.4
	2	173	0.5	0.3
	1	151	0.3	0.2
HW			Slack	Slack
After HW	1	021	0.3	0.2
	2	358	0.5	0.3
	3	353	0.6	0.4
	4	356	0.5	0.3
	5	359	0.4	0.3
	6	098	0.3	0.2

From the chart

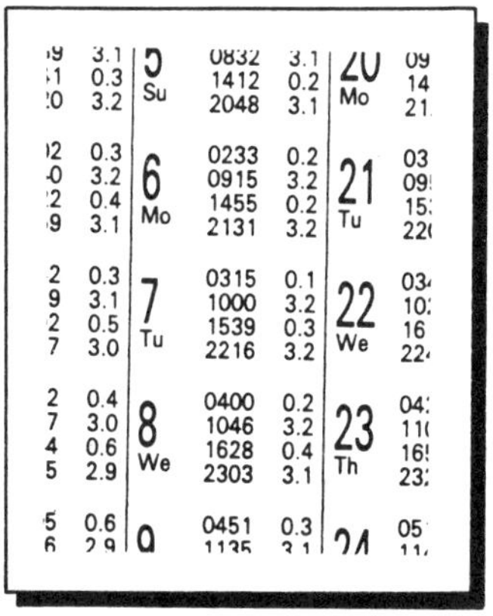

5 Su	1412	0.2
	2048	3.1
6 Mo	0233	0.2
	0915	3.2
	1455	0.2
	2131	3.2
7 Tu	0315	0.1
	1000	3.2
	1539	0.3
	2216	3.2
8 We	0400	0.2
	1046	3.2
	1628	0.4
	2303	3.1
9	0451	0.3

From the tide tables

At Auckland, the port of reference, on *Tuesday 7th* high water is at 1000 with a height of 3.2 metres. Elsewhere in the tide tables we are informed that at Auckland 3.2m is a *spring* tide.
At 1000 (*HW*) the tidal stream at 'A' will be slack.
At 0900 (*1 hour before HW*) the tidal stream at 'A' will be setting 151° true at 0.3 knots.
At 1200 (*2 hours after HW*) the tidal stream at 'A' will be setting 358° true at 0.5 knots.

Monitoring the boat's progress

If the boat's position is fixed at frequent intervals, progress is recorded on the chart and any effects of wind, tide and errors of the compass will become evident. When the boat is shown to be wandering progressively from the required course line, course can be adjusted in the opposite direction to compensate for this drift.

By measuring the distance travelled between fixes, the boat's speed can be assessed. Intervals between fixes should be regular for this reason. Depending on the closeness to the shore, chart scale and the boat's speed, fixes at 15, 20 or 30 minutes should be used.

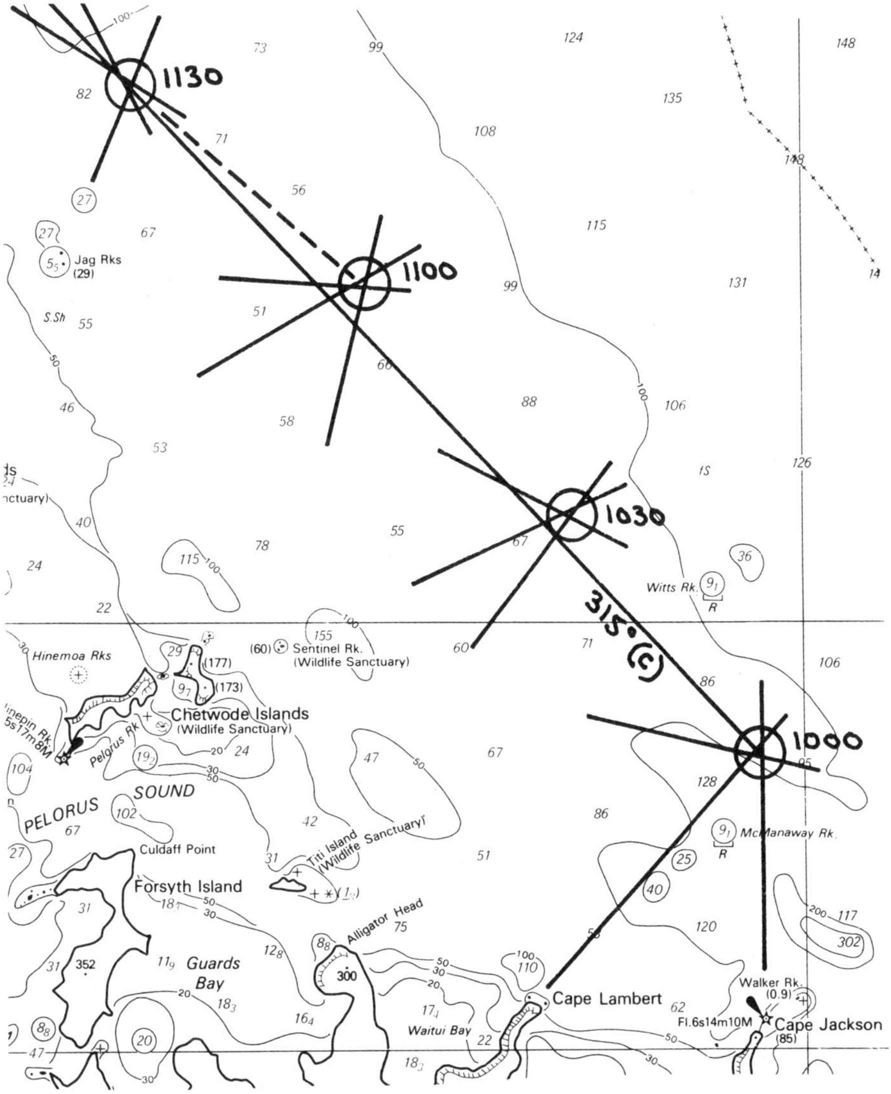

Monitoring the boat's progress

Position is fixed by bearings at 1000 and a compass course of 315° is set towards the boat's destination. Fixes at 1030 and 1100 show the boat to be drifting progressively off her courseline, and at 1100 course is adjusted to bring the boat back to her original course line.

Transits

When two landmarks are in line with each other, they are in transit. A transit provides an excellent position line on the chart, and can also be used as a quick check on the compass.

If the compass bearing is taken of the objects in transit and compared with the true bearing as found from the chart, the difference is the compass error.

Clearing marks

Fixed landmarks that are clearly visible can be used to guide you clear of dangers that may not be visible. The landmarks used are clearing marks, and are ideally objects that are in transit. Clearing marks may be shown on a chart, or may be selected by the navigator for his own use.

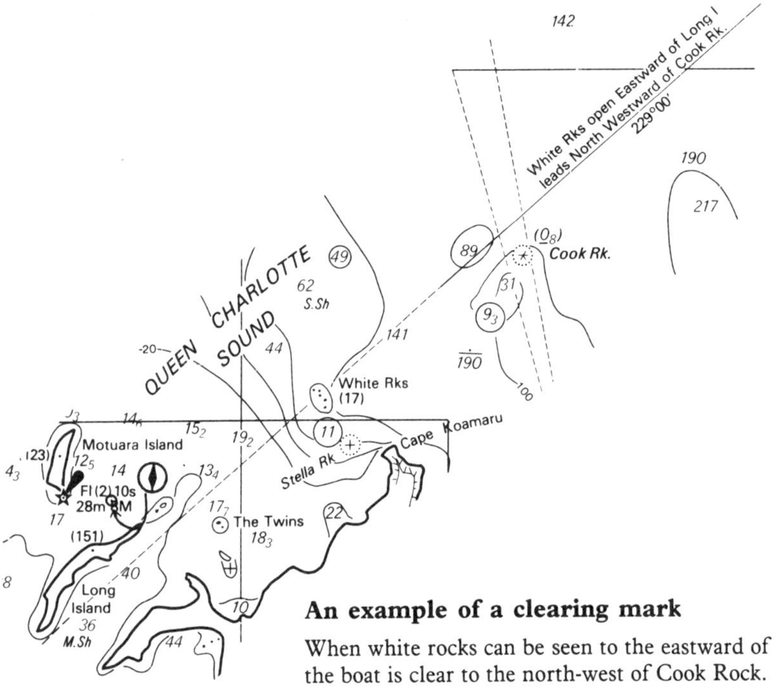

An example of a clearing mark

When white rocks can be seen to the eastward of Long Island, the boat is clear to the north-west of Cook Rock.

5

THE WEATHER

A wet sheet and a flowing sea,
A wind that follows fast
And fills the white and rustling sail
And bends the gallant mast.
— Allan Cunningham

More than any other factor the weather will determine whether your boat trip will be pleasant or unpleasant. A simple knowledge of meteorology, and of how to obtain information about the weather, is therefore necessary — not only to make your boating pleasant but to keep it safe.

Pressure systems

Air will move from an area of higher pressure towards an area of lower pressure. As the air moves we feel this movement as a wind, but its movement will also cause changes to occur within the air: it may cool down or heat up; it may increase or decrease its humidity; it may become unstable and begin to rise to form large masses of cloud, or it may remain at the same level and form sheets of cloud.

An important feature of a weather map is therefore the distribution of pressure areas, for once the locality of the pressure systems is known it is possible to trace the history of the air and determine the weather it is bringing with it and to predict how the air will move and modify in the future, and the type of weather that will result.

Isobars

An isobar is a line on a weather map joining places of equal pressure, hence revealing areas of high and low pressure in much the same way as map contours show areas of high and low ground. Atmospheric pressure is measured in hectopascals (hPa) or in millibars (mb); the units have identical values.

Owing to the earth's rotation, the flow of air is not directly from an area of high pressure to an area of low pressure, but in a circular motion that gives a flow almost parallel to the isobars.

Anticyclones

An anticyclone is an area of high pressure and is shown on a weather map as a series of closed and ascending isobars. In the Southern Hemisphere the wind blows anticlockwise around an anticyclone, the wind angling slightly outwards across the isobars.

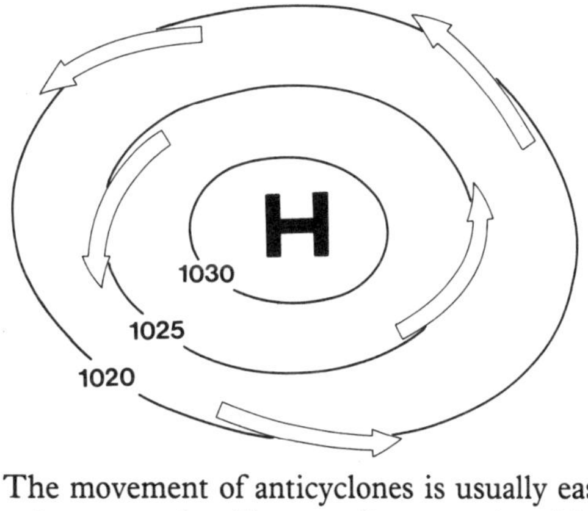

The movement of anticyclones is usually eastwards across the Tasman Sea, crossing New Zealand at intervals of about seven days. At their centres they bring fine weather with warm sunny days but cooler nights; winds are light and variable.

Depressions

A depression is an area of low pressure and is shown on weather maps as a system of closed and descending isobars. The isobars are usually closer together than those of an anticyclone. In the Southern Hemisphere the winds blow clockwise around a depression, the wind angling slightly inwards across the isobars.

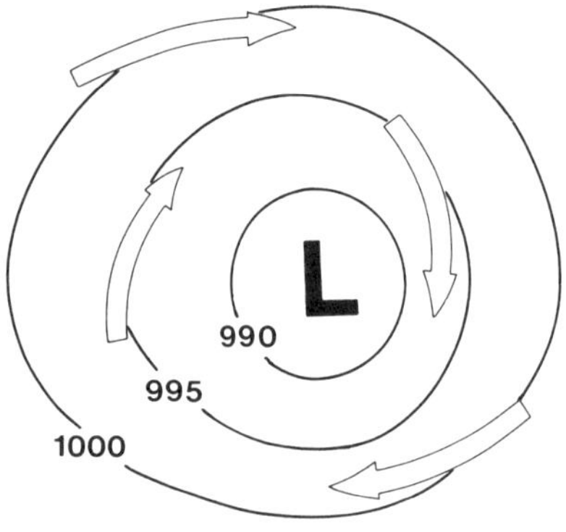

Depressions also generally move eastwards, positioned between the anticyclones. As a depression approaches, the sky will cloud over and rain will usually commence. As the depression passes, the rain may ease to intermittent showers or may cease altogether.

The barometer

The instrument used to measure atmospheric pressure is the barometer. Of particular interest is how the barometer is moving, and in this respect is a valuable weather-forecasting tool. If the barometer moves up (rising), an anticyclone is approaching; if it moves down (falling), a depression is approaching.

The wind

Wind direction is governed by the isobars, as shown above, but there is also a definite relationship between the spacing of the isobars and the strength of the wind. The closer the isobars, the greater the pressure difference, and so the stronger will be the wind.

Wind directions are given in compass points, according to the direction *from* which the wind is blowing. Thus a northerly is coming from the north.

As pressure systems move across land or sea, the direction of the wind that is being experienced will alter. The wind *backs* when it changes in an anticlockwise direction (for example, if the wind changes direction from north to north-west). The wind *veers* if it changes in a clockwise direction (for example, from north to north-east).

Wind speeds may be given in knots, or as a wind force as determined by the Beaufort wind scale.

Wind gusts

Wind speeds are not constant. Airflows that are disturbed by the shape of the land, such as when eddying around headlands, hills and ranges, or when funnelling through straits, valleys or gorges, will fluctuate considerably in strength.

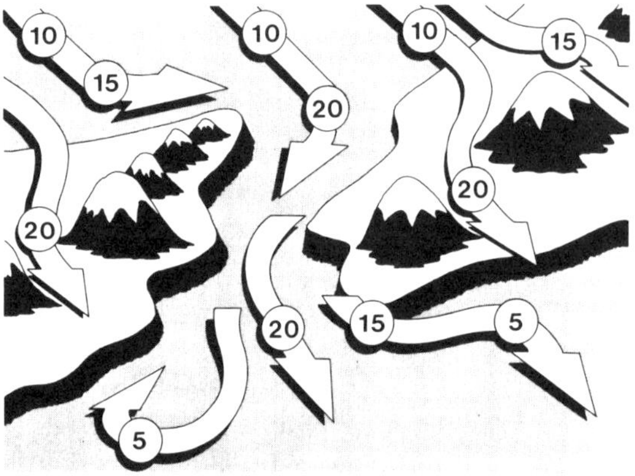

Some areas will experience increases in wind strengths, as gusts; other areas may experience lulls. Wind directions will also be affected. In strong wind conditions, beware of gusts on the leeward side of high land.

Fronts

The circular motion of air around anticyclones and depressions brings cold air from polar regions towards the north, and warm air from tropical regions towards the south. A front is the boundary between air masses that have come from different regions.

A warm front occurs where warmer air is advancing and displacing colder air. The advancing warmer air slides gently over the colder air, and as it does so, cools to form a vast area of layer (stratus) cloud. Light persistent rain may fall from the thicker areas of the lower cloud.

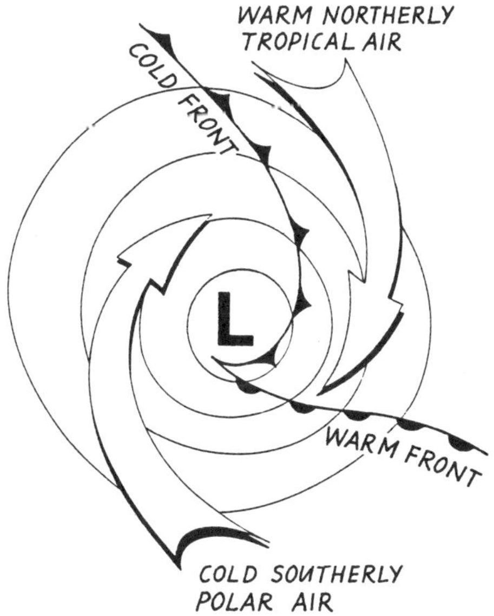

As the front approaches, the cloud level will progressively lower, and as the cloud thickens the likelihood of rain will increase. The passage of the front will bring a rise in temperature, and the rain may then ease or cease altogether.

A cold front occurs where colder air is advancing and displacing warmer air. The colder air undercuts and lifts the warmer air vertically to form heaped clouds (cumulus or cumulonimbus), which can produce heavy rain and perhaps hail and thunder.

An approaching cold front can be detected by a falling barometer, and its arrival is heralded by the towering cloud, often dark in colour and appearing to roll towards you across the surface. Squalls may be present just before the front and its accompanying rain arrives. The passage of the front is marked by a sharp fall in temperature, more noticeable than the change of temperature experienced at the warm front. The front may pass fairly rapidly, and the heavy rain may then clear to isolated showers.

Advance of a warm front

Advance of a cold front

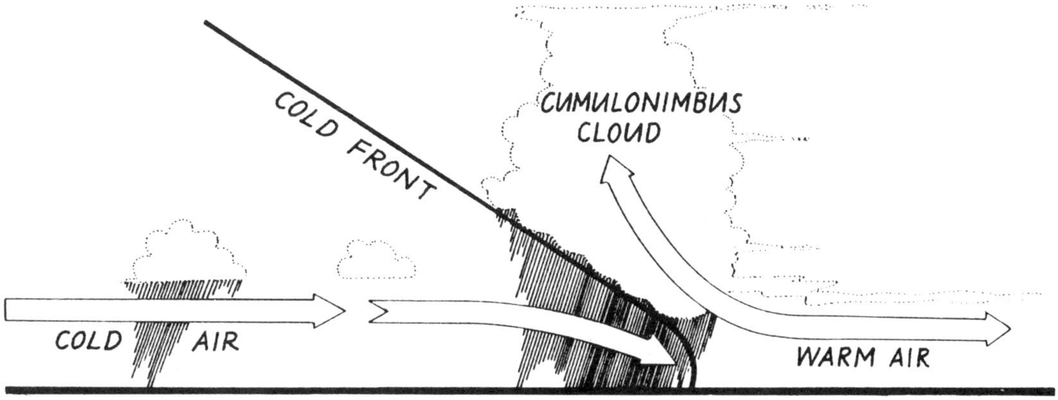

Reduced visibility

Visibility may be reduced at any time because of rain, drizzle, mist, fog or haze. Fog and mist each result from the air being cooled below its condensation temperature through a variety of reasons.

Radiation fog

This occurs over the land at night in the calm conditions of an anticyclone. With clear, cloudless skies and little or no wind, the atmosphere cools rapidly, which may be sufficient to condense out the water vapour in the air. The likelihood of fog is increased if the ground is wet, as is often the case in valleys, riverbeds, or swamps.

Essentially a land fog, it may however drift over the sea but is short-lived and usually disperses with the arrival of the morning sun.

Advection fog

This occurs when warm air passes over a surface sufficiently cool to condense out the water vapour. It may be experienced over the land or sea in spring and summer when air moves from the warmer land to the colder sea; or in winter when warmer air moves over a colder land or sea surface. Unlike radiation fog, advection fog can be quite persistent.

Land and sea breezes

The wind patterns formed by anticyclones and depressions may be modified around the coasts by temperature differences that develop between the air over the sea and the air over the land.

Wind strengths will depend on the wind conditions prevailing before modification. The winds set up may increase the strength of the prevailing wind, or may oppose the prevailing wind to give calmer conditions.

By day, particularly under the clear skies of an anticyclone, the land will heat more rapidly than the sea. The warmed air over the land rises, and cooler air moves in from the sea to replace it.

This is the sea breeze, often setting in before midday. Winds of up to 20 or 30 knots may be produced, which may affect conditions up to

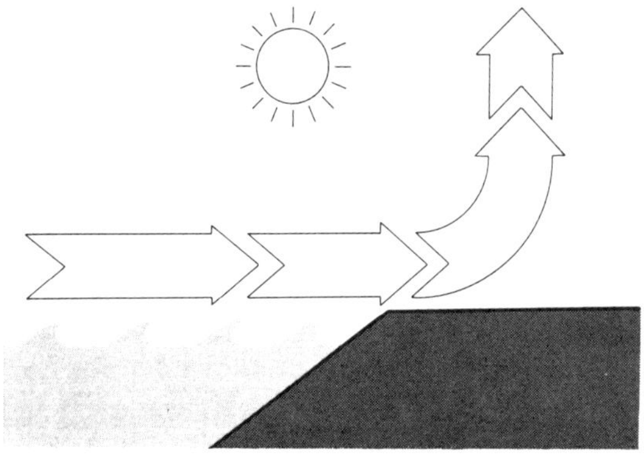

SEA BREEZE

about 20 miles off the coast, but these will rapidly die away after sunset.

At night the land may cool more rapidly than the sea. The cooled air over the land descends and flows out over the sea to displace the warmer air there. This is a land breeze. It is less noticeable than the sea breeze, and does not reach the same strength.

LAND BREEZE

Katabatic winds

On cloudless nights, such as during anticyclonic conditions, the land cools rapidly and thereby cools the air over the land surface. On steep-sided coasts, hillsides and valleys, the denser cold air flows down the slope under the influence of gravity. This cold flow of air down the slopes is a katabatic wind.

On steep-sided coasts, and where mountain valleys stretch down towards the coast, strong winds and gusts can be expected that may extend

KATABATIC BREEZE

well to seawards. Such winds are most noticeable at night, but may set in shortly after the sun loses its afternoon heat.

Weather forecasts

Most of New Zealand's weather approaches from the west. A study of a weather map of the area to the west will give an indication of what is to come, and this can be verified by watching the barometer.

On-the-spot forecasting has its merits, and one should learn to recognise the symptoms of an approaching depression or front, but this should never substitute for a professional forecast.

Obtain a forecast before you put to sea, and while at sea continue to monitor the weather by observing the barometer and the sky, and by listening to the marine forecasts. However, never forget that a forecast is simply a prediction of what is expected to happen — not a guarantee.

Form of forecasts

Each marine forecast is broadcast in a certain format:

(1) *Time of issue.* This is the time the forecast was issued by the weather office, not the time it is broadcast.

(2) *Warnings.* If existent, warnings are always given preceding the general forecast. The warning may be a

— gale warning (winds of force 8 or 9);

— storm warning (winds of force 10, 11 or 12);

— hurricane warning (tropical cyclone with winds of force 12);

— squall warning, to warn of the sudden onset of strong winds which may exceed gale force for a few minutes only;

— strong wind warning, to warn of wind gusts of 33 knots or greater.

(3) *Situation.* A general description of the pressure arrangement over the area, and the localities of the various weather systems.

(4) *Area forecasts.* Forecasts for each area are given, predicting the weather usually for a period of 18 hours. The areas are given in anticlockwise order. Radio New Zealand broadcasts start in the North Island with Plenty, finishing with Nick. The South Island areas start with Foulwind and finish with Clarence and then Chatham.

(5) *Outlook.* A brief prediction for a further 18 hours following the forecasted period.

Obtaining a forecast

Weather forecasts are available from a number of sources:

■ Radio New Zealand and private radio stations frequently conclude their news bulletins with weather forecasts. Times of broadcasts, and the stations and radio frequencies on which the broadcasts are made, are listed in the *Listener.*

■ Weather forecasts are given continuously or at scheduled times on VHF and radiotelephone from certain Coastguard and marine radio stations. Times, channels and radio frequencies of these broadcasts are listed in the latest edition of the *New Zealand Nautical Almanac.*

■ Recorded telephone forecasts are available through the Coastal MetPhone service, an 0900 service provided by Telecom. Telephone numbers for each coastal area are given in the *New Zealand Nautical Almanac*, and details of local weather forecasts by telephone will be found in your local telephone directory.

■ Weather maps and land area forecasts are given daily on television following certain news programmes. Details of broadcast times are in the *Listener.* Area forecasts are also provided through the Teletext service.

■ Many local and national newspapers carry a weather map and forecasts, but remember these forecasts are generally for land areas and may be many hours out of date.

■ Radio facsimile transmissions of weather maps may be obtained if a radio fax receiver is fitted aboard the boat. Details and frequencies of transmissions are given in the *New Zealand Nautical Almanac*, and a schedule of transmissions is broadcast twice daily or is available from Met-Service.

New Zealand weather forecast areas

The New Zealand coast is divided into 23 areas, each extending to about 30 miles from the land.

Coastal weather forecast areas

Areas are named by recognised coastal features.

6

THE SEA

Roll on, thou deep and dark blue Ocean — roll!
— Lord Byron

Whether your boating or allied water sport is done on, in or under the sea, a knowledge of the sea's behaviour will go a long way towards ensuring that your activities will be safer. The condition of the sea, together with its movement, is frequently a direct result of the weather, and an understanding of how weather and water interact with each other is necessary for those who go to sea.

Waves

When the wind blows over the water, it imparts energy into the surface layers of the water to create waves; driving them in the same direction as the wind, and gradually increasing their size. As the wave grows, the crests become more pointed and the troughs more rounded until a height is reached that is dependent upon the wind speed. Waves that are caused directly by the wind are called sea.

The greater the wind speed, and the greater the distance over which the wind has blown to create the waves (known as the wind's fetch), the larger the waves will be. Wave heights and lengths are expressed in metres, but wave height may also be given as a descriptive term, used internationally, to describe waves of given heights.

Descriptive term	*Average height of larger well-formed waves*
Calm (glassy)	0 metres
Calm (rippled)	Up to 0.1 m
Smooth (wavelets)	0.1–0.5 m
Slight	0.5–1.25 m
Moderate	1.25–2.5 m
Rough	2.5–4 m
Very rough	4–6 m

The direction of the wind will eventually change, as it curves around a high- or low-pressure area. Or the wind may decrease in strength and perhaps eventually die altogether. However, once generated, a wave will continue in more or less the same direction. Waves generated by a wind that is no longer with them, and approaching upon a local area, are known as swell.

Without their supply of energy from the wind, swell waves will gradually weaken, but can nevertheless travel tremendous distances before

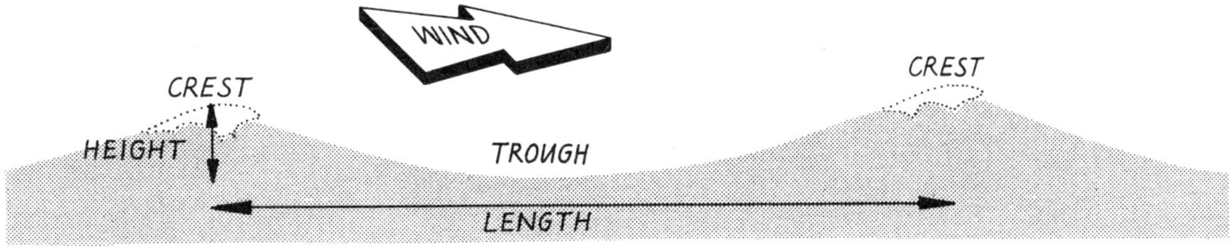

finally disappearing. While travelling they assume a lower, longer form. Swell waves tend to have less steep sides and longer wavelengths than sea waves. Different descriptive terminology is used to indicate swell heights.

Descriptive term	*Average height from trough to crest of well-formed swell waves*
Low swell	0–2 m
Moderate swell	2–4 m
Heavy swell	Over 4 m

Wave interaction

The sea surface is composed of numerous wave trains, each combining and intermixing to form new wave trains. Wave heights are therefore rarely uniform. Where wave crests coincide, a wave of greater height is formed; where a crest coincides with a trough, a smaller wave results. In this way, waves are usually found to travel in groups, some larger than average, some smaller than average. It is possible for these groups to combine to produce, on rare occasions, exceptionally large waves.

If sea and swell waves are travelling in the same direction they will superimpose and combine to form longer waves, interspersed with occasional breaking waves. If travelling in different directions, a more confused sea surface results. If travelling in opposite directions, a more 'choppy' sea develops, giving shorter waves that are steeper sided with a greater tendency to break.

If the sea or swell runs with a current or tidal stream, longer waves will be produced. If the current or tidal flow runs in a direction opposite to the waves, a shorter choppier sea will form, with increased wave heights and steeper sided waves travelling at slower speeds.

The motion of the water

If you watch a piece of flotsam you will see it move up and down as the waves pass, but it will move only very slightly forwards. This is because waves are not so much a movement of water itself, but rather a disturbance moving *through* the water. A closer look at the flotsam will show that its movement is actually circular.

On the crest of the wave the flotsam moves in the same direction as the wave, but in the trough it moves back in the opposite direction. The flotsam is prescribing a circular orbit, completing each orbit in the period taken for each wave to pass. This same orbital motion is prescribed by each particle of water in the wave, and explains many maritime phenomena.

Surf

As waves move into shallower water, friction with the seabed slows the waves down, causing them to bunch up and give greater wave heights. Greatest friction occurs in the trough, since that part of the wave is nearest the seabed. The water particles in the crest will now travel faster than those in the trough. As the wave slows further, the water in the crest overtakes the rest of the wave, and it breaks onto the beach.

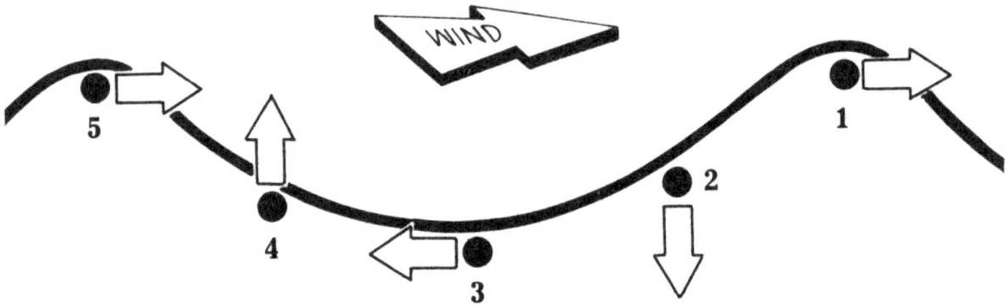

As the wave passes a spot, each particle of water on the surface moves; first forwards on the wave crest **(1)**, then downwards on the back of the passing wave **(2)**, backwards along the trough **(3)**, upwards on the leading edge of the next wave **(4)**, and then forwards again on the next crest **(5)**.

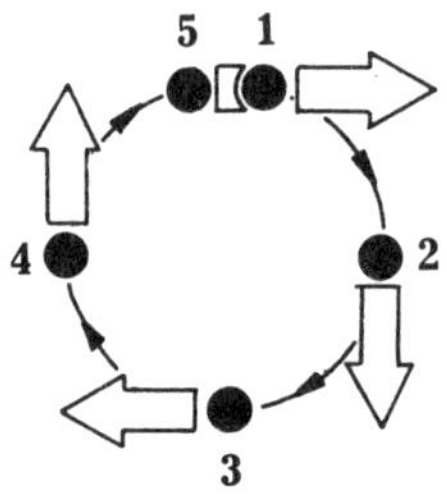

The water on the surface thus prescribes a circular orbit, completing an orbit with each passing wave.

The breaking of a wave

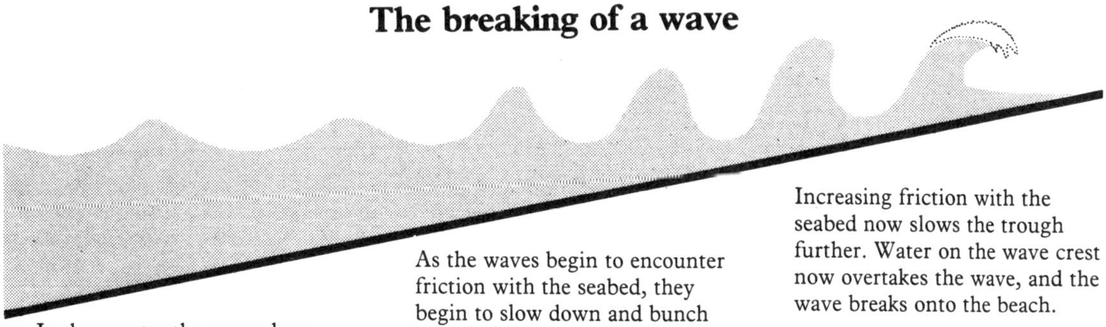

In deep water the waves have long low troughs, with sharper wave crests.

As the waves begin to encounter friction with the seabed, they begin to slow down and bunch up. Wave lengths reduce, but wave heights increase.

Increasing friction with the seabed now slows the trough further. Water on the wave crest now overtakes the wave, and the wave breaks onto the beach.

Surfriding

The water particles at the crest of a wave are travelling in the same direction as the wave. Those on a breaking wave are travelling forwards as fast as, or faster than, the wave itself. Thus, as long as a surfboard remains on the wave crest, it will be given forward impetus by the motion of these particles.

Broaching

This occurs when a boat gets into waves, particularly breaking waves, one end of the boat being on the wave crest and the other end of the boat in the trough. That end of the boat on the crest is taken by the water particles in one direction, while that end of the boat in the trough is taken in another.

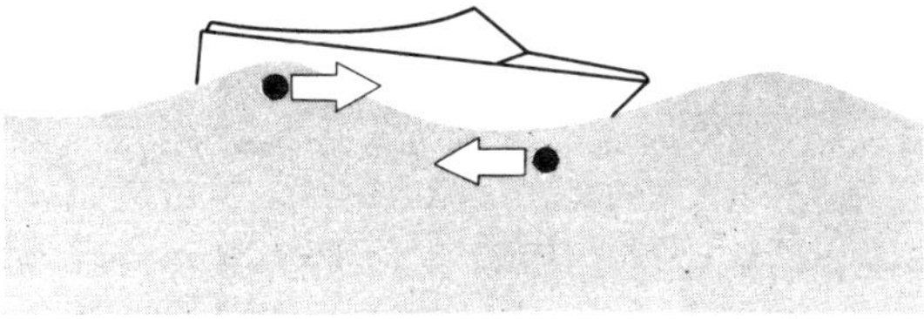

As a result, the boat slews broadside on to the waves, and is then in imminent danger of being rolled over by the next incoming wave.

If it is absolutely necessary to bring a boat through surf, broaching can be prevented by paying out an anchor or sea anchor from the seaward end of the boat to arrest any tendency to slew.

Yawing

This occurs when a boat is travelling in the same direction, or in nearly the same direction, as the waves. The waves are following, approaching the boat from astern. As the stern rises onto a wave crest, it speeds up and tries to overtake the bow. As the wave passes, the stern then drops back into the trough, where it slows down again. This gives the boat an uncomfortable corkscrew motion among the waves.

Alteration of the boat's course may reduce yaw. Excessive yaw, and perhaps the danger of broaching, may be prevented by trailing a length of line in the water from the stern to arrest the boat's movement.

Wave refraction

When waves approach a coastline diagonally, those parts of the wave in shallow water reduce their speed of advance, while those parts in deeper water are not so affected. Thus the waves refract, swinging around and approaching the beach almost head on.

This can be misleading and sometimes dangerous when approaching a beach by boat. Offshore the waves will be travelling in the same direction

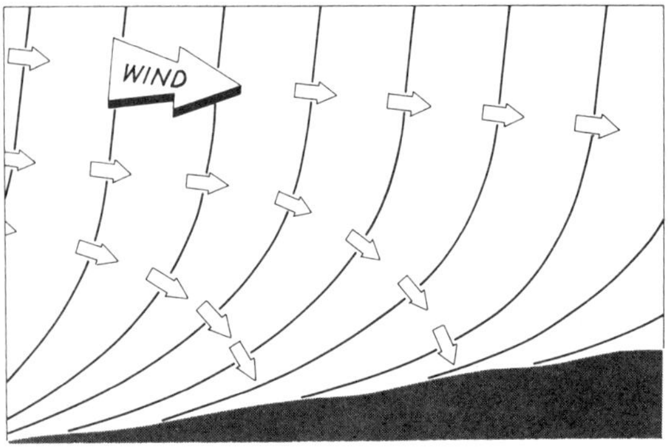

as the wind, but inshore the waves may be running across the wind, bringing a chop to the surface and possibly increasing the risk of broaching.

Rips and undertows

Because of wave refraction, and the varying slopes of the seabed along a coast, waves may concentrate and pile up in certain areas. There must be a route for water to escape from these areas of concentration. The water may escape along the beach as a long-shore current, or directly back towards the sea.

If the flow is seawards beneath the incoming waves, it is felt as an undertow. If the flow is an isolated narrow surface current, it is known as a rip current.

Rips and undertows may be identified by the effect they have upon the sea surface. They may tend to reduce the surf and wave height, thus producing an unfortunate and dangerous invitation to bathers. Or water movement and waves may combine to form very short choppy waves, which are particularly dangerous to boats.

Currents

A current is a horizontal flow of water, which may be due to the prevailing winds or to a gradient in the water's level, density or temperature. The currents affecting New Zealand are predominantly those caused by the prevailing winds, known as drift currents.

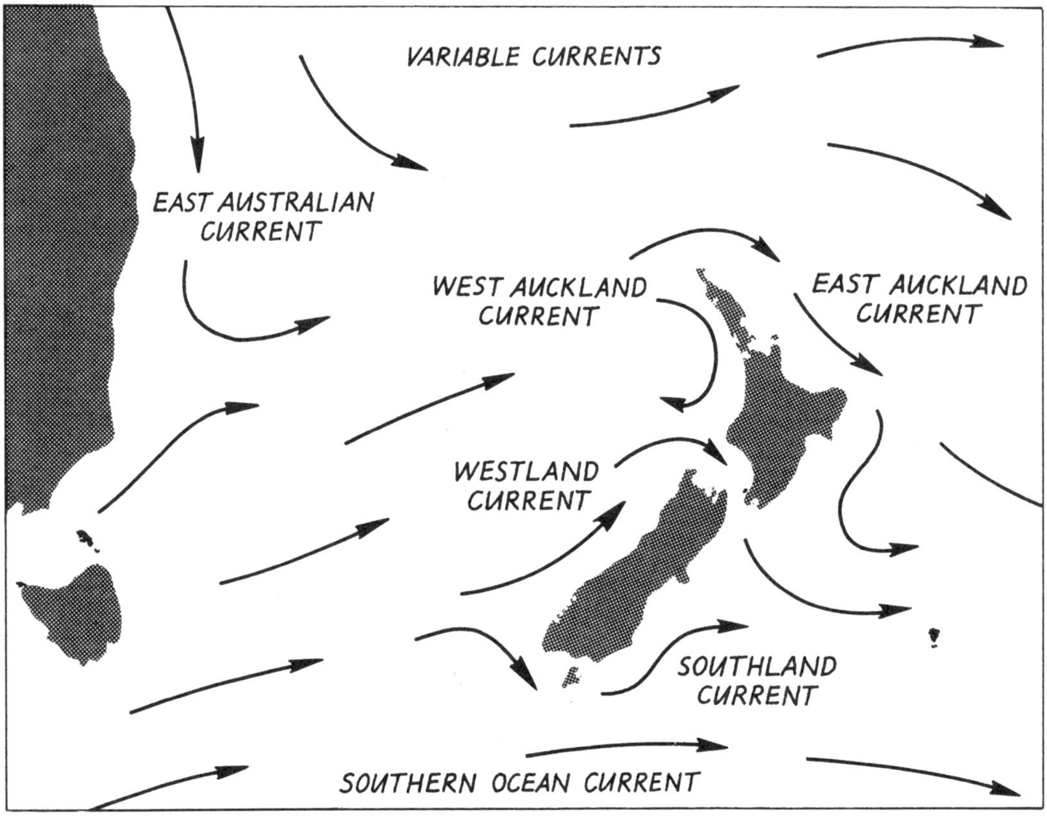

Unlike wind directions, a current direction is the direction towards which the current is moving, called the set. The current's speed, usually measured in knots, is its rate. The drift is the distance in nautical miles that the current takes you over a specified period of time.

Tides

A tide is a vertical movement of water, the water moving up and down under the daily influence of the sun and the moon. This vertical movement does, however, cause horizontal water movements, called tidal streams. As the water level rises, there is a water flow into harbour known as a flood tide. As the water level lowers, there is a flow of water out of harbour, known as an ebb tide.

The cause of tides

Tides are caused by forces of gravity. The earth's gravitational force keeps us and the sea on its surface, but the sun and moon also exert a gravitational force, which is felt on the earth as they pass overhead. As the moon passes around the earth, it pulls the sea surface towards it, producing a high water directly beneath its overhead position. Centrifugal effects will cause another high tide on the earth's opposite side. On the remaining two sides, where the moon's gravity has the least effect, there is a low water. In a period of about a day, any place will experience two high tides and two low tides as the earth and moon rotate.

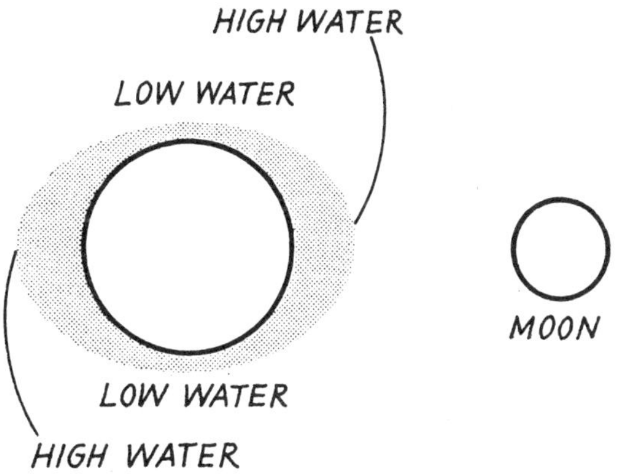

Spring and neap tides

In the same way, the sun also affects the heights of the water, but because it is further away, its influence is less than half that of the moon.

If both sun and moon are acting together in the same place, higher tides than normal are produced, with corresponding lower tides. These are called spring tides and occur at about the times of new moon and full moon.

If sun and moon are acting against each other, high tide is not as high as normal and low tide is not as low as normal. These are neap tides, and occur at about the times of half-moon.

These tidal movements are not entirely regular, for the paths of the sun and moon across the sky vary throughout the year. However, because the movements of earth, sun and moon are predictable, the times and heights of tides can be calculated. These predictions are contained in tide tables.

Spring tides

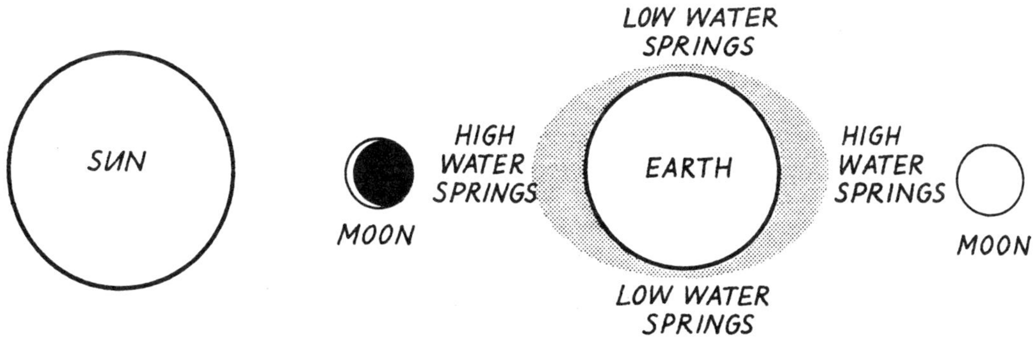

Neap tides

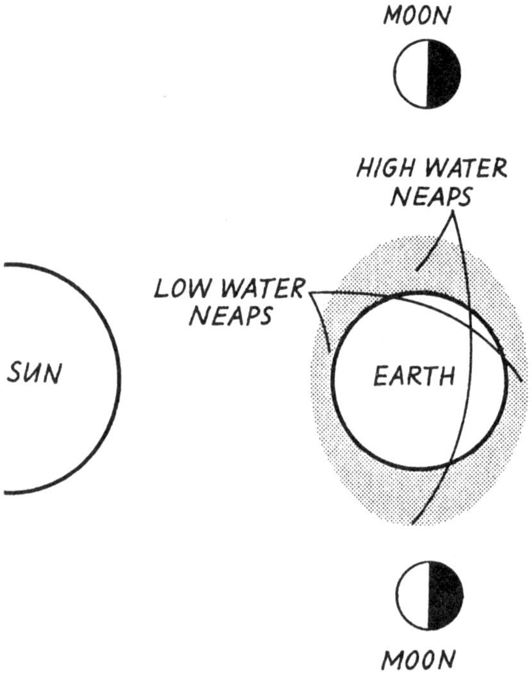

Reading the water

In rivers and shallow water, the surface of the water is often affected by the shape of the seabed. If you boat in such waters, learn to read the water and to recognise the signs that may indicate hidden danger.

In clear water, shallows can usually be seen or detected by the colour of the water. A shallow patch may appear darker or lighter than the surrounding water, depending on whether the seabed is covered with weed or light sand. Often it is the change of colour that is significant.

If water is running rapidly over a shallow area, the waves may appear to stand still. The faster the water flow and the deeper the water, the larger the standing waves. In very shallow water the standing waves are small and closer together, appearing as stationary ripples.

An isolated standing wave, which may be breaking or not, indicates a rock or similar submerged obstruction. The obstruction will be slightly upstream of its wave.

Confused waves can indicate a number of different conditions, and because of the uncertainty about their cause, they should be given a wide berth. A wide area of confused sea could be due to interaction between wind and sea, but if concentrated in a small area, confused waves may originate from the merging of cross-currents, interaction between a current and a cross-wind, or disturbances in a flow caused by an uneven seabed.

Smooth water does not necessarily indicate deep water. The smooth patch may be a pool isolated from a current, so that no waves are formed.

An isolated smooth patch can occur on the lee-side of a floating obstruction, perhaps a partially submerged log or debris, or it may be due to a patch of weed just beneath the surface.

7

THE ENGINE

engine. *Mechanical contrivance consisting of several parts working together . . .*
— The Concise Oxford Dictionary

Engineering is a subject as complex as boating itself and cannot be fully covered here. If your knowledge of engines is limited, you would do well to enrol in a basic engineering course — there are many offered that concentrate on boat engines, both outboard and inboard.

You should at least have a basic understanding of how the engine is working; how to keep the engine and its associated machinery in a safe condition; and how to troubleshoot and deal with minor problems in case of breakdown. Be able to recognise whether your own engine is running comfortably before you start learning how to overhaul it.

Remember that there are no service stations out there on the water. So you must be able to recognise engine problems before they start, or at any early stage. Concentrate on trouble prevention first. A well-maintained engine that has been checked thoroughly before you put to sea is less likely to cause trouble at sea.

Remember also that the engine, its fuel tanks and exhaust system is a prime source of fire. A well-maintained engine and a clean engine compartment will not only reduce the likelihood of mechanical problems, it will also reduce the risk of fire and explosion.

The following sections contain checklists of precautions that need to be observed for your engine, electrical system and batteries, cooling system, propeller and shafting, exhaust and fuel systems.

The engine

■ An alarm system, warning of overheating and low oil pressure, should be fitted.

■ Ensure that drip trays are fitted beneath the engine and gear box to prevent any fuel or oil collecting in the bilges. Frequently inspect the bilges and drip trays for water, oil, fuel or rubbish.

■ Do not allow any spinning part of the engine or shaft to pick up oil from a drip tray to be sprayed around. All rotating parts of the engine and the shaft should be suitably guarded as a protection against injury. The engine should be covered.

■ If a bilge-pumping system is fitted, it should be regularly inspected and tested. A non-return valve should be fitted so that flooding cannot occur, and the valve must be kept clean to prevent failure.

■ The area around the engine should be protected so that oil will not permeate woodwork and cause a fire hazard.

■ Flame arrestors must be fitted to carburettor air intakes.

■ Run all fuel piping well clear of the electrical system, and the exhaust system — preferably on the opposite side of the engine.

■ Use only the fuel and oils specified for your engine. If necessary, change the oil for winter grade if boating during colder seasons.

■ Follow the makers' recommendations for cleaning and replacing oil filters, fuel line filters, and sea-water filters.

■ Frequently check that all hose fittings and connections are tight and leak-free.

■ Frequently check that belt drives are not worn and are at the correct tension.

■ Use a recommended cleaner for cleaning the engine. Do *not* use petrol or kerosene for cleaning purposes.

■ Keep your engine compartment free of inflammable rubbish. Cleaning rags, oil, grease, etc., must be properly stored away from any likely fire source, or disposed of immediately.

Electrical system and batteries

■ Frequently check all wiring for chafe, any breakdown in insulation, or signs of burning or overloading.

■ A heavy-duty master electrical switch should be fitted. When the boat is not being used, and when refuelling, the switch should be open.

■ Each electrical circuit on the boat should be protected by a fuse of the correct rating.

■ Know how to remove spark plugs, how to clean and set the correct spark gap and distributor points, and how to check for spark failure. Never test for a spark without first checking that the engine area is gas-free.

■ Keep all electrical parts, especially the ignition system, clean, dry and well protected from oil and the effects of salt spray.

■ Place batteries as high in the boat as is practicable, and always above floorboard level. If low down, they will be the first to suffer in the event of flooding.

■ The batteries should be well secured to prevent movement, and protected against vibration.

■ A battery should be in a covered box. The cover must be non-conductive and protect the battery and its terminals from spray or dropped tools that may cause short-circuiting. Ensure that the box is well ventilated for the removal of gases produced when the battery is charging; ventilation should not be into the engine space.

■ Check the water level in the battery frequently, and look for any electrolytic corrosion around the terminals. (Electrolytic corrosion may be prevented by coating the terminals with Vaseline, or a similar non-conductive grease.)

Cooling system

■ Check that the sea intakes and outlets are free of corrosion and marine growth. All inlets and outlets should be fitted with sea cocks. Bilge-pump outlets should be fitted with non-return valves to guard against flooding.

■ Keep filters and strainers clear of weed, silt or debris.

■ If the engine is cooled by a closed-circuit water system, place a corrosion inhibitor in the water. If boating during colder weather with a closed circuit cooling system, use a suitable anti-freeze.

■ Thoroughly check and overhaul all sea cocks regularly and frequently. Ensure that they are closed while the boat is unattended.

■ Carry spare impellers for water pumps.

Propeller and shafting

■ Check the propeller frequently for damage to the blades. Chipped or bent blades will cause excessive vibration, which will in turn cause problems in shaft and engine bearings.

■ Grounding or sudden impact to the boat may cause the engine to shift, resulting in mis-alignment of the shaft. Check the stern gland for signs of leaking or overheating.

■ Always carry a spare shear pin or drive pin.

■ Learn how to check, adjust and re-pack the stern gland (stuffing box). Do not overtighten, and do not overgrease.

Exhaust system

■ All exhaust piping should be run clear of any woodwork or bodywork liable to catch fire. Pipes should be lagged to reduce the transfer of heat to surrounding areas.

■ Regularly inspect all exhaust pipes and keep them in good condition so that exhaust fumes cannot leak and gather in living spaces.

Fuel system

■ There must be at least one isolating valve between the fuel tank and the engine in case of a broken fuel line or an outbreak of fire and to enable filters to be changed.

■ The upper end of a filling pipe should be at an open deck, so that any overflow will run overboard and not back into the boat. The filling pipe cap should be in place, with a good tight fit to prevent the ingress of dirt or water.

■ All fuel lines should be well secured and made of heavy-gauge steel or copper or other approved materials. Flexible lines should be heavy-duty and metal-braided.

■ Frequently check all tanks, fuel lines, valves and connections for signs of movement, looseness and corrosion. A leak caused by a corroded tank or fitting should be remedied by replacement of the corroded part, rather than by trying to patch it up.

■ Ensure that each fuel tank has a vent and that it is not blocked. The vent pipe should lead from the top of the tank to outside the boat, with a wire gauze covering at its outer end, and be of adequate size.

■ Observe the re-fuelling procedures listed on page 47.

Before starting the engine

■ Check that your fire extinguishers are in place, charged and in top working order.

■ Inspect the bilges and drip trays for water, oil, fuel or rubbish. Check the bilge-pumping system, and that the non-return valve is clean.

■ Check all enclosed spaces and bilges for petrol fumes. Open the boat and thoroughly ventilate all spaces, particularly the engine compartment and associated bilge spaces.

■ Ensure that the gas detector is operating, and indicating a gas-free atmosphere.

■ Check oil levels in the engine and gearbox, and, if applicable, the water level in the header tank.

■ Visually check the engine: belt drives, the electrical system, hoses, connections and drip trays.

■ If the engine is an outboard, ensure that it is properly and securely fastened to the transom, that the fuel tank is correctly attached and the fuel line is the correct way around, and that the control grip is in the start position.

■ Check that all control wires and pulleys are greased and secure.

■ Check that the gearshift is in neutral.

■ Open the sea cocks.

■ Check the stern gland for water seepage, and that the propeller is clear to turn.

■ Ensure that there is sufficient fuel and water for your journey, with allowance for unforseen circumstances.

■ Check that the fuel-tank vents are clear.

■ Open the fuel valves.

After starting the engine

■ Check that the cooling water is circulating, and look over the side to see that it is discharging.

■ Check the oil pressure, and that the battery is charging.

■ Visually check the engine for signs of fuel leaks, overheating, excessive vibration, etc.

■ Allow the engine to warm up slowly. Do not apply full load to the engine until it is properly warmed.

■ Before stopping the engine, allow it to idle for a few minutes to allow it to cool down.

8

ROPEWORK

Too late he looks back to the land when, the rope being loosed, the curved keel rushes into the deep.

— Ovid

Rope types

Manufacturers often give their ropes trade names and brand names, each with individual characteristics and colours, but all are manufactured from the same raw materials. Ropes may be made from natural fibres or from synthetic fibres.

Common natural fibre ropes in use at sea are manila and sisal. Jute and hemp ropes are more flexible and have a softer texture. Less common are cotton and coir ropes.

There are four basic types of synthetic materials commonly used for ropes: nylon (chemically known as polyamide), polyester (also known as terylene), polypropylene (commonly called polyprop) and polythene (or polyethylene). Kevlar, a very low-stretch rope, is becoming widely used on racing yachts but is very expensive.

The construction of ropes

All natural fibres are staple fibres; that is, they are of limited length. Almost all synthetic fibres are continuous in length; some are very fine, in which large numbers of filaments are grouped together to form a yarn known as multifilament yarn.

The fibres are first twisted into yarns, the twist binding the fibres so that friction holds them together. Several yarns are then combined as a strand, and these are then laid to form the rope.

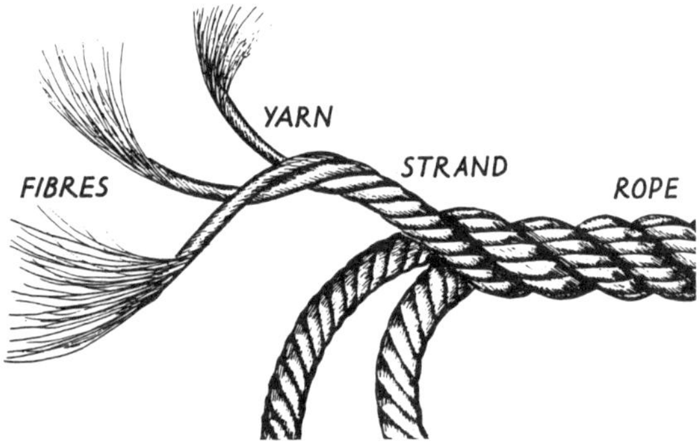

Laid ropes

These have their strands twisted in the familiar spiral form. Three strands laid in this way form the hawser-laid rope, commonly used; four strands form the less common shroud-laid rope, which is weaker in comparison. The lay is usually right-handed, but it can be left-handed. The twist of a right-handed rope is in the same direction as the thread of a screw.

RIGHT-HANDED

LEFT-HANDED

Braided ropes
These generally consist of smaller strands, plaited together. A braided rope has more stretch and less strength than a laid rope, but it is more pliable, does not kink, and its smoother surface is easier to handle and allows it to run smoothly through leads and blocks.

BRAIDED ROPE

Rope size
Ropes are available in various lengths. The size of a rope, however, refers to its diameter in millimetres.

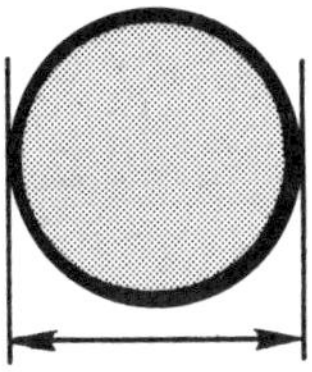

Rope characteristics

Strength
Rope strength is usually expressed as a breaking strain — the strain measured in kilograms that the rope will endure before breaking. Much will depend on how the load is applied; a rope may well hold a weight if the load is applied gradually, but break if the same weight is applied as a shock loading. Synthetic lines are stronger than natural fibre ropes of equivalent size, nylon possessing the greatest strength.

For safety, the working load on a rope should never exceed one-sixth of its breaking load.

Stretch
All ropes stretch if under strain, but synthetic lines, particularly nylon, have a greater degree of stretch.

The high stretch of nylon may make the line potentially dangerous. A stretched rope will whip back like an elastic band if it breaks or is suddenly released from a heavy strain.

The immense strength of nylon is frequently underestimated. The line's strength may well exceed the strength of the fitting to which it is attached. There is a very real danger that, if placed under heavy load, the line may not break but the fitting will pull loose. On a violently recoiling line, the fitting could then be a lethal missile.

The amount of stretch also depends on the rope's construction. A braided rope will have greater stretch than a laid rope, and a loosely laid rope will stretch more than a tightly laid rope. Continual and excessive stretching will eventually weaken any rope.

Durability
Whatever their type or construction, all ropes will wear in time, but synthetic lines, particularly polyester, offer the best resistance to abrasion. Dampness, mildew and marine growth will all cause a loss of strength and eventual rotting of a natural fibre rope, but synthetic ropes are unaffected.

A particular enemy of all ropes is direct sunlight. Prolonged exposure to the ultra-violet rays of sunlight will cause brittleness and the eventual breakdown of the rope fibres. Polypropylene is most affected, while polyester offers the best resistance. Darker-coloured ropes will suffer less than lighter-coloured ropes.

Behaviour in water
Polypropylene and polythene ropes float in water, which makes them useful for some purposes but unsuitable for such purposes as anchor lines. Natural fibre ropes absorb water, increasing their weight and often causing the rope to swell and stiffen. Synthetic ropes absorb little or no water and suffer no loss in flexibility.

Which rope?

Synthetic ropes in particular offer a wide range of properties, which make certain rope types suitable for certain tasks and unsuitable for others. Your choice of rope must match the work you intend it to do. By examining the requirements of the task, it should be possible to select a rope with characteristics that match these requirements.

Halyards
Ropes used for halyards require high strength and minimal stretch. Polyester is recommended, but polypropylene may be used on smaller boats. Use a laid rope rather than a braided rope, because of its lesser stretch.

Sheets
These require low stretch but must be easy to handle. Use braided polyester line on larger boats, but polypropylene will suffice on the smaller boat.

Anchor line
A strong line is needed, with high-stretch capability to absorb sudden loading and prevent the shock being transmitted to the anchor. Nylon is best suited. Remember the advantage in also using a length of chain. Avoid using polypropylene or polythene as anchor warps. Because of their buoyancy they may foul or be cut by a propeller.

Mooring lines
Polyester is best suited to the larger vessel, but polypropylene or polythene will be sufficient for most smaller boats.

Water-ski towline
A low-stretch line is required, with the ability to float. A braided polypropylene or polythene line is therefore recommended.

Handling ropes

A rope lying around the deck is both untidy and dangerous. Even the end of a rope not in use should be coiled neatly. This keeps it readily available in a condition that will not produce unwanted kinks or tangles.

To coil a rope, lay it out as straight as possible, and then coil it down in loops, one on top of the

A guide to ropes and their properties

Use this information as a comparative guide only.
Always seek the supplier's specifications and recommendations.

	Natural fibre		*Synthetic fibre*			
	MANILA	*SISAL*	*POLYAMIDE (Nylon)*	*POLYESTER (Terylene)*	*POLYPROPYLENE*	*POLYTHENE (Polyethylene)*
TEXTURE	Bristly. Coarser than synthetics.	More flexible than manila, and lighter in colour.	Very smooth and glossy. Has an oily texture when new.	Softer and easier to handle than nylon.	A waxy texture. Less slippery than other synthetics.	Shiny plastic texture. More slippery than other synthetics.
STRETCH	20%	15%	46%	25%	35%	35%
BUOYANCY	Does not float (S.G. 1.48)	Does not float (S.G. 1.48)	Does not float (S.G. 1.14)	Does not float (S.G. 1.38)	Floats (S.G. 0.91)	Floats (S.G. 0.95)
WATER ABSORPTION	30%	33%	4%	Nil	Nil	Nil
BEHAVIOUR IN WATER	Swells and stiffens. Suffers a loss in strength of about 45%	Swells and stiffens. Suffers loss in strength of about 45%	Does not swell. Equally as flexible. Loses 5 to 10% strength whilst saturated.	Does not swell. Equally as flexible. Equally as strong.	Does not swell. Equally as flexible. Equally as strong.	Does not swell. Equally as flexible. Equally as strong.
MELTING TEMPERATURE	None	None	250°C	265°C	165°C	125°C
BREAKING STRAIN (10 mm line)*	705 kg	635 kg	2080 kg	1590 kg	1425 kg	930 kg
WEIGHT per 100 m (10 mm line)*	6.8 kg	6.6 kg	6.8 kg	8.0 kg	5.7 kg	6.1 kg

*Three-stranded laid rope.

other, with the loops as large as space permits. Right-handed rope must be coiled in a clockwise direction, and left-handed rope in an anticlockwise direction. Braided ropes may be coiled in any direction, but are usually coiled clockwise. To prevent a loop from forming an '8', give the rope a twist between finger and thumb. (If the rope persistently forms '8's as you coil it, leave them in the coil. This will prevent the line from kinking as you later take the rope off the coil.)

A coil should be wholly turned over if the end to be used first is underneath. The running end of the rope must always be on top of the coil.

New ropes
Depending on their size, rope lengths may be supplied in a coil or on a spool. Larger ropes are invariably in coils, sometimes with lashings and sacking around the coil to keep it in shape. To remove some rope, the coil should be placed so that the tail of rope inside the coil is at the top. Cut the lashings, but do not remove the sacking. Take the rope from the coil, commencing with this inner end, so that the rope uncoils in an anticlockwise direction.

Smaller cordage is often supplied on a spool. To remove rope from the spool, place a stick through the spool so that it revolves as the rope is drawn off.

Making fast to a cleat
A cleat enables a rope to be secured and released while it is under strain. Correct securing of the rope is therefore essential to avoid jamming, and to allow the rope to be slackened off under strain.

Lead the rope to the end of the cleat furthest away, so that the standing part of the rope does not lead under the nearer end of the cleat. Take one complete turn, and then two or three figure-of-eight turns. Don't smother the cleat with turns. A final turn pulled tight, rather than a locking hitch, is sufficient to secure the rope on the cleat.

Making fast to a bollard
If a bight is made in the end of a line by making an eye-splice or by tying a bowline, this can be slipped over the bollard. As an alternative, pass the end of the line around the bollard and back on board. This will make it easier to release later.

If you wish to moor to a bollard already in use, spare a thought for the first user. To enable either line to be removed without disturbing the other, put your mooring through the eye of the first line before placing it over the bollard.

Knots and hitches

Countless knots and hitches have been designed over the ages, many of them ornamental rather than functional. What the boatman must acquire initially is a knowledge of the basic knots in common use — the others are optional extras.

The right knot for the job
Each knot has a purpose. It is as important to know which knot to use as it is to know how to tie the knot. A knot may be beautifully tied, but if it is the wrong knot for the task, it will be of little or no use.

Tighten the knot
The knots illustrated here have been loosely tied for demonstration purposes. After you have tied a knot, tighten it by hand before putting the knot to work.

Allow plenty of tail
Once a load is applied, a knot will work itself tight, perhaps by taking up some of the free rope in the knot's tail. If there is insufficient length to the tail, the end of the line may work itself through the knot and allow the knot to free itself. Because of the inherent slipperiness of synthetic lines, extra tail should be allowed when tying knots in these lines. Polythene is the most slippery, polypropylene is the least slippery. As an extra safeguard, the tail may be secured by binding it to the standing part of the rope.

The strength of knots
No matter how well you tie your knot, and even if it is the right knot for the job, the ultimate strength of the line will be reduced by the knot. A knot may reduce a line's strength by up to 40

per cent. Several knots in a line will seriously reduce its strength. Continual knotting and unknotting will also weaken a line by wear on its strands.

The figure-of-eight knot

This is used as a stopper knot, to prevent the rope end from disappearing through a lead or block, or it can be tied in the end of a newly cut line to prevent the line from unlaying.

The reef knot

A knot designed originally to bind sails down to reduce sail area ('reefing'). It is therefore more suited to smaller cordage than larger ropes, and is of limited use. It should not be used for joining different lines together. Ensure that the two tails of the completed knot emerge on the same side as their own standing parts. If they emerge on different sides you have tied a 'granny' knot, which will slip and perhaps untie itself when under strain.

The sheet bend

A particularly useful knot for joining lines of equal or different sizes, and different materials. It is a good knot for synthetic lines; it does not jam, and is easily untied. The larger of the two lines should be used to form the eye, and the smaller line passed through the eye to form the knot. The two rope ends should emerge on the same side of the knot, otherwise the knot may prove unreliable.

The double sheet bend

A very reliable knot that is also easy to untie. It may be used to join two lines of the same or different sizes, types, or construction. It is tied in the same way as the sheet bend, but then the smaller line is taken around a second time and is again tucked beneath its standing part. This extra turn makes the knot more secure, especially if one rope is considerably larger than the other.

The bowline

A knot designed to form a bight, or loop, at the end of a line. This is an indispensable knot in any seaman's repertoire because it is reliable, quick to tie, never slips and is easily untied. It has a multitude of uses where a non-slip loop is required — in mooring lines, or where a foot- or handhold is needed at the end of a line; or it can be tied around a person's waist to help him or her out of the water.

To tie the knot, first take a small notch in the standing part of the line at that point where the knot is to be made. Then pass the end of the line through this notch, around the back of the standing part, and then back through the notch to complete the knot.

The clove hitch

Used for making a line fast to a spar or post, such as a painter to a side rail. It can be tied quickly but tends to slip sideways along the spar when subjected to a sideways pull. It may jam if wet, but may also work loose if heavy loads are intermittently applied. Allow plenty of free tail and use as a temporary measure only.

The rolling hitch

A hitch made in the same way as the clove hitch, but with an extra locking turn to make it more secure. It is less likely to slip sideways if subjected to a side strain, and is less likely to work itself free.

The round turn and two half-hitches

Used to secure a rope to a spar or ring. A reliable hitch that is quickly and easily tied. It will tighten its grip as a load is applied but is less likely to jam than other hitches, and is easier to release. The knot is made by taking a complete round turn around the spar, and then two half-hitches (overhand knots) are taken around the standing part.

The anchor bend

Also known as a 'fisherman's bend', this is used to secure a rope to a spar, or a rope to the ring of an anchor. It is a strong and reliable knot that will not slip, but is more difficult to release than the round turn and two half-hitches. The knot is made in the same manner as a round turn and two half-hitches, except that the first half-hitch is taken through the round turn.

The use of ropes

■ You will often find that one end of a rope is used more than the other end; perhaps with the result that a rope may have to be replaced because one end is worn out. Therefore, occasionally end-for-end the rope. By distributing the wear you will get a longer life from the rope.

■ Although tough, synthetic lines are affected by certain chemicals. Nylon is attacked by all mineral acids and some organic acids, and is weakened by contact with bleaches. Polyester is resistant to most acids, bleaches and solvents, but is attacked and weakened by alkalis. Polypropylene and polythene are very stable and resistant to most chemicals, but may be weakened by some strong industrial solvents.

■ When using synthetic lines on a winch, extra turns may have to be taken to prevent slipping. But do not allow the rope to surge on the winch drum; frictional heat may melt the rope or cause the fibres to fuse. The low melting temperatures of polypropylene and polythene make these lines particularly susceptible to frictional fusing.

■ Synthetic lines will not rot like natural fibres, but will not last forever. Examine your ropes frequently for wear, chafe and damaged fibres. A synthetic line may 'fur' with age, but this will generally help to protect the inner fibres of the rope. Open the strands and inspect the inner fibres. If you find a powdery substance, this indicates internal wear and the rope should be replaced.

■ Never stand close to or in line with a line under strain, particularly a synthetic line.

■ Synthetic lines are not attacked by marine organisms or seaweed. If, however, you wish to remove any marine growth from the rope, allow it to dry, then flex the rope and rub the growth off gently by hand. Do not use harsh brushes or abrasives.

■ Never underestimate the strength of a synthetic line. A line will always break at its weakest point; this may be the fitting to which it is attached.

■ Do not tie a left-handed rope to a right-handed rope. They will unravel when placed under strain.

■ Stow your ropes out of direct sunlight, and avoid using them near sand, grit and rust.

■ When splicing synthetic lines, include at least two extra tucks to allow for the slipperiness of the line.

■ A simple method of identifying the type of line is to burn a small sample. Nylon burns with an acrid smell and emits white smoke. Polyester has a waxy smell and emits a dense black smoke. Polypropylene and polythene give off a lot of smoke, and melt into molten globules. Natural fibres will char or burn, but will not melt.

■ When cutting a rope, place a whipping on the rope end to prevent unravelling. This is done by binding the rope with a few turns of light twine. A stopper knot, such as the figure-of-eight, may be placed in the line as a temporary measure. The fibres of a synthetic line may be fused together by melting over a flame.

■ A natural fibre rope will generally give a warning that it is about to part — it will groan and creak, and the fibres often part individually. A synthetic line generally gives no warning — it parts with a bang.

9

BOAT STABILITY

. . . If you would keep afloat, you
must know what you are about;
unless a man is worthy, the sea
will surely find him out.
— Hans Hendrick Andersen

A boat that has been pushed from its upright position by an external force, such as the wind or waves, should return to the upright position. If it does so, the boat is stable. If the boat does not return upright, it is unstable. A well-designed boat has adequate stability built into it. However, any changes made to the boat, or any changes made to her loading, will upset that stability — perhaps to the extent of making the boat dangerous.

We must be able to recognise the signs of impending instability of the boat, and we must know the measures needed to correct this. In the long term this may involve consultations with a surveyor or a naval architect, but in an emergency at sea more immediate measures may have to be taken and these will only be safe and effective if we have a basic understanding of the fundamental forces that govern a boat's stability.

The two forces governing boat stability are buoyancy, provided by the water, and gravity.

The centre of buoyancy

As a boat is lowered into the water it appears to lose weight. The water is exerting an upward thrust on the hull called buoyancy. When the boat is floating free in the water, this upward thrust is equal in value to the weight of the boat and everything aboard it.

Buoyancy acts over the entire submerged surface of the hull. The centre of its force is called the centre of buoyancy (**B**), and through this point the force of buoyancy always acts directly upwards. The centre of buoyancy is always at the geometric centre of the boat's underwater volume. When the boat is on an even keel, this is on the centreline.

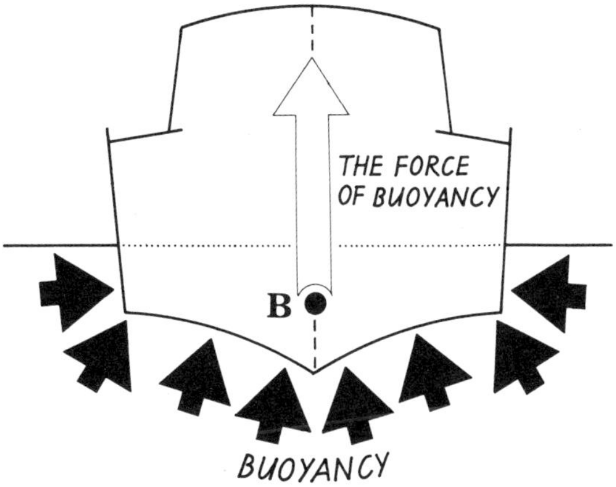

Rolling
If the boat rolls, the centre of buoyancy will take up a new position to port or starboard of the centreline, but always at the centre of the underwater portion of the hull with the force of buoyancy acting directly upwards.

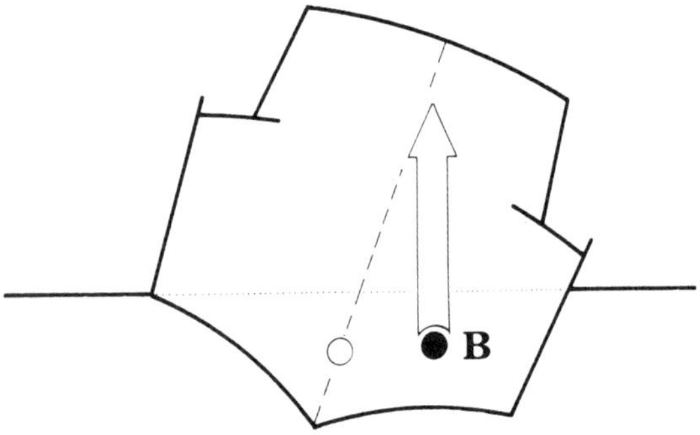

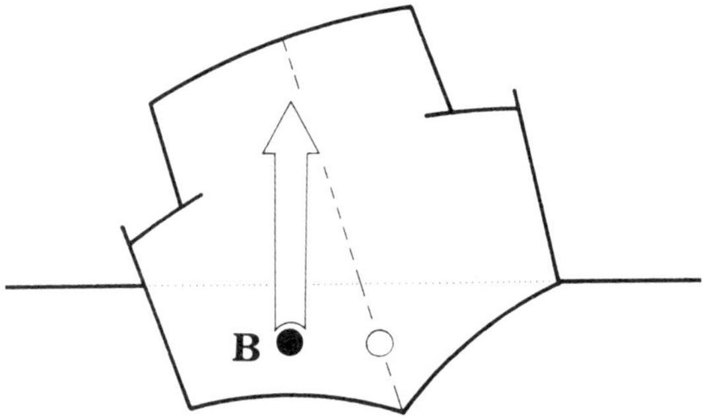

The centre of gravity

Gravity is the force that gives everything weight. If it were possible to suspend a boat so that it balanced perfectly in all directions, the point of suspension would be its centre of gravity (**G**). Thus the whole weight of the boat, and everything aboard it, is considered to act through this point vertically downwards.

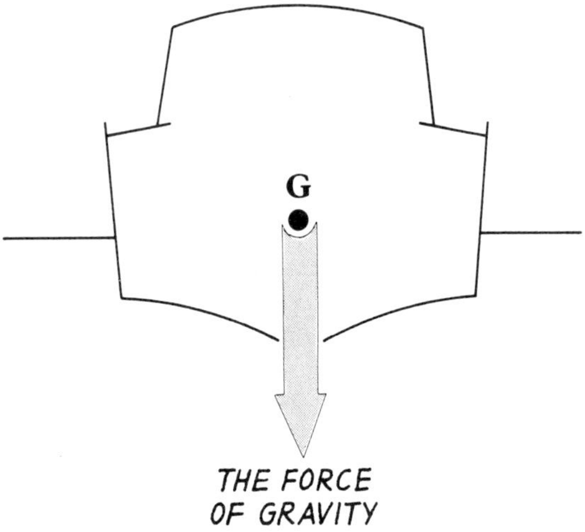

A well-designed boat has its centre of gravity as low as possible. Heavy weights, such as the engine and storage tanks, are placed in the bottom of the boat to help achieve this.

Movement of weights

If any weight is moved within the boat, the balance is upset, and therefore the centre of gravity must also move to maintain its position at the centre of balance.

If a weight is moved horizontally across the boat, the centre of gravity will also move horizontally in the same direction. If a weight is moved vertically, the centre of gravity will also move vertically in the same direction. The distance moved by the centre of gravity will depend on the amount of weight shifted — the heavier the weight, and the further it is moved, the further the centre of gravity will shift.

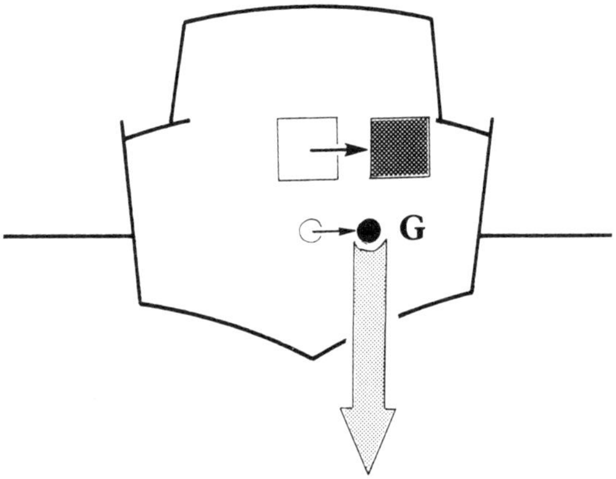

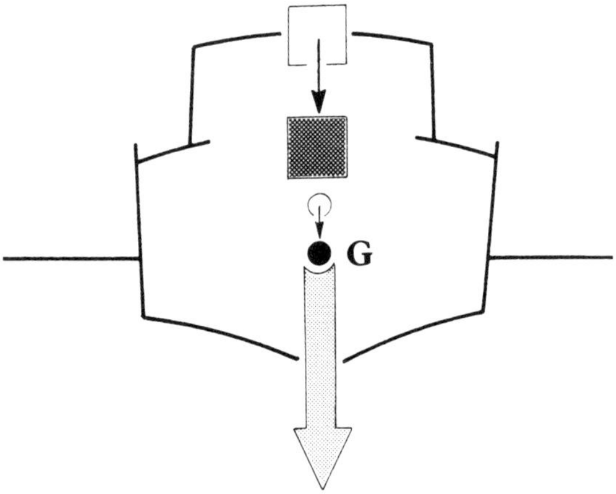

Addition or removal of weights

If a weight is added to the boat, the centre of gravity will move directly towards the added weight. If a weight is removed, the centre of gravity will move directly away from the former position of that weight.

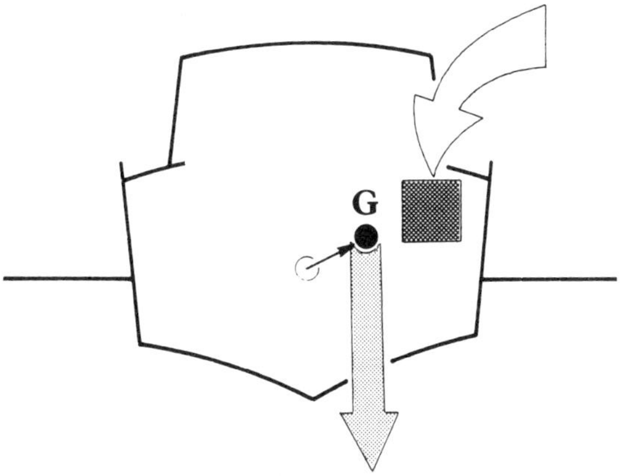

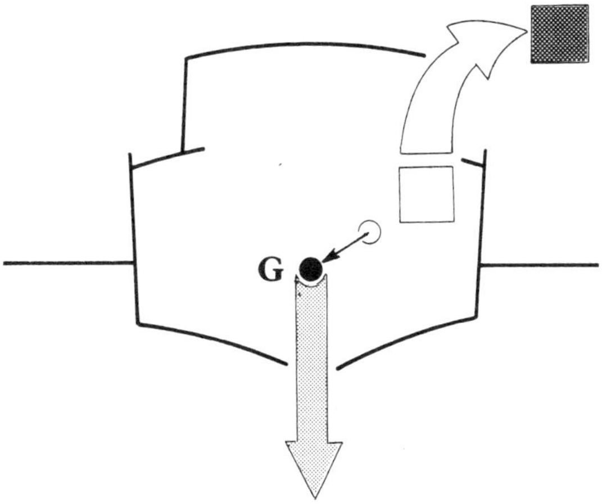

The distance the centre of gravity will shift will be proportional to the amount of weight added or removed, and its distance from the boat's original centre of gravity.

Interaction between gravity and buoyancy

When a boat is heeled over by the effects of wind and sea, it will try, if it is stable, to return to an upright attitude. This is brought about by an interaction between the forces of gravity and buoyancy.

In a stable boat, which has evenly stowed weights within the boat, the centres of gravity and buoyancy are on the centreline, and the boat rests in an upright position. This is because the forces of gravity and buoyancy are acting in opposite directions but in the same vertical line.

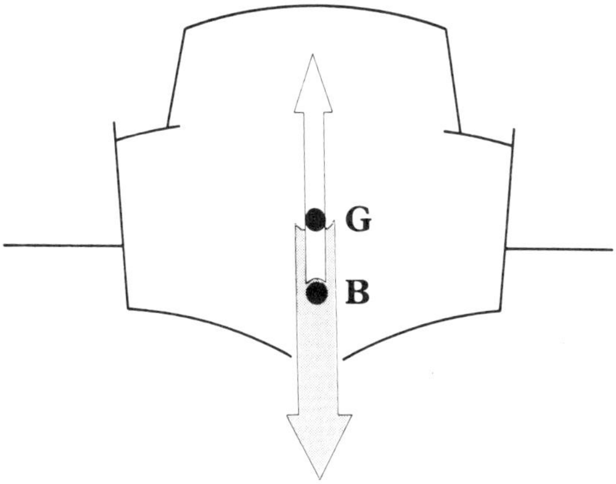

If the boat is now heeled by the wind, there is an immediate change to the shape of the hull's underwater portion. Since the centre of buoyancy is always at the centre of the underwater volume of the hull, it will move to take up a new position further towards the lower side of the boat. The forces of gravity and buoyancy now form a couple, acting to return the boat to an upright attitude.

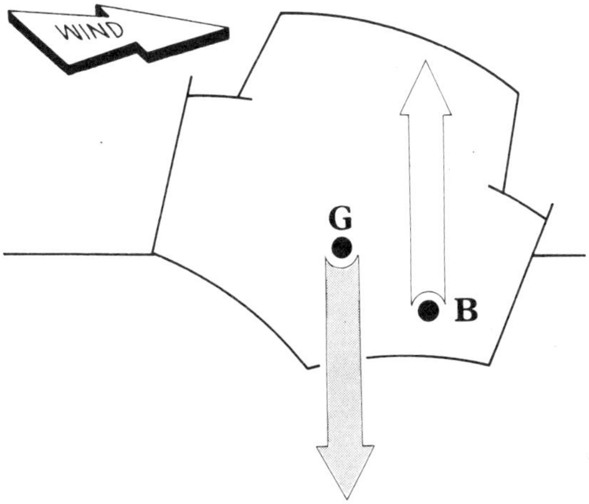

List

An athwartship change in the boat's attitude caused by the wind is called heel, but if the boat leans to one side because of an uneven distribution of weight aboard, the boat is said to have a list.

If, for example, a weight is moved across to the starboard side of the boat, the centre of gravity will also move to starboard. The two forces of buoyancy and gravity have now been put out of balance, and the resulting couple tips the boat to starboard.

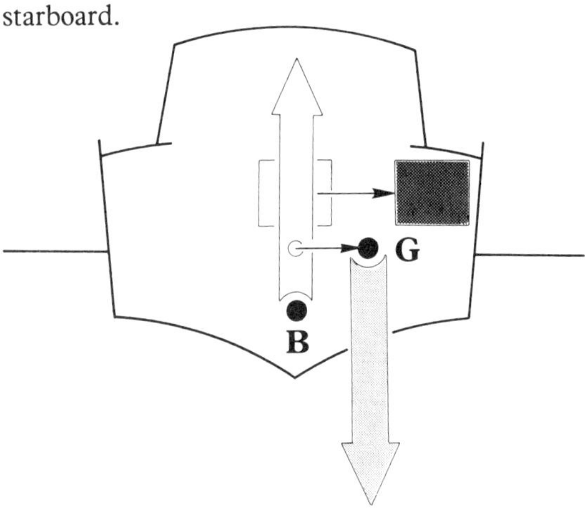

As the boat tips, the underwater shape changes, and the centre of buoyancy will move over to starboard to assume its new position at the centre of this shape. The centres of gravity and buoyancy are now both to starboard of the centreline, with their forces acting in the same vertical line. No righting couple is formed, and the boat will therefore rest in this attitude, listed to starboard.

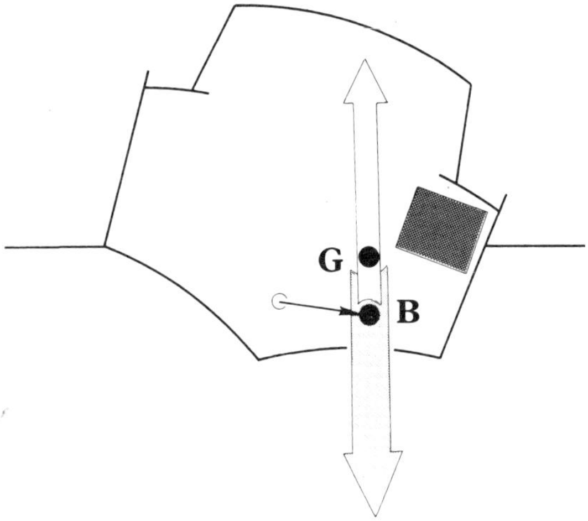

Stiffness and tenderness

The height of the centre of gravity within the boat can be gauged by the manner in which the boat rights itself.

If the centre of gravity is low, the forces of gravity and buoyancy exert a large righting couple to return the boat upright.

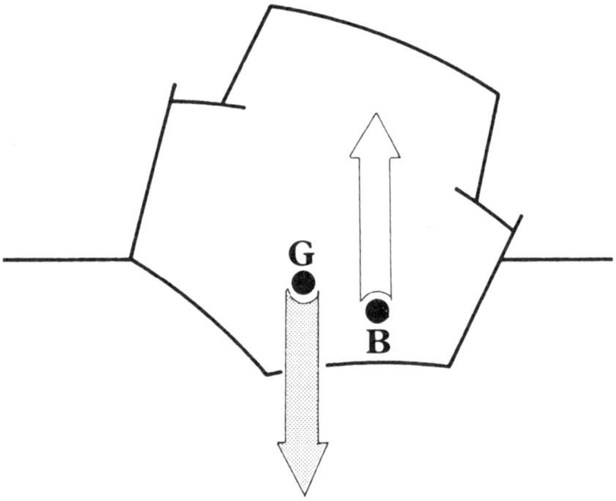

A boat in this condition is very stable and returns to the upright position rapidly. This boat is said to be stiff.

If topweight on the boat raises the centre of gravity, the righting couple trying to return the boat to the upright is reduced. A boat in this condition is not so stable and returns more slowly to the upright position. This boat is said to be tender.

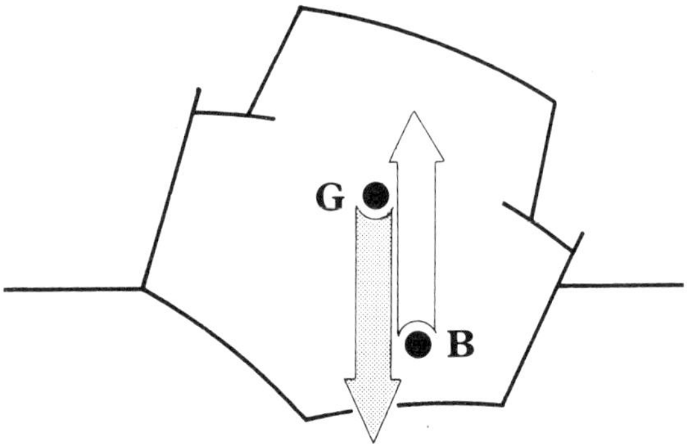

The stiffness or tenderness of a boat is usually indicated by the way in which it rolls. A stiff boat rolls quickly, almost uncomfortably, as it tries to keep upright. A tender boat has a much slower period of roll — if it is very tender it may 'hang' at the extreme of the roll before swinging back.

Instability

If the amount of topweight on the boat causes the centre of gravity to become too high, the boat will be unstable. In this condition the forces of gravity and buoyancy are forming a couple that will cause capsize.

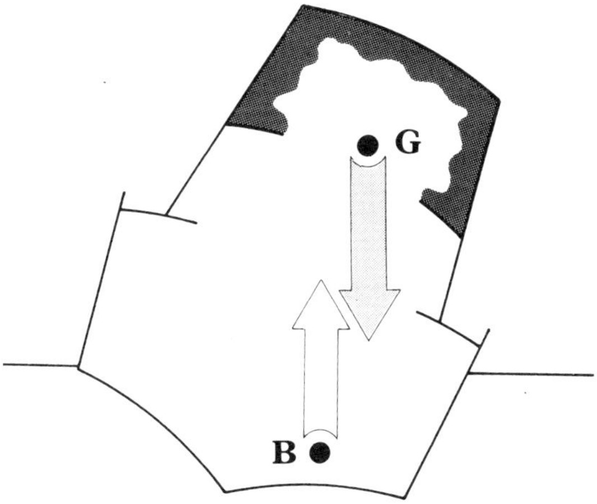

Loll

A situation may arise in which the centre of gravity is at a height where the forces of gravity and buoyancy neither return the boat to the upright nor cause it to roll further. In this condition the boat has no righting couple. It will therefore flop over and take up an angle of loll.

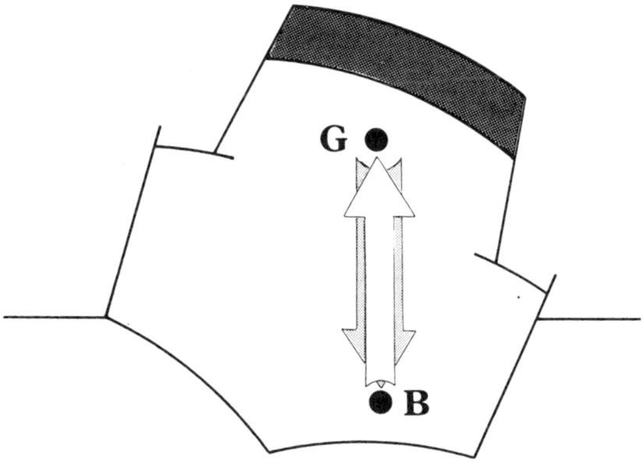

This boat is now at neutral equilibrium, a dangerous situation because it could capsize very easily. The immediate remedy is to lower the boat's centre of gravity.

It is important that any action taken to correct loll is taken at once, and that the corrective action is safe. Do not mistake loll for list. List can be corrected by placing weight on the opposite side of the boat, but loll must never be corrected in this way. Placing a weight on the higher side of the boat will raise the centre of gravity further, and create an unstable situation. The boat will simply flop over in the opposite direction and capsize.

If the boat should ever develop a lean to one side for no apparent reason, and adopts a sluggish, rolling motion, suspect loll. Act quickly to lower the boat's centre of gravity. This can be done by reducing topweight and increasing bottom weight, or by restowing weight from the top of the boat into the bottom of the boat.

Loose water (free surface)

A particular hazard to a boat's stability is any water within the boat that is able to move around. As the water moves from side to side with the rolling motion of the boat it has the effect of reducing the boat's ability to right itself.

If the water in the bottom of the boat is unable to move, the boat's centre of gravity will not move as the boat rolls. The righting couple is large enough to return the boat quickly to the upright.

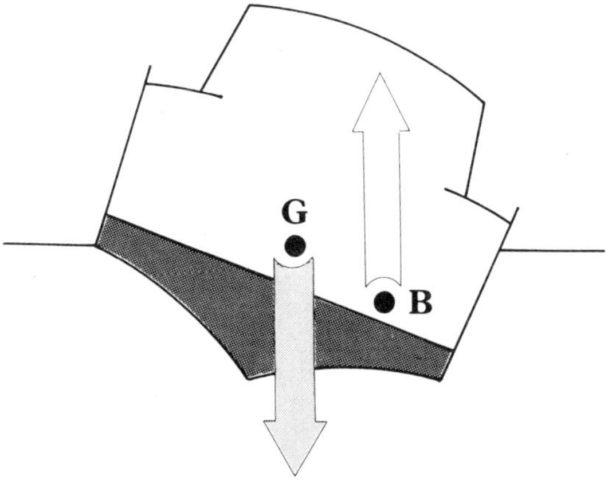

If the water in the bottom of the boat is able to move, it will move towards the low side. Because weight has shifted within the boat, the boat's centre of gravity will shift, also towards the low side. The righting couple is now considerably smaller, perhaps non-existent.

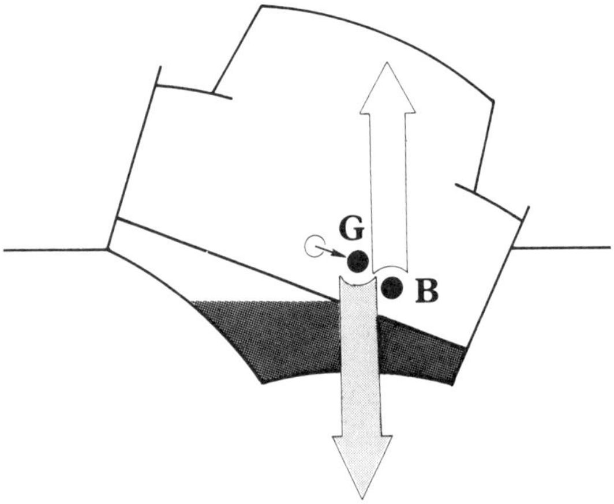

Loose water or fuel in storage tanks will cause a similar reduction in stability. Movement within tanks can be reduced by fitting baffles, otherwise ensure that tanks are kept fully topped up or completely empty. A similar loss in stability can also be caused by loose equipment rolling around in the boat, and this will present the added danger of damage to the boat and injury to the boat's occupants.

Increasing a boat's stability

There are a number of preventative measures that can be taken to improve a boat's stability or corrective measures if loss of stability is suspected. In each case the object is to lower the boat's centre of gravity, and to prevent the ingress of water that may cause loose water effects.

■ Deck scuppers and freeing ports should be kept clear to help the escape of any water taken on the deck. Water on deck causes a two-fold danger to stability: the extra weight on deck raises the centre of gravity, and the movement of the water across the deck with the rolling motion of the boat seriously affects the boat's righting ability.

■ Avoid carrying equipment on deck. In addition to raising the centre of gravity, it will impede the escape of water off the boat.

■ Know your boat's natural rolling period. Be alert to any change to this period, especially a lengthening in the period, which may suggest reduced stability.

■ If the boat appears to be becoming unstable at any time, jettison weight from the top of the boat or restow those weights lower in the boat — even positioning your crew lower in the boat will have an immediate effect.

■ Never place weights (or crew) on the high side of the boat to correct a loll. Place weight in the bottom of the boat.

■ If considering making alterations to your boat, always consult an expert with regard to its seaworthiness and stability.

■ When stowing gear aboard the boat for a voyage, stow heavy gear as low as possible, and spread the weight towards the outer parts of the boat. All gear should be secured to prevent movement.

10

BOAT HANDLING

A boat that will not obey her helm will have to obey the rocks.

— A Cornish proverb

Handling a boat, like handling a car or an aeroplane, is an acquired art. It is a skill that must be learnt by practice and observation. Only after experiencing for yourself how the propeller affects the heading of the boat, and how the boat reacts to her rudder, will you have an insight into the art of boat handling. Experience for yourself the effects of wind and current on the control of the boat and you will then have a better understanding of how you can work with the wind and current to acquire better control over your boat.

The propeller

The direction in which the propeller rotates to drive the boat ahead can be clockwise or anticlockwise. If the propeller turns clockwise when viewed from aft, it is named a right-handed propeller; if it turns anti-clockwise, it is a left-handed propeller. Most single-screw boats have right-handed propellers.

A boat fitted with twin propellers usually has the propellers outward-turning; that is, the port propeller is left-handed and the starboard propeller is right-handed. Inward-turning propellers give slightly more speed, but do not give the same degree of manoeuvrability.

A boat's hull is designed to give a smooth flow of water towards and into the propeller. For this reason a propeller works most efficiently when the boat is moving ahead; when moving astern, the water flow through the propeller is much more disturbed.

Propeller pitch

The blades of the propeller are angled like the blades of a fan. The angle made by the blade with the plane in which the propeller is turning is called the angle of pitch.

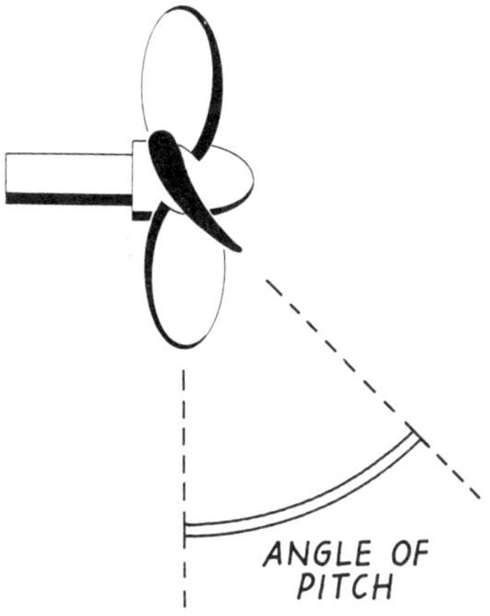

Propeller thrust

When the engine is put ahead, the propeller thrusts the water astern, causing the boat to move ahead. But because the propeller is turning transversely, some of the water is paddled sideways.

Axial thrust is the component of a propeller's thrust acting to move the boat ahead or astern, that is, along the boat's fore-and-aft axis.

Transverse thrust is the component of a propeller's thrust acting sideways. Because of the 'paddle-wheel' effect of the propeller, the stern is paddled to one side.

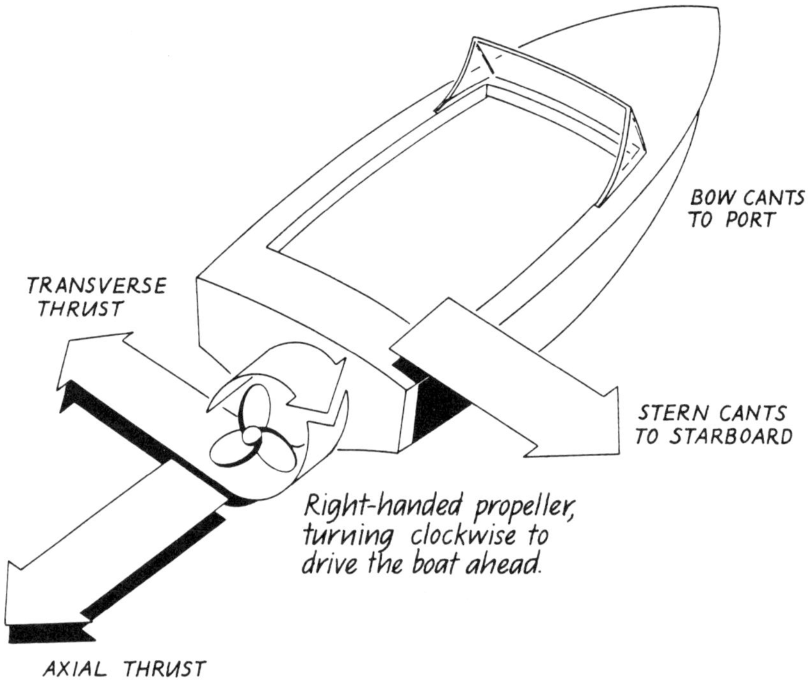

When a right-handed propeller is put ahead, the stern is paddled to the right, canting the boat around to port. This is most noticeable as the boat begins to gather way; however, as the boat increases speed and the rudder and hull line become more operative, the effect becomes negligible.

When the same boat is put astern, the opposite occurs and the boat is canted to starboard. This time there is no smooth flow of water into the propeller and the effect is usually more pronounced.

The effects of transverse thrust vary between different boats. On high-speed boats with high-pitch propellers it can be particularly noticeable, even a problem, at slower speeds, especially when manoeuvring astern. Boats with twin propellers rotating in opposite directions are not affected, because the transverse thrust from each propeller cancels out.

Cavitation

When a propeller rotates, it sucks in water from one side and expels it from the other. Thus, if the engine is going ahead, on the face of each propeller blade there is an increase in water pressure, thrusting the water away from the propeller, and on the back of each blade there is a reduction in pressure as the propeller sucks in water. As propeller speed increases, pressure builds up on the blade faces and reduces on the backs. Water pressure can be increased indefinitely, building up the propeller's thrust, but eventually the reduction in pressure on the backs of the blades becomes low enough for the water to vapourise and vapour pockets, or 'cavities', begin to form along the backs of the blades. This is called cavitation and is visible as a mass of vapour-pocket 'bubbles' around the fast-rotating propeller.

As soon as cavitation occurs, the propeller's efficiency decreases. The propeller loses its grip on the water. Engine revolutions increase, perhaps causing the engine to race, and the propeller thrust reduces dramatically. In addition, as the vapour pockets collapse onto the blades, uncomfortable levels of vibration and noise are produced, and pitting and erosion of the propeller blades may result. Cavitation may occur if moving either ahead or astern.

Propeller performance can also be affected if the propeller is operating too close to the surface, so that air bubbles are sucked down into it. These bubbles create the same problems as cavitation. Most outboard engines have anti-cavitation plates fitted horizontally above the propeller to reduce the inflow of air bubbles from the surface.

The rudder

Rudder action relies on the flow of water past the rudder. If the boat is moving, or if the propeller is pushing water past the rudder, it will be effective; but if there is no water flow across the rudder surfaces, it will have no effect.

On a moving boat with the rudder amidships the water flow is equal on both sides of the rudder. If the rudder is turned, this flow is disrupted to create pressure differences on each side of the rudder. It is this pressure differential that causes the rudder to be displaced sideways, and with it, the stern.

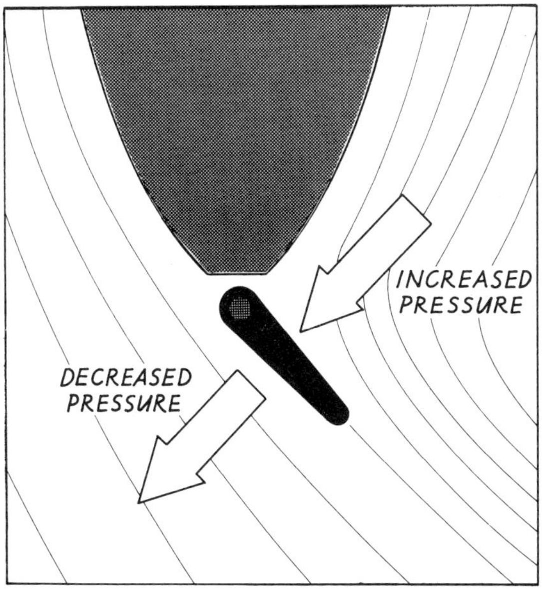

If the rudder is turned to starboard, an area of higher pressure is created on the starboard side of the rudder, and lower pressure on the port side. This pressure differential leans on the rudder, pushing and pulling it to port.

One important aspect of this movement should be noted: the stern moves away in the opposite direction to which we wish to turn. Unlike the movement of a turning car, in which the front wheels pull the car around, the rudder of a boat pushes the stern outwards so that the bow will move around in the intended direction.

Stemming the tide

For the rudder to be effective there must be a flow of water past it. This means that to be able to steer your boat it must be moving; you will lose steerageway if your speed is insufficient to provide this flow. You can manoeuvre your boat at slower speeds if you are travelling against the tidal flow ('stemming' the tide), for then the tidal flow will provide an additional flow of water past the rudder. You will have greater speed but less control if moving with the tide astern.

The pivoting point

When turning, a boat pivots around a point forward of the amidships position. The exact pivoting point varies with the hull shape, but for a displacement craft it will be located at a position approximately one third of the length from the bow. Faster boats have their pivoting point further forward; a boat on the plane pivots around a point some distance ahead of the bow.

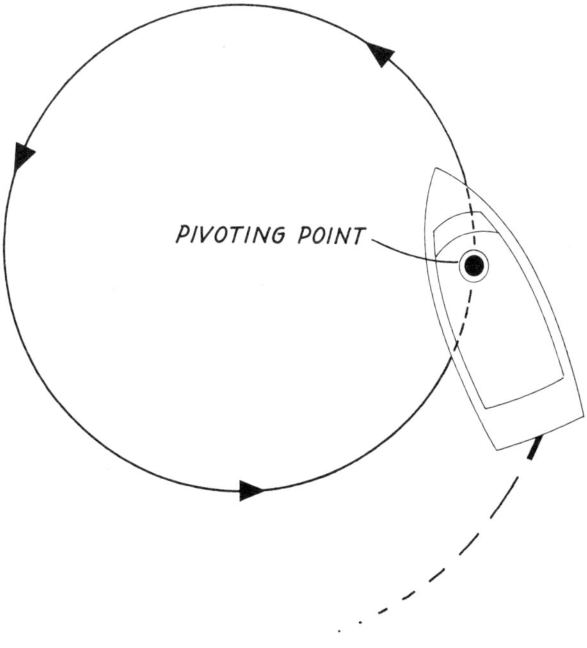

When a boat is moving astern, its pivoting point moves well aft, usually to a point between the stern and a third of the length from the stern.

The turning circle

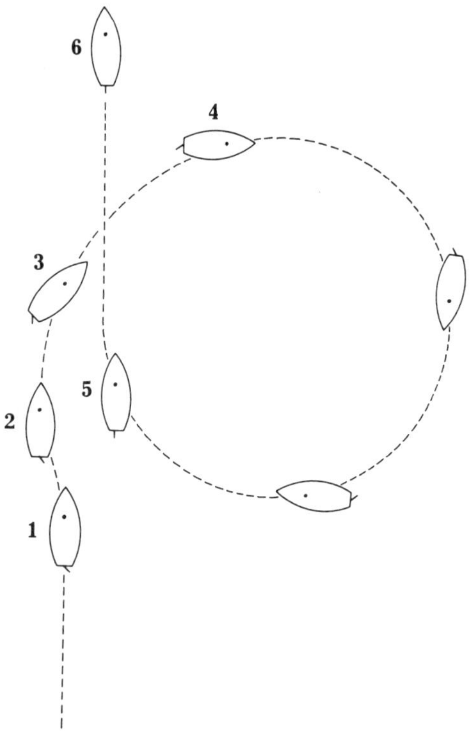

How a boat reacts to its rudder when put through a turn. With a right-handed propeller, a boat's turning circle to port will be slightly smaller than the circle to starboard, because of transverse thrust.

1
The rudder is put to starboard.

2
Forward momentum and inertia carry the boat a short distance, and then the entire boat sideslips to port before it commences turning.

3
The stern of the boat moves out to port as the boat enters the turn.

4
The boat turns about its pivotal point, its bow inside the path of the turn and its stern outside the path.

5
The turn is completed and the rudder is returned amidships. Course is resumed.

6
The boat resumes its course, usually on a line inside that of its original line.

The current

A current or tidal stream carries the boat bodily in the direction of the flow, so that the boat's track over the ground can be quite different to the course and speed through the water.

This water movement has no effect on the boat's handling characteristics but must be considered when carrying out any manoeuvre. Remember the advantages of increased control at slower speeds when stemming the tide. Water movement will, however, affect your navigation, for the boat's course, as indicated by the compass, is not the same as that being made over the ground; and the boat's speed and distance covered, as indicated by the log, is the speed and distance through the water and not across the ground.

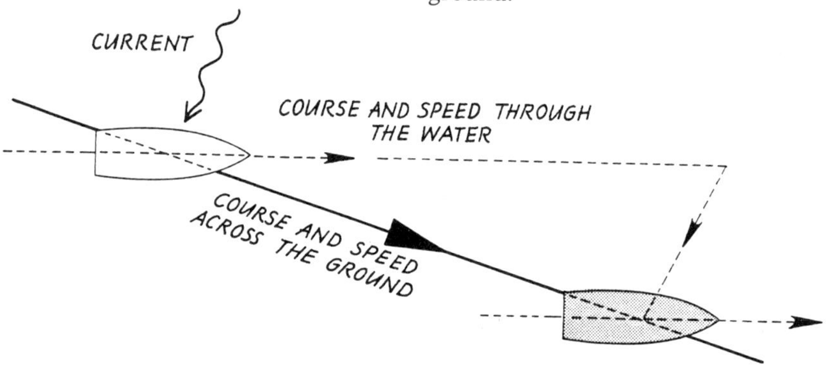

When carrying out a manoeuvre, assess the water flow by observation. The direction in which a buoy is lying to its mooring, flotsam or weed moving past the pile of a jetty, and eddies around the downstream side of a fixed obstruction all give an indication of the direction and strength of the water flow.

The wind

The effects of wind vary considerably between boats. Much depends on the shape of the hull and where its pivotal point lies, but it is the exposed topsides of the boat that finally determines how the boat will handle in a wind.

A boat stopped in the water and left to its own devices generally comes to rest broadside to the wind. While moving ahead, if the area of topsides aft of the pivoting point is larger than forward, the boat will try to 'round up', or turn towards the wind. If there is more topside area forward of the pivoting point, she will try to 'pay off', or turn away from the wind. When the boat is moving astern, the pivoting point moves well aft. Because the majority of the topsides area is then behind the pivoting point, the boat invariably tries to bring its stern up into the wind. Generally this effect is more pronounced than when moving ahead, often making a manoeuvre astern in the wind particularly difficult or perhaps impossible.

Leeway

Leeway is the amount by which the boat is pushed off her intended track by the wind. The angle of leeway is the angle between the boat's head and the track actually being followed through the water. It is more easily determined by looking aft and comparing the boat's fore-and-aft line with the wake.

The amount of leeway varies with a boat's form and depends on the strength of the wind and its direction relative to the course. A beam wind causes the maximum leeway. A heavy boat with a deep keel makes very little leeway compared with a lighter boat that has a large amount of windage.

Shallow water

A boat's handling characteristics can change dramatically as it enters shallow water, and these changes are usually detrimental to good control. With the close proximity of the hull to the seabed there is a restriction in the flow of water towards the propeller and rudder, and the boat's response to them decreases correspondingly. The boat becomes sluggish and less sensitive to adjustments of speed and rudder. There is also the danger of weed, stones and mud being drawn into the propeller and cooling system.

Displacement boats

What seems sufficient depth on the chart sometimes turns out to be insufficient for displacement craft, because of the phenomena of settlement and squat. The reduced space available between the bottom of the boat and the seabed causes the water flow to increase and a venturi effect develops; the increase in flow causes a decrease in water pressure beneath the boat. The boat now drops, or 'settles' into this decreased

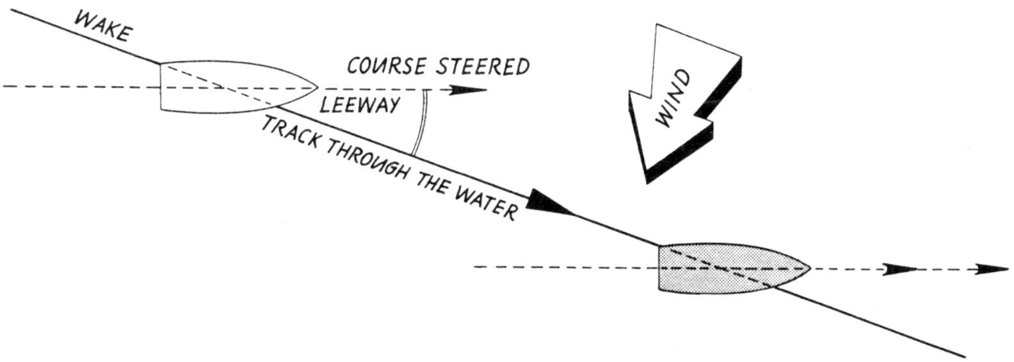

pressure area. The faster the boat is moving, the greater the effect, and the more chance there is of grounding. As well as settling bodily into the water, the trim of the boat can also alter, with the stern squatting lower into the water than the bow.

A boat gives its own warning signs of settling in shallow water. Bow and stern waves increase in size in proportion to the boat's speed and the shallowness of the water. A loss in speed is experienced, and sometimes excessive vibration can be felt.

Planing boats

It is generally found that a boat planes more efficiently over shallow water than over deeper water, and it is able to maintain a planing attitude at slower speeds. This negates the need to negotiate shallows at high speeds — less speed will give you more time to study the water ahead. Learn to read the water, and to recognise the signs of hidden dangers. (See page 70.)

Interaction

The same venturi effect that causes a boat to settle closer to the bottom in shallower water can also draw your boat towards a nearby boat or structure as you pass. It is also particularly noticeable as you pass a moored boat, which is drawn along with the moving boat in a surge that may be severe enough to cause damage or carry away moorings.

The effects of interaction increase with speed, so reduce speed well before passing to avoid upsetting boats and tempers.

Anchoring

■ Study your chart to select the most suitable spot for anchoring, taking into account the depth of water in relation to your draught and the length of your anchor line; the nature of the bottom in relation to the type of anchor you are using; and the shelter provided by the anchorage in relation to the present and expected weather.

■ Consult your chart for good landmarks on your approach to the anchorage, and so that your position can be verified while at anchor.

■ Check from your chart that the seabed is clear of wrecks and cables. Avoid 'prohibited' areas, and select an anchorage well clear of shipping lanes.

■ Prepare your anchor in good time. Ensure that the anchor is connected to the anchor line (not as silly as it sounds!), and that the inboard end of the line (the bitter end) is secured to the boat. Have the line laid out ready to run out as the anchor is let go.

■ Hang the anchor ready over the bow, or in the anchor leads.

■ Approach the anchorage at slow speed, stemming the tide or wind so as to give maximum control at minimum speed. If in doubt about the direction of approach, line up your boat in the same direction as other anchored boats.

■ As the point of anchorage is reached, put the engine into neutral. Allow the tidal flow (or use the engine, if necessary) to give the boat a little sternway.

■ As the boat gains sternway, lower the anchor to the seabed until it just touches bottom (see **1** on page 93). Do not pay out all your anchor line at once, it will lie over and foul the anchor.

■ As the boat continues moving astern, slowly pay out the anchor line. The aim is to lay out the chain in a line along the seabed (**2**).

■ When sufficient line has been paid out, secure the line and allow the boat to come up on it. This will 'dig' in the anchor. If necessary, give the engine a short burst astern to help dig in the anchor (**3**).

■ Check that the anchor is not dragging by watching or feeling the anchor line. When the boat is settled comfortably to its anchor, it is said to be 'brought up'.

■ Take bearings of suitable landmarks and check the depth with echo sounder or lead line to confirm your position. These can later be used to check that you have not dragged anchor.

Laying the anchor

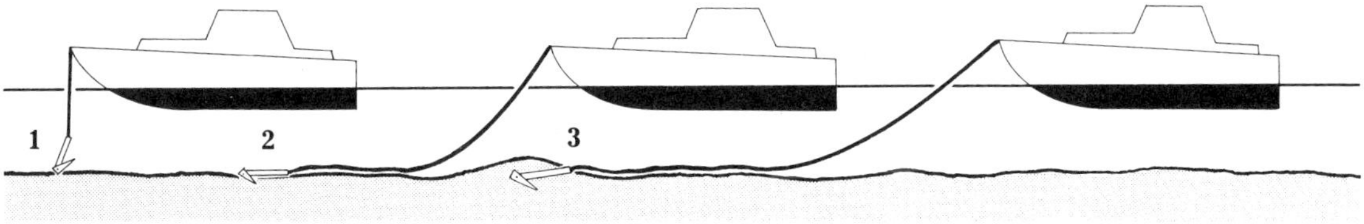

Weighing anchor

Before weighing anchor, have your engine running. If the boat is lying in the wrong direction, bring it around to the desired heading, using the engine and rudder, before weighing anchor. You may find it necessary to use a stiff brush to remove the mud from your anchor before it is brought aboard. Should a strong tide be setting, come gently ahead on the engine to ease the tension on the line.

Foul anchor

You may be unfortunate to discover that the anchor has fouled an obstruction on the seabed. If the obstruction feels solid, take the boat across the anchor and heave it from another direction. You may have to try pulling from several directions, and perhaps try engine power to pull the anchor out. If these attempts fail and you are unable to dive to clear the anchor by hand, your only alternative may be to 'slip' the anchor by cutting the line and buoying it for later retrieval.

Securing a boat to a berth

The number of lines used to secure a boat alongside depends on the size of the boat, the strength of the wind and current, and the rise and fall of the tide. Each line serves a purpose — all or only some may be necessary, depending on circumstances. In severe weather you may have to double up on some lines. Fenders will also be necessary to prevent damage to the boat as it moves or surges at its berth.

The headline and sternline prevent the boat from surging back and forth along the quay. The greater the rise and fall of the tide, the longer should be the lead on these lines.

The breastlines hold the boat bodily alongside. Unless they can be tended constantly, they should not be used if there is a large rise and fall of tide.

The springs act with the headline and sternline to prevent surging along the jetty. The headspring acts with the headline to hold in the bow, and the backspring acts with the sternline to hold in the stern.

Springing a boat off a berth

The headspring (or backspring) can be used to 'spring' one end of the boat away from the berth, particularly if manoeuvring space is limited.

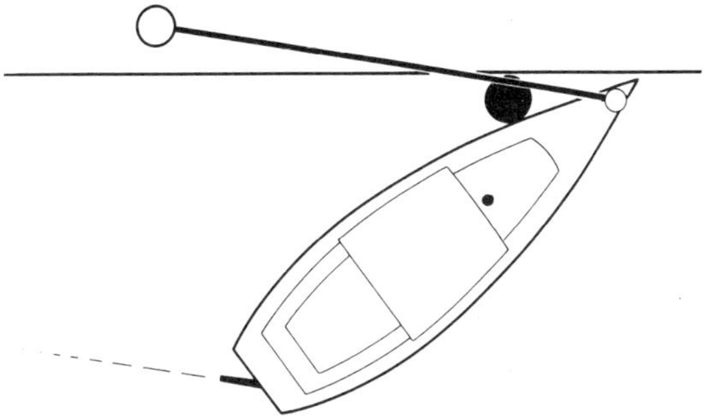

Use the boat's engine, or the wind or current, to move the boat's stern while the spring holds in the boat's bow. Once the stern is sufficiently clear of the berth, the engine can be used to move the boat astern to clear the berth.

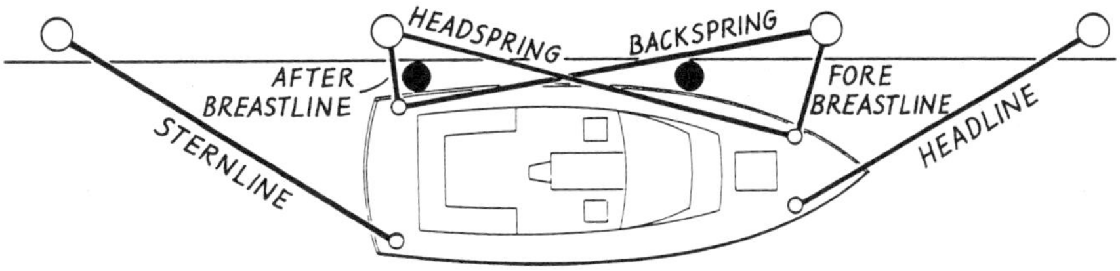

Turning short round

The effects of transverse thrust can be used to advantage when turning a boat around in a confined space.

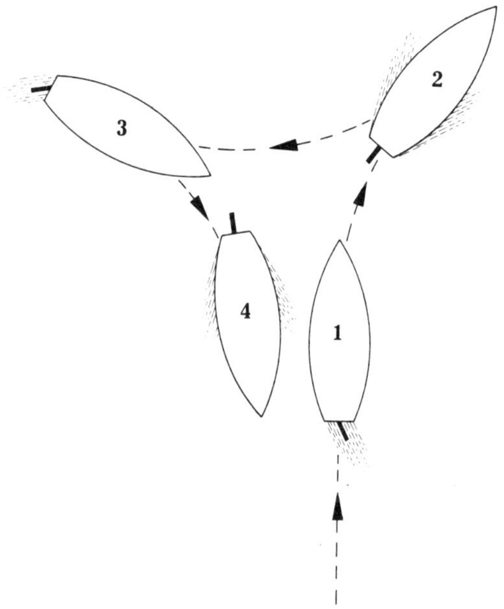

1
The boat is first stopped in the water. The rudder is then put hard over to starboard (for a right-handed propeller) and the engine put ahead.

2
Immediately the boat begins making headway, swinging to starboard, the rudder is brought amidships and the engine put astern. Transverse thrust now cants the boat further around to starboard.

3
When the boat begins to move astern and loses its cant, the rudder is put hard over to starboard with the engine ahead again.

4
The process is now repeated; as headway begins the engine is stopped, rudder put admidships, and the engine put astern. Transverse thrust will again cant the stern further to starboard.

This is repeated as many times as necessary to bring the boat around. More effect from transverse thrust will be gained if the headway is kept to a minimum on each occasion.

The Williamson turn

This turn is designed to bring the boat through a 180° turn so that it returns to its original course line. It is a particularly useful manoeuvre for power boats in a man-overboard situation. Full speed is maintained throughout the turn.

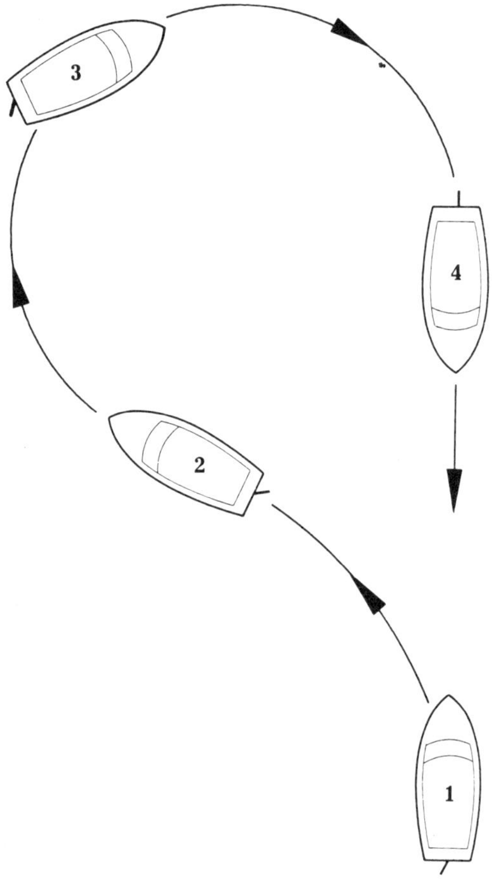

1
To commence the turn, the wheel is put hard over to port or to starboard. In the case of a man overboard, the initial direction of helm is preferably to the side from which the person fell.

2
As the turn begins, the compass heading is noted. After the boat has swung about 60 to 70 degrees from her original course, the rudder is put hard over to the opposite side. (The amount of swing before reversing rudder direction varies with the speed, size, and type of boat. With pleasure boats it is usually found to be about 70 degrees, but a few

practice manoeuvres will determine this for your own boat.)

3
The boat now swings in the opposite direction, and this turn is maintained with full rudder until the reciprocal of the original course is reached.

4
The rudder is now used to steady the boat onto the reciprocal course. The boat should now be proceeding back along its former track.

Man overboard

This is probably the most common emergency situation, and should certainly be the most rehearsed of your emergency manoeuvres.

Alert the remaining crew to the situation by shouting 'Man overboard!'

Throw something into the water for the victim to hang on to. Ideally this should be a lifebuoy kept on deck for just such an emergency, but a buoyant cushion, a spare lifejacket or any other buoyant object may do. This will also mark the position in the water if the victim has gone under.

Never lose sight of the person in the water. Even in slightly choppy water a small head can quickly be lost to view among waves. If you have the crew available, have someone stand high on the boat to point to the person in the water to keep him or her in sight.

The return manoeuvre to bring the boat back to the person in the water is a matter of choice. You may make a full-powered turn to the spot, or use the Williamson turn. If under sail, you may choose to gybe and take the boat downwind so that the approach can be made head to wind; or perhaps forget the sails and use the engine. If time is needed to reduce sail, leave a path of floating objects in the water so that you can retrace your track. On a powered boat, throttle back on your final stage of the turn so that you can approach at slow speed. Never stop and back up.

Mind your propeller! The chance of a falling person being caught in the propeller of a boat moving ahead at speed is remote. If the boat is travelling at high speed, the victim may not even hit the water until you are well past, and even on a slower-moving displacement boat the waves will probably push the person clear. The greatest moment of danger is when you return to the spot and manoeuvre for a pick-up.

Your approach to the victim is the part of the manoeuvre that requires all your skill in boat handling. You must ensure that the victim does not get near to the propeller. In very light conditions it may be preferable to place your boat upwind of the victim, stop engines, and gently drift broadsides down to him. In anything other than light conditions you must maintain maximum control by approaching head to wind — the current is not important. Approach at slow speed; if you are moving too fast you may run past, and putting your engine astern may have fatal consequences. If at all possible, throw a line to the victim and pull him to your boat rather than attempt a tricky manoeuvre to come alongside.

Retrieval from the water is easiest if made at the stern or quarter where there is the least amount of freeboard and plenty of cockpit space. Ensure that the propeller has stopped turning. On many boats the propeller turns even if the engine is in neutral — it is safer to stop the engine completely.

Wet clothes and lifejacket add considerable weight to anyone who has fallen overboard, and you may find that a bight of line or a fender over the side to act as a foothold will help. If the person is disabled or unconscious, extra help may be provided by having someone else in the water. It may be necessary to use your winch, with a loop of rope under the victim's armpits, to help the victim aboard.

Darkness presents additional problems, likewise if the person went over the side without being noticed. In such cases the Williamson turn is especially useful, for it will return the boat to its original track. A marker, preferably an illuminated signal, should be dropped into the water to provide a reference position. Even in daylight a marker or danbuoy should be dropped if it is apparent that the search may be a lengthy one.

Your radio can be used to summon further help, perhaps from a nearby vessel or from professional or voluntary services ashore.

Heavy weather

Maintaining control of the boat and ensuring its seaworthiness in bad weather requires constant effort and concentration. If any crew are seasick, the degree of effort and concentration will be appreciably impaired. Establish a heavy-weather routine aboard that will keep your crew occupied in preparing the boat to meet the elements, and that will give them confidence in the seaworthiness of the boat and in your own ability as skipper.

Shelter

As skipper, you must decide by weighing up the pertinent facts whether to run for shelter or stay where you are and heave to. Verify your position on the chart — the chart may indicate suitable sites for shelter, but you must also consider the time and distance it will take to reach your chosen refuge and the seas you must travel through to reach it. Shallows and tidal streams frequently produce more dangerous seas closer to the shore and in harbour and bay entrances than further out to sea. Cliffs and islands may provide shelter on their lee side, but they can also cause areas of confused and violent seas and strong wind gusts. If you have no local information, remember that your radio can put you in touch with someone who has.

Rolling

Maximum rolling occurs if the waves strike the boat from abeam, and can be excessive if the wave period synchronises with the boat's natural rolling period. If possible, adjust the boat's course and speed to reduce the rolling. If the boat is stationary, stream a sea anchor to bring the boat's head to the waves.

Stability

Make sure your boat remains stable and seaworthy. Keep it dry inside by securing all hatches and accesses. Any water that does enter the boat must be quickly removed. Ensure all loose gear is stowed as low as possible, and that it is unable to move around.

Running with the sea

If the boat is running at the same speed as the waves, water flow past the rudder is considerably reduced and steering may be extremely difficult. There is also the added danger of broaching. A long line trailed in the water over the stern will help prevent broaching, and help to keep the boat on a steady course.

Running into head seas

Driving the boat into head seas can also present problems with steering. When the boat is in a trough there is relative shelter, but as it mounts the crest of a wave there is the possibility of the bow being knocked or blown sideways. Constant attention is required to prevent this, if necessary by turning to meet each wave crest directly head-on rather than at an angle on the bow.

Speed will also require constant attention. A boat driven too hard into head seas can suffer structural and mechanical damage; pounding into a wave under power could smash the boat to pieces, and constant lifting of the propeller out of the water will cause the engine to race.

On the other hand, many boats rely on their speed to lift the bow — at slow speed the boat may sit with its head low in the water and may well plough through a wave rather than lift over it. This could have serious consequences in an open boat.

Heaving-to

If conditions become too severe it may be necessary to heave to and ride out the bad weather. You must place the boat in an attitude that takes as much strain as possible from it and the crew. This may be achieved by stopping the engine and lying to an anchor or sea anchor, or by making slow headway with the sea on the bow. Yachts vary in the most suitable rig for heaving-to. You must experiment to find the most comfortable rig for your boat.

Lying to an anchor or sea anchor virtually leaves the boat to look after itself, but attention must still be given to keeping it stable and dry. Although a sea anchor will reduce drift, leeway will still be made, and care must be taken to see that the boat is not driven onto a lee shore (a shore onto which the wind is blowing). Verify your position frequently.

Emergency propulsion

A well-equipped boat will always have some alternative means of getting home should its primary system of propulsion fail. This may be in the form of another motor, an auxiliary outboard, or perhaps simply a paddle. Even if no alternative method of propulsion is fitted, it is surprising how a little ingenuity will provide a solution. Many a disabled power boat has been sailed home, its makeshift sail fashioned from sheets or curtains.

Emergency steering

Failure of a boat's steering, although inconvenient, does not necessarily render the boat unmanageable. Twin-screw craft can still be steered by varying the speeds of the individual engines, and a yacht may be able to be steered by constant adjustment of the sheets. Any craft can be brought home with an improvised steering arrangement.

A paddle or oar over the stern will suffice as a makeshift rudder, but anything dropped over the side to drag one side of the boat around will also provide a means of steering the boat. A bucket, or similar drogue, on a length of line should be sufficient.

Running aground

An unintentional grounding of the boat may be serious or not, depending on the type of boat, the nature of the ground touched, and the state of the sea. Grounding on a muddy or sandy bottom is likely to cause little or no damage, but if the boat is among waves, pounding onto the bottom may be dangerous.

A small boat running aground will quite possibly present no problem, for its crew may simply be able to step over the side and lift it back into deeper water. The problems associated with the stranding of a larger boat, however, may be more complex.

Let someone know of your plight. Although you may not be in any immediate danger, you may require assistance later. If the boat is damaged, it may be better to stay where you are rather than attempting to refloat it.

Damage

Before attempting to refloat, check for damage. Make a thorough inspection of the boat's hull, not only up forward where the impact occurred, but throughout the boat's length. Water in the bilges may give an indication of damage, but the absence of water does not necessarily mean that the hull has not been strained. Look for visible signs of sprung timbers, cracks or fractures — these may appear in an area remote from the point of contact. Check the engine mountings and the propeller shaft. The force of impact may have upset the shaft alignment; water seeping through the stern gland may give an indication of this.

The seabed

Have a good look around over the side, perhaps by diving, to see what the boat has grounded on and where it is fast. Look for a deeper area in which to refloat, and note any rocks or boulders that may have to be avoided.

The sea

If waves are running, or perhaps surf, immediate measures may have to be taken to prevent the boat being slewed broadside to the sea. This is done by laying out an anchor or ground tackle. Cross-currents or cross-winds may also require similar measures.

The tide

Check the tide tables to find whether the tide is rising or falling, and the expected range of the tide. If the tide is rising, you may not have to wait long but if it is falling, use the extra time sensibly. On a keeler you may have to consider bracing the boat to prevent it settling onto its side as the water level lowers.

Using the engine

This must be done only after careful check of the engine, shaft and propeller, and only if you are quite sure that the boat is not damaged. A short burst of stern power may be sufficient to pull the boat off, but persistent use of the engine may only make matters worse. Your propeller could be stirring up the seabed causing damage to the propeller and choking of the cooling water system.

Slewing the boat

On softer bottoms it is frequently only suction between the hull and the seabed that holds the boat fast. Slew the boat with the rudder or rock the boat gently to release this suction as you use the engine.

Altering trim

Transferring weights aboard may also help to lift the grounded portion of the hull off the bottom. If the boat is aground forward, it is not necessarily a shift of weight to the stern that will have the desired effect — this may only increase the length of keel on the bottom. Experiment by transferring weight to the bow. Keel yachts have often been refloated by using another boat to pull the top of the mast sideways, heeling the boat to reduce its draft.

Ground tackle

If engine power alone is insufficient to refloat the boat, put out ground tackle to pull the boat off. One or more anchors should be placed, either by walking the anchor out manually or by rowing it out by dinghy. By pulling on the anchor line, manually or with a winch, the boat may float off easily, but if not, leave the anchor there until a rising tide comes in to help.

A tow from another boat

If assistance is available, use as long a towline as possible, and take care that when passing the towline the other boat does not also ground. The towing boat can use its own anchor to prevent being driven ashore; this anchor may also serve as a useful purchase while pulling. Only attempt pulling the boat off in this way if you are sure the boat is not seriously holed, and that the pull off the bottom will not further damage the hull.

Rescue at sea

Rescuing the occupants from another boat requires careful and considerate boat handling to ensure you do not lose control of your own boat and end up in the same predicament as those you are attempting to rescue. No two rescues are the same, and you must be guided by common sense and the prevailing circumstances. However, the following points should always be borne in mind.

Use your radio to inform others of your intended rescue, and to find out as much as you can about the boat in trouble. Find out the number of people aboard, and whether they are injured or non-swimmers. How long is the disabled boat expected to remain afloat? How much sea room is there, and what is the state of the sea? What lifesaving equipment does the disabled boat have aboard? A dinghy or liferaft is useful for transferring persons between boats.

Never endanger your own boat by putting it in a position where it could be blown or set onto the disabled boat or the obstruction in the water that caused the trouble in the first place. Remember, as long as your own boat is moving through the water you have control over it; the moment you stop, unless you have an anchor down, you lose control.

If the other boat is afloat, current will affect both boats and is therefore of no concern unless there is a risk of being swept onto some other danger. You will probably find that the wind is the factor requiring most attention. In very light conditions it may be preferable to place the boat upwind, perhaps offering lee, and then allow the boat to drift slowly down broadsides to the disabled boat. In anything but light conditions make your approach head to wind, and try to keep the boat in this attitude — if necessary by using an anchor or sea anchor. If you stop and your boat falls away from the wind to lie broadside to wind and sea, rolling will make conditions aboard more difficult.

Transferring people from one boat to another must be done with extreme care. Unless the sea is perfectly calm, do not put your boat alongside and expect people to jump across. Movement of the two boats, especially in heavier seas, will cause damage to the craft and could be fatal if anyone were to fall or get a limb caught between the boats. A dinghy or inflatable liferaft should be used if available, otherwise people should be transferred through the water. Endeavour to pass a line between the boats, but keep it well clear of the propeller at all times.

If transferring people between boats through the water, watch your propeller. Stand sufficiently apart from the other boat to maintain enough searoom for manoeuvring. If the other boat is not drifting and other conditions allow, put an anchor down to hold your own boat and to give you more freedom to attend to the survivors. Bring the people along the line, but never have more than one person in the water at a time.

Remember the difficulties involved in retrieving people from the water, and have a ladder or foothold over the side to help them aboard. If they have been in the water or adrift in a disabled boat for some time, they could be suffering from hypothermia — once aboard keep them below and have blankets and spare clothing ready.

A dinghy or liferaft is ideal for ferrying people between boats. If you are to use your own, bring your boat upwind of the disabled boat and float the raft or dinghy down on a line. Once the survivors have boarded, it can then be hauled back to your own boat. If using the other boat's dinghy or raft, the survivors should board it and allow it to drift downwind of their boat on a line. You can then bring your own boat alongside the raft or dinghy, and bring its occupants aboard.

Towing

When one boat is towing another, the handling characteristics of both boats change completely. There are bound to be problems, and you will inevitably find that tempers will fray as quickly as ropes. Common sense and courtesy dictate that the person offering the tow should be in charge of the manoeuvre, so follow instructions.

The towline

Ideally, the longer the line the better. Extra length will reduce the strain on the line, and it is less likely to become suddenly taut during the tow.

When making a longer sea tow, experiment to find the most suitable length of line. In a swell it is better to adjust the length to a multiple of the wavelength so that both boats are moving up and down in unison without the line continually working slack and taut.

Remember that nylon's elasticity and immense strength could prove extremely dangerous should the line part or be stronger than the fittings to which it is secured.

To prevent sudden shock loading of the line as it comes taut, place a weight mid-length in the line. A sandbag or a length of chain will do, its function being to keep the line down in the water, acting rather like a spring or shock absorber.

Securing the line

Ideally the towing boat should tow from its pivoting point, to allow the rudder to move the stern and allow the boat to manoeuvre, but this is seldom practicable on a pleasure boat.

Nevertheless, always endeavour to lead the towline from the centre of the stern and not from one of the quarters. A lead that is not centrally placed will cause the towing boat to sheer continually to one side. If no central fairlead is fitted to the boat, lead the towline from a bridle.

In calmer weather and more confined waters it may be easier to bring the towed boat alongside rather than to tow astern.

Whatever arrangement is used, remember that the usual cleats and fairleads on a pleasure boat are not generally designed to take heavy loads. A towline is only as strong as the fitting it is made fast to — the towline may not break but the cleat may pull out. If you doubt the strength of the fittings, do not make the towline fast to one single point, spread the load; take turns with the line around several points so that the strain is dispersed.

Similar precautions must be taken aboard the towed boat. If necessary, spread the load to more than one point. The line should be centrally led over and attached at the stem rather than over one side of the bow, or the towed boat may sheer and upset the manoeuvrability of both boats.

Handling the towing boat

When commencing the tow, take up the tension on the line gradually and thereafter try to maintain a steady speed to prevent unnecessary slackening and tightening of the line. Plan any manoeuvre well ahead, as your turning circle will now be considerably larger. The boat and towline in the water behind will restrict the use of the engine to slow or stop your boat.

With the weight of the tow behind, speed will naturally be reduced, but your engine will be working just as hard, or harder, than usual. Check frequently that it is not overheating, especially if the cooling system relies upon the flow of water past the hull.

A boat with a flat-bottomed planing hull will have poor directional properties when moving at these slower speeds, and will most likely wander considerably, making course-keeping difficult. A deeper-keeled displacement boat should be more manageable. When towing a boat larger than your own, the increased windage of the towed boat will also complicate course-keeping; in a cross-wind the larger boat will constantly pull your stern downwind, giving your own boat a tendency to point itself closer to the wind.

A jetboat, or one propelled by outboard or sterndrive in which the steering is effected by the direction of the propeller thrust, will not, as a rule, experience steering problems. The engine will be turning faster with the increased load, and steering should be more definite.

Handling the towed boat

Being under tow does not necessarily mean you can sit back and let the other boat do all the work. Many boats tow well, but just as many do not, sometimes sheering considerably at the end of the towline. At slower speeds you may well find the rudder has insufficient effect to control the boat's sheer. Correction of sheer, or preventing it by attending to the trim of the boat, will increase the manoeuvrability of the towing boat.

The ideal attitude for the towed boat is to be well trimmed by the stern. A boat down by the head will wander off course and will resist the pull of the towline to bring it back again. Even the transference of the crew's weight to the back of the boat may be all that is needed to dig the stern deeper into the water and lift the bow. On boats with outboards the motor should be left down to increase water resistance aft. If these methods fail, consider paying out a length of line over the stern.

Launching a boat from a trailer

Before backing the trailer and boat to the water's edge, park at a convenient place clear of the ramp and assess the launching area. Watch other boats being launched, and note the effects of wind and tide during their launch and immediately the boats are waterborne. Check for any overhead power lines in the vicinity of the ramp, and their clearance. If any lines are present, do not raise and rig the mast until the boat is waterborne and clear of the lines.

Prepare your boat for sea. Check the underside of the hull and the keel or centreboard in case of road damage, and make sure the boat's bungs are in. Place the outboard in the fully raised position, and if the boat has a rudder, either unship it or fully raise it for the launch. Prepare a bow line (painter) for holding the boat after it has left the trailer.

Remove the boat's tie-downs and preventers, and disconnect the trailer's electrical system from the car. Have some chocks ready to prevent the car wheels from slipping on the ramp. Do not load the boat with unnecessary weighty gear until it is in the water.

Now back the trailer and boat down the ramp to the water's edge. It should be possible with a tilt-trailer to keep the wheels dry, but always endeavour to keep the wheel hubs and bearings out of the water. Stop the car, apply the handbrake, and chock the wheels. Appoint a crew member to hold the bow line, and release the winch brake and remove the towing hook from the bow of the boat. Now ease the boat off the trailer and into the water, controlling the boat with its bow line as it leaves the trailer.

Once the boat is waterborne, the car and trailer should be quickly removed from the ramp to a suitable parking area. Using the bow line, the boat should be taken clear of the launching area to a nearby beach or alongside a jetty for loading and rigging.

Retrieving the boat to a trailer

It is preferable to approach a ramp head to wind; an onshore wind may make retrieval more difficult. If necessary, wait clear of the ramp and watch others retrieve their boats. Note the effects of wind and tide on their retrieval, and any difficulties they may be experiencing.

Place the boat's trailer at the water's edge, preferably with the trailer's wheel hubs out of the water and with the car's wheels chocked. Run the winch cable out, and attach the cable end to the boat's winching point. You may have to place someone in the water at the stern of the boat to help align the boat with the trailer's rollers and guide the boat onto its trailer. Stand well clear of the winch cable when it is under tension.

Beaching

It is sometimes required to land a boat on a beach. In smaller boats, this may be desirable for purely recreational purposes, but beaching may be a necessary manoeuvre if the boat has suffered serious damage or is taking in water and is in danger of foundering. The process of beaching the boat and the precautions to be observed are essentially the same in each case.

Before approaching the beach, check the largest scale chart for any hazards in the area, and that the beach is suitable for your purposes. Check the state of the tide. Note the wind direction to see if it is onshore or offshore, and if there are waves or breakers onto the beach.

During your approach, continually monitor the depth by echo sounder or a boat-hook. If approaching a populated beach, watch carefully for swimmers and other water users. Under the Water Recreation Regulations, your speed must not exceed 5 knots within 30 metres of swimmers or within 200 metres of the shore. Have an anchor ready, and a bow line rigged and ready for your landing. Reduce sail if necessary and be ready to lower the sails, raise the centreboard or tilt the motor as you enter shallower water. A crew member will need to be at the bow, ready to jump into the water on landing and hold the boat head to wind.

In a smaller boat, approach the beach at right angles to the wave crests. During the final approach, bring the boat's head into the wind while there is still sufficient water to float the boat but shallow enough for the crew member to stand in the water.

When landing on a beach, whether approaching bow- or stern-first, there is a danger of broaching. Measures should be taken to prevent this, particularly if the boat is disabled and has no control. The rudder alone may not be sufficient to correct a broach, but steering ability may be improved by using a paddle or an oar.

In larger boats, or if there is a stronger sea running, consider turning the boat head to sea further offshore and dropping the anchor. By progressively paying out the anchor line you can then allow the boat to approach the beach stern-first, the anchor maintaining the boat's head to wind and waves.

Probably the most dangerous moment during beaching is when the boat first touches bottom. Unless checked, the boat may then quickly slew around, and subsequent waves may roll the boat. There is also the powerful effect of undertow when surf is running, which could carry the boat seawards into the next oncoming wave. In smaller boats, have crew members ready to jump over the side to manhandle the boat further up the beach. In larger boats, the offshore anchor will help to prevent slewing, but have extra lines or another anchor ready to take up the beach and brace the boat in position.

11

BUOYAGE

A great ship asks deep waters.
— Proverb

Buoys and beacons are the signposts of the sea. As such they must be recognised and understood if you are to find your way safely from place to place.

In 1977 the International Association of Lighthouse Authorities (IALA) introduced a maritime buoyage system for international use, which has two regional variations. New Zealand has chosen the Region A variation of this system, known as the IALA Buoyage System, Region A, or the Combined Cardinal and Lateral System (Red to Port). Other markers are also used to mark areas of local significance, such as water-ski areas, underwater cables, etc.

Local harbour authorities or port companies place buoys and beacons in the waters within their jurisdiction, under the guidance of the Maritime Safety Authority. Full details of the system may be found in *The System of Buoyage and Beaconage for New Zealand*, published by the Maritime Safety Authority.

The markers

A buoy is a floating mark, secured to the seabed by mooring chains, whereas a beacon is a mark permanently fixed upon the seabed. The significance of a mark is revealed by its colour, shape, topmark and light.

The region A system used in New Zealand for lateral marks uses the colour coding red to port and green to starboard, when travelling in the buoyage direction. Other markers each have their own specific colours, as shown here.

There are five basic shapes of buoys, and the shape may give an indication of the correct side on which the marker is to be passed when travelling in the buoyage direction.

A buoy may be identified by name, letters or numbers painted upon its side. By convention,

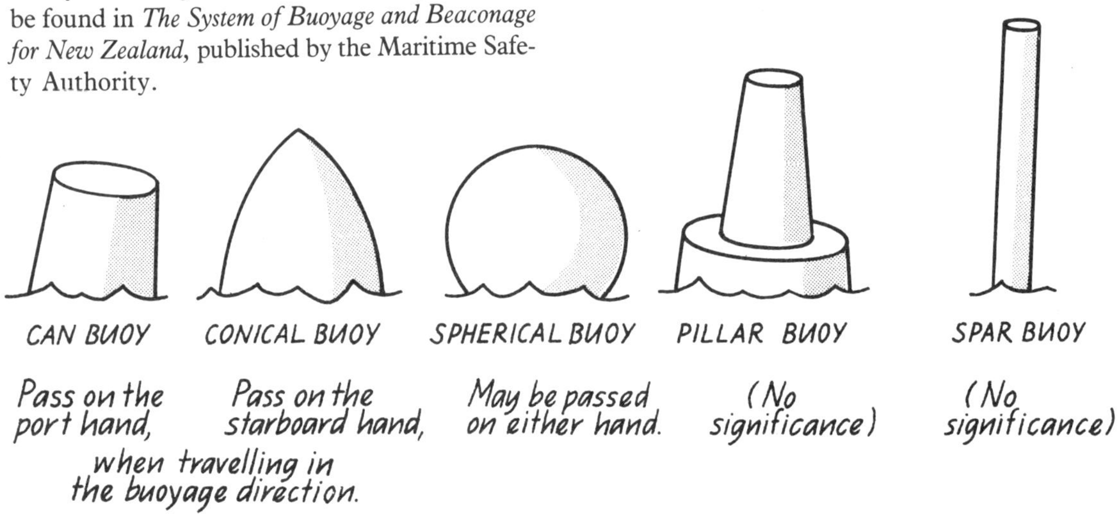

buoys are numbered so that port-hand buoys have even numbers, and starboard-hand buoys have odd numbers.

A topmark is an additional shape placed on top of the marker. If the shape of buoys cannot indicate the side to pass, a can or cone topmark may be used to convey this information. Some buoys and beacons, such as the cardinal marks, are required to carry double topmarks because they convey important information but on some markers the carriage of a topmark is optional.

Important markers are lit with red, green, white or yellow lights, showing a distinctive characteristic as shown here. An unlit marker may be marked with retro-reflective strips; the colour of the strips will be the same colour as prescribed for that marker's light, if it had been fitted.

The positions of all buoys and beacons are charted, together with their colours, shapes, markings, topmarks and characteristic lights. When you are passing any marker it should be positively identified and compared with the charted symbol as a check on the boat's position, and as a check on the significance of the marker and the position of the feature or danger it is marking.

Lateral marks

A lateral mark is intended to guide the mariner in a certain direction, that direction known as the buoyage direction. Two types of markers are used to mark the sides of the channel, known as channel markers. A port-hand channel marker must be passed on your port hand (that is, on the boat's port side) when travelling in the buoyage direction; and a starboard-hand channel marker is passed on your starboard hand (that is, on the boat's starboard side).

The buoyage direction

The direction of buoyage in most countries is by convention, usually chosen to coincide with the direction taken by a flood tide.

The conventional buoyage direction in New Zealand is either that direction approaching a harbour, estuary or waterway from seaward; or when travelling clockwise around the North Island or clockwise around the South Island, as shown here.

When travelling in the buoyage direction, the markers are passed on their correct sides. When travelling in the opposite direction, against the direction of buoyage, the side to pass is reversed.

Port-hand markers
To be passed on the port hand when travelling with the buoyage direction.

Colour: red.
Shape: can, pillar or spar.
Topmark: (if any) a red can.
Light: (if any) red, any rhythm, other than that prescribed for a preferred channel marker.

Starboard-hand markers
To be passed on the starboard hand when travelling with the buoyage direction.

Colour: green.
Shape: conical, pillar or spar.
Topmark: (if any) a green cone.
Light: (if any) green, any rhythm other than that prescribed for a preferred channel marker.

Preferred channel marks

Preferred channel marks, also known as bifurcation marks, are used where a channel divides to indicate on which side the preferred channel lies. The preferred or main channel lies on the named side of the mark, and a secondary channel lies to the other side.

Preferred channel to starboard
Preferred channel to starboard of the mark (secondary channel to port).

Colour: red with a green band.
Shape: can, pillar or spar.
Topmark: (if any) a red can.
Light: (if any) red composite group flashing Fl(2 + 1).

Preferred channel to port
Preferred channel to port of the mark (secondary channel to starboard).

Colour: green with a red band.
Shape: conical, pillar or spar.
Topmark: (if any) a green cone.
Light: (if any) green composite group flashing Fl(2 + 1).

Cardinal marks

These marks are used to indicate the side of a danger (or any other feature) on which it is safe to pass. They may also show where to find the deepest water in an area, or may draw attention to a bend or junction in a channel, or mark the end of a shoal.

Cardinal marks take their name from the cardinal points of the compass and should be passed on the named side of the mark. For example, pass to the north of a north cardinal mark.
Lights: All cardinal marks carry a white light which may be quick flashing (60 or 50 flashes per minute), or very quick flashing (120 or 100 flashes per minute) in the characteristic shown here. The concept of 3, 6 and 9 and is easily remembered if associated with a clock face.

Cardinal marks

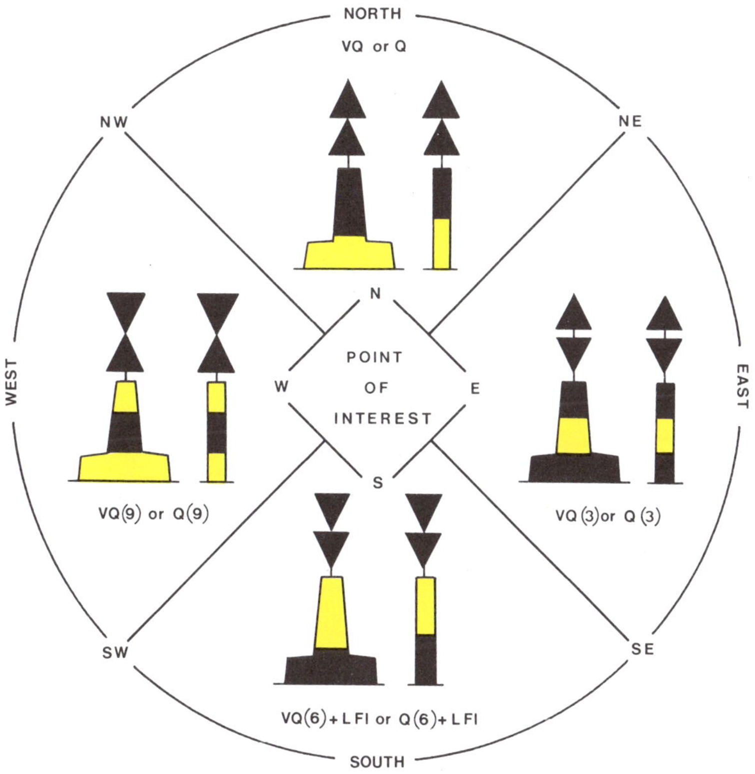

Isolated danger marks

These mark a danger of small area, with navigable water all around it.

Colour: black with red bands.
Shape: usually pillar or spar.
Topmark: two black spheres.
Light: (if any) white, group flashing Fl(2).

Safe-water marks

These do not mark a danger but are used, for example, as landfall marks or mid-channel marks. There is navigable water all around the mark.

Colour: red and white vertical stripes.
Shape: spherical, pillar or spar.
Topmark: (if any) single red sphere.
Light: (if any) white; occulting, isophase, 1 long flash every 10 seconds, or morse code 'A'.

Special marks

Special marks are used to indicate an area of special significance, such as spoil ground, a cable or pipeline area, a military exercise area, or an ODAS (Ocean Data Acquisition System) mark.

Colour: yellow.
Shape: optional, but in accordance with the conventional navigational shapes.
Topmark: (if any) a single yellow 'X'.
Light: yellow, any rhythm other than those used for cardinal marks, isolated danger marks, or safe-water marks.

Local marks

Water-ski lanes

Each side of the lane is marked on the shore with transit posts of orange and black. Noticeboards are placed ashore to warn bathers. In the water, in line with the transit posts, orange and black buoys may be placed to mark the sides of the lane.

Surfing lanes

Each side of the lane is marked on the shore with transit posts of orange (or yellow) and blue. Noticeboards, to warn bathers, are also displayed.

Submarine cables

Marked where the cable enters or leaves the water with white painted beacons and topmarks. Similar markers are used to indicate submarine pipelines, and appropriate wording appears on the triangle.

Overhead powerlines

When passing beneath an overhead powerline, whether the boat is in the water or being trailered ashore, there is a danger of electric shock if the mast or rigging touches or passes close to the line.

Allow sufficient clearance between the masthead and the powerline. Remember that the power can arc from powerline to mast, especially if high tension exists in the line, and if the boat provides a good earth, and if the mast or rigging is wet or the atmosphere humid. Observe the recommended safe clearance; it is that between the high-tide level or river level and the lowest part of the cable.

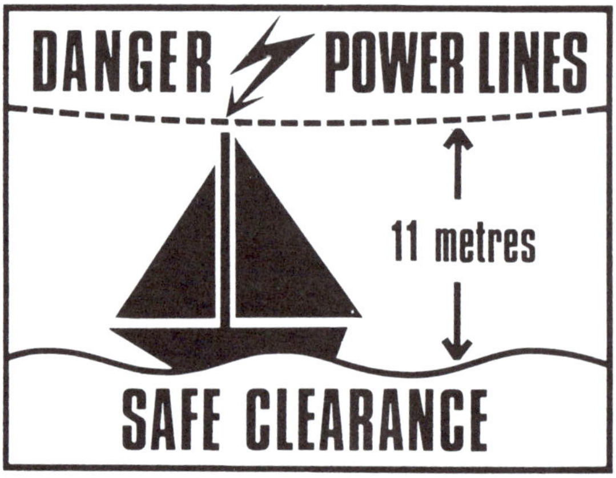

Example of a buoyage system

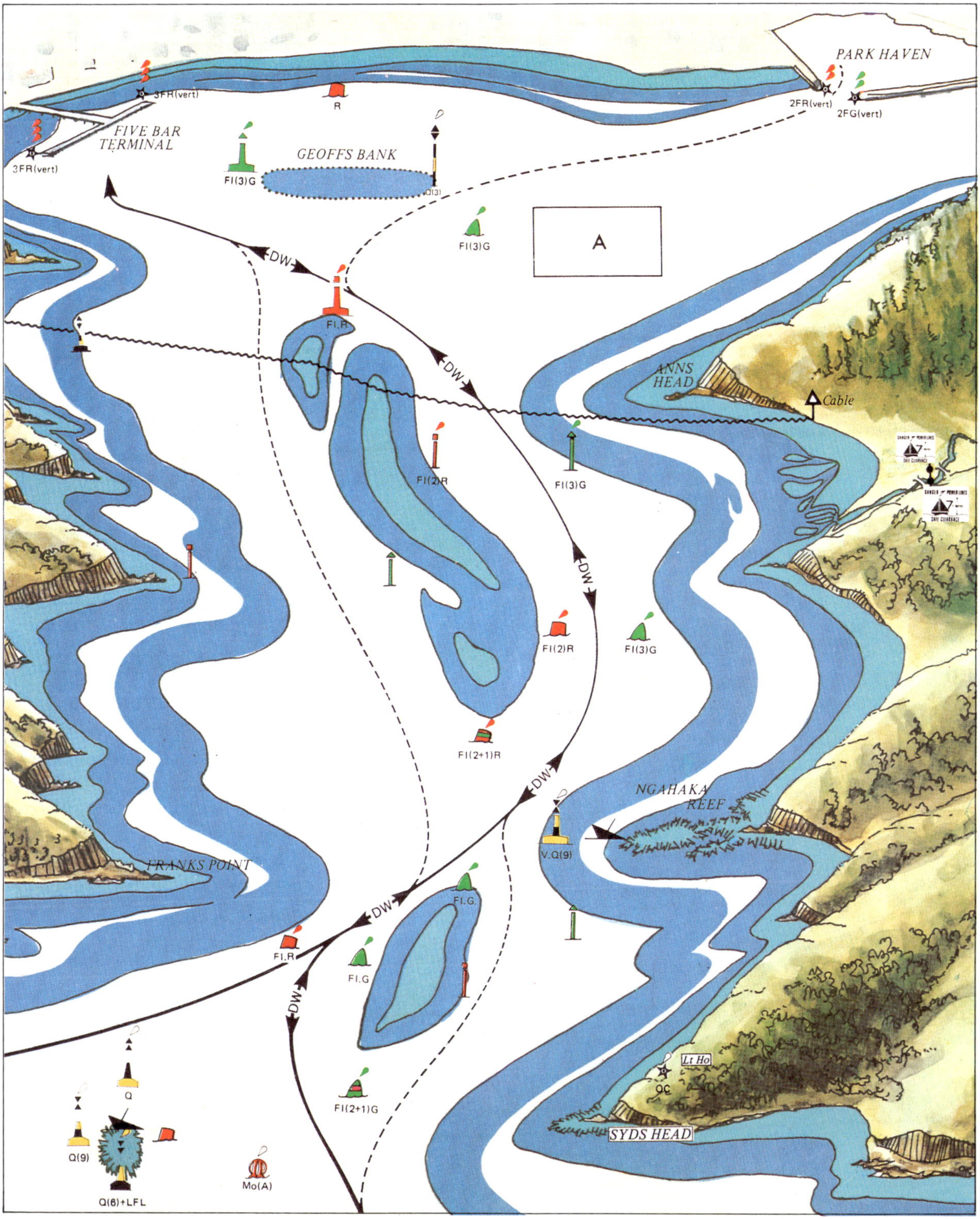

12

RULES OF THE ROAD

These rules shall apply to all vessels upon the high seas and in all waters connected therewith navigable by seagoing vessels . . .
— The Collision Regulations

Although you may have taken up boating to get away from rules and regulations ashore, there are still some rules and regulations at sea. Just as there must be a highway code on the roads, there must also be a highway code for the roads at sea.

The New Zealand boatman has to take account of three sets of rules. First there are the international Collision Regulations, observed by all vessels wherever they are and whatever their size. Next there are New Zealand's own regulations, which are applicable to all vessels within New Zealand waters. These include the Water Recreation Regulations, and the General Harbour Regulations. Finally, there are the bylaws drawn up by individual harbour boards for waters within their jurisdiction.

Copies of the Collision Regulations and the Water Recreation Regulations are available from GP (formerly Government) Bookshops. The Coastguard Federation booklet *Rule of the Road at Sea* contains the Collision Regulations together with illustrated explanations.

Comprehending regulations is never easy. What follows in this chapter is not intended as a substitute for the regulations, but as an aid to their understanding.

The Collision Regulations

These regulations are internationally recognised and apply to all vessels, regardless of type, size or occupation, when upon the high seas, rivers, lakes, harbours or inland waterways. If you contravene these regulations, you commit a crime.

Identification of vessels

The Collision Regulations specify a system of lights and shapes that enables various vessels to be readily identified.

By day
Certain vessels are required to carry shapes, painted black.

By night
Vessels are identified by the pattern of lights they display. These are generally called navigation lights.

Commercial vessels are regularly surveyed to ensure that the correct identification signals are fitted and shown. However, any boat, whether used for commercial purposes or for pleasure-boating, must comply with the regulations; it is your responsibility to see that your boat is displaying the correct lights and shapes, in their correct positions, and at the correct times.

Lighting-up time
Navigation lights must be shown from sunset to sunrise; and by day or night during conditions of restricted visibility; and at any other time when considered necessary. During these times boats should show no other lights that could cause confusion or prevent recognition, or interfere with the keeping of a good lookout.

Navigation lights

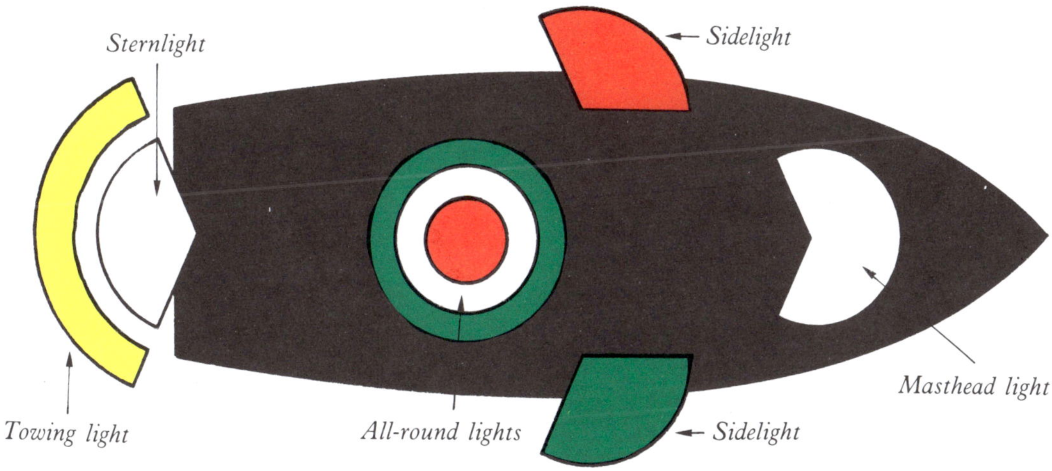

Masthead light
A white light carried by power-driven vessels. Placed over the fore-and-aft centreline to show an unbroken light from right ahead to 22.5° abaft the beam on either side of the vessel.

Sidelights
A red light on the port side and a green light on the starboard side, each showing an unbroken light from right ahead to 22.5° abaft the beam on its respective side.

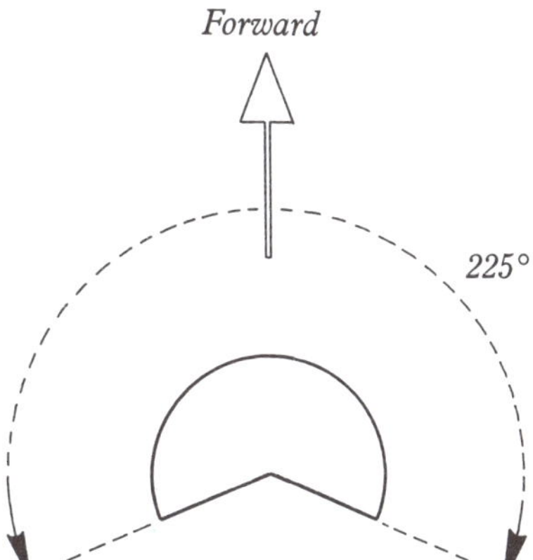

Masthead light

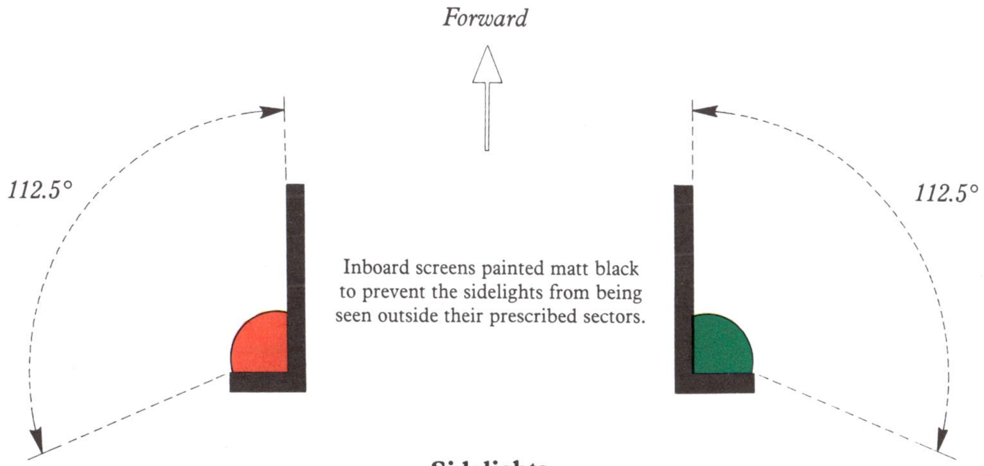

Sidelights

Sternlight
A white light placed as nearly as practicable at the stern, showing an unbroken light from right aft to 22.5° abaft the beam on each side.

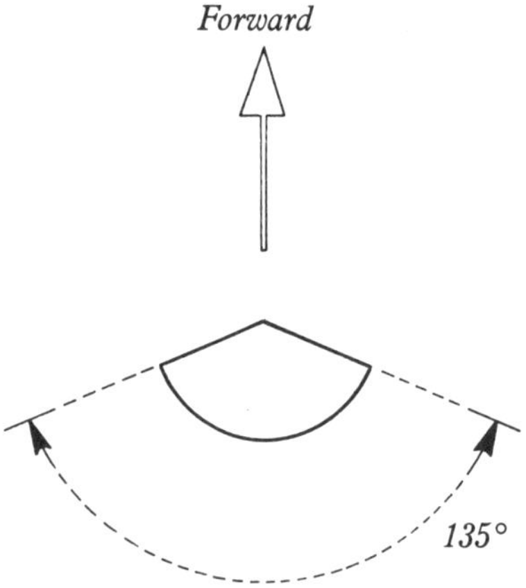

Sternlight

Towing light
A yellow light shown by vessels towing, having the same characteristics as the sternlight.

All-round light
A light, which may be of any specified colour, showing an unbroken light over an arc of 360° of the horizon.

It is important that the lights on your boat be correctly placed and displayed, so that others may recognise you. The exact positioning of these lights is prescribed in Part C and Annex I of the Collision Regulations.

If you are under oars
You may carry the same lights as a sailing vessel, or simply carry a torch or lantern showing a white light. Show this light in sufficient time to prevent collision.

If you are at anchor
If your boat is less than 50 metres in length you must show an all-round white light where it can best be seen, and by day a black ball in the forepart of the vessel where it can best be seen. (See page 122.)

If your boat is less than seven metres in length, and anchored away from channels, fairways or anchorages where other vessels normally navigate, you are not obliged to show these signals.

Under sail and power
If you are under sail and under power at the same time, you are considered a power-driven vessel and must obey the rules for such vessels. By night you must show the lights for a power-driven vessel of your length, and by day a black cone, point downwards, in the forepart of the vessel where it can best be seen. (See page 117.)

Visibility of lights

	Length of vessel			
Light	*Under 12 metres*	*12–20 metres*	*20–50 metres*	*50 metres or more*
Masthead light	2 miles	3 miles	5 miles	6 miles
Sidelights	1 mile	2 miles	2 miles	3 miles
Sternlight	2 miles	2 miles	2 miles	3 miles
Towing light	2 miles	2 miles	2 miles	3 miles
All-round	2 miles	2 miles	2 miles	3 miles

Power-driven vessels

Sidelights at a height above the uppermost continuous deck of not greater than three-quarters of that of the masthead light. If 20 m or more in length, the sidelights must not be in front of the masthead light.

Sternlight as nearly as practicable at the stern.

White masthead light

If more than 20 m in length: Placed not less than 6 m above the uppermost continuous deck, and if the breadth exceeds 6 m then at a height not less than such breadth, but need not exceed 12 m in height.

If 12 m to 20 m in length: Placed at a height above the gunwale of not less than 2.5 m.

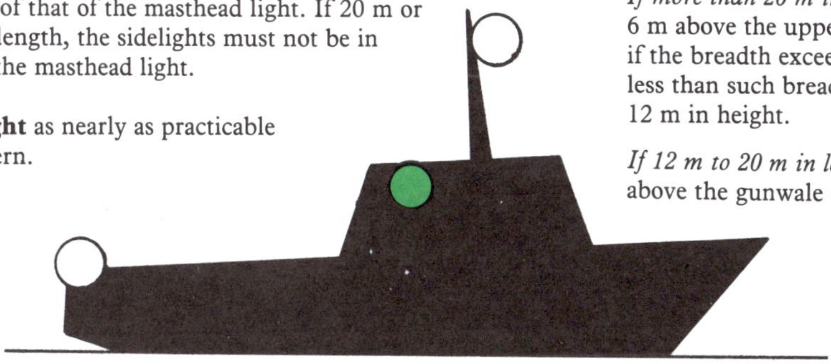

If less than 12m in length

An all-round white light may be shown instead of a masthead light, with sidelights but no sternlight.

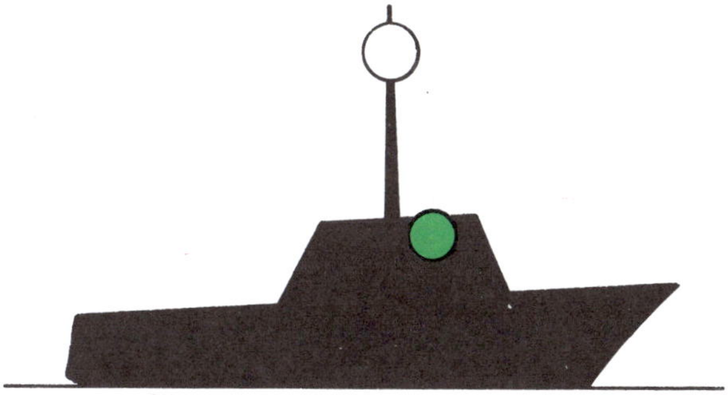

The uppermost light may be less than 2.5 m above the gunwale, but if it is a masthead light it must be at least 1 m higher than the sidelights.

If less than 7 m in length and maximum speed does not exceed 7 knots

May, instead of the above, show an all-round white light. If practicable, sidelights should also be exhibited.

If less than 20 m in length

The sidelights may be combined in one lantern, carried on the fore and aft centreline of the vessel.

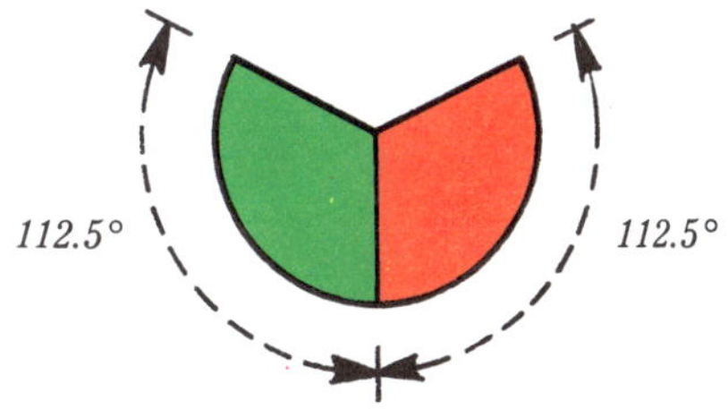

The combined lantern must be not less than 1 m below the masthead light.

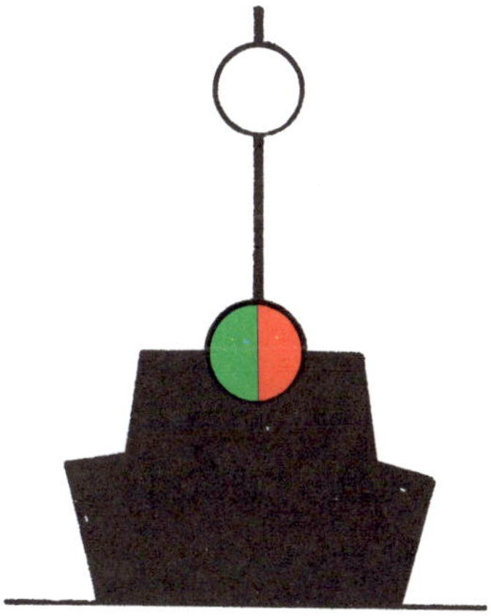

Sailing vessels

Any sailing vessel

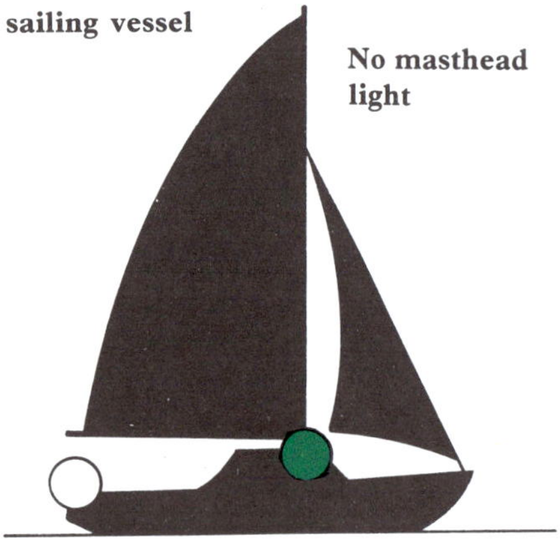

May also show optional red over green all-round lights. They are carried at or near the top of the mast, where they can best be seen.

If 20 m or more in length they are to be not less than 2 m apart, with the green light at least 4 m above the hull.

If less than 20 m in length they are to be not less than 1 m apart, with the green light at least 2 m above the hull.

If less than 7 m in length

If practicable, show the sidelights or tricoloured lantern. If not, have at hand a white torch or lamp and show it in time to prevent collision.

If less than 20 m in length

The sidelights may be combined in one lantern, carried on the fore and aft centreline of the vessel. A separate sternlight must also be shown.

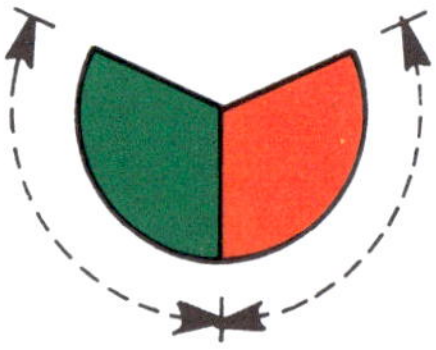

The sidelights and sternlight may be combined in a tricoloured lantern, carried at or near the top of the mast.

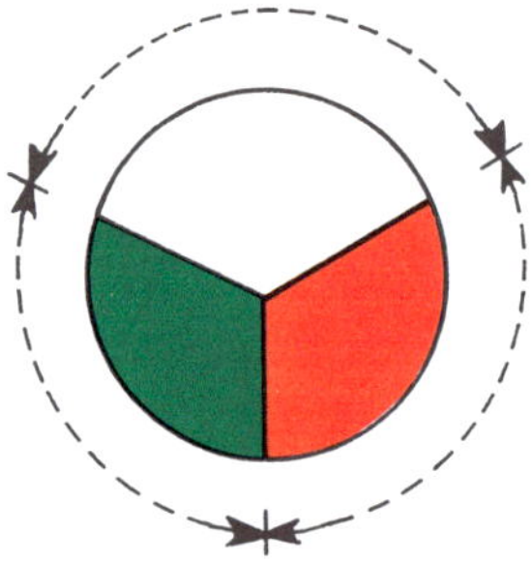

The tricoloured lantern must not be shown with the red over green all-round lights.

This lantern must not be used with a masthead light when under power.

Recognition of vessels

A POWER-DRIVEN VESSEL
underway (Rule 23a)

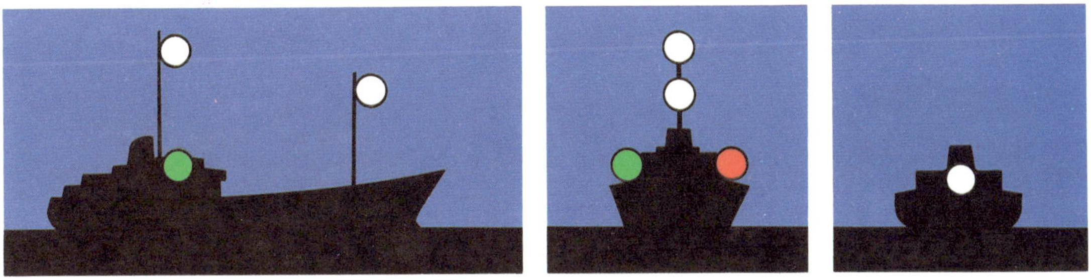

Starboard side *Ahead* *Astern*

A vessel of less than 50 m in length is not obliged to exhibit the aft masthead light, but may do so.

A POWER-DRIVEN VESSEL
less than 50 m in length, underway (Rule 23a)

Starboard side *Ahead* *Astern*

If less than 20 m in length, the sidelights may be combined.

AN AIR-CUSHION VESSEL (HOVERCRAFT)
in non-displacement mode, underway (Rule 23b)

Starboard side *Ahead* *Astern*

An aft masthead is exhibited if 50 m or more in length.
The yellow light flashes at a frequency of 120 or more per minute.
If less than 20 m in length, the sidelights may be combined.

A POWER-DRIVEN VESSEL (Rule 23c)
less than 12 m in length, underway

Port side *Starboard side* *Ahead* *Astern*

An all-round white light may be exhibited instead of the masthead light and sternlight. Sidelights may be combined.

A POWER-DRIVEN VESSEL (Rule 23c)
of less than 7 m in length and whose maximum speed does not exceed 7 knots, underway

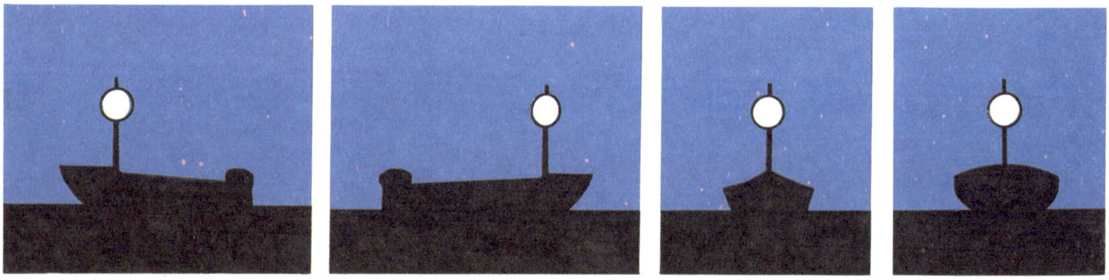

Port side *Starboard side* *Ahead* *Astern*

An all-round white light. Sidelights are also shown if practicable.

A POWER-DRIVEN VESSEL WHEN TOWING (Rule 24a)
Length of tow less than 200 m

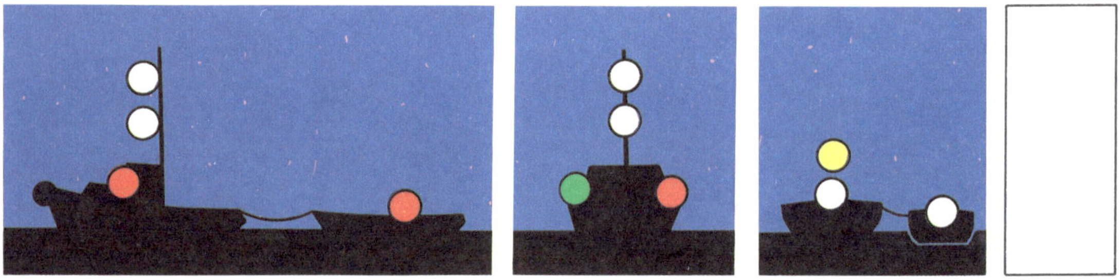

Port side *Ahead* *Astern* *No day signal*

An aft masthead light is shown on the towing vessel if it is 50 m or more in length.
The towed vessel shows only sidelights and sternlight.

A POWER-DRIVEN VESSEL WHEN TOWING (Rule 24a)
Length of tow exceeds 200 m

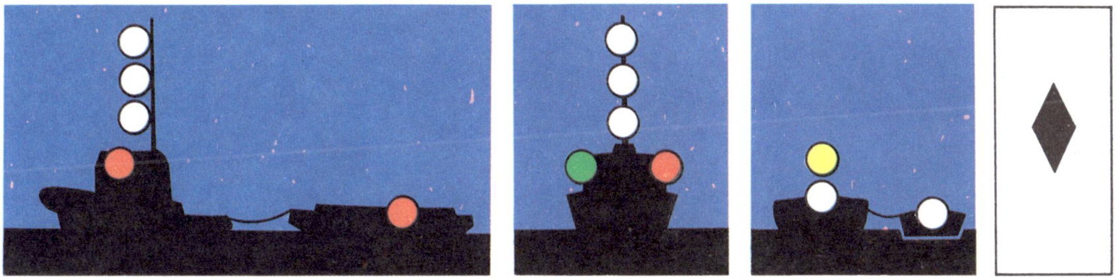

Port side *Ahead* *Astern* *Day signal*

An aft masthead light is shown on the towing vessel if it is 50 m or more in length.
The towed vessel shows only sidelights and sternlight.

Shown on the towing and on the towed vessels

A VESSEL TOWING AN INCONSPICUOUS OR PARTLY SUBMERGED VESSEL OR OBJECT (Rule 24g)

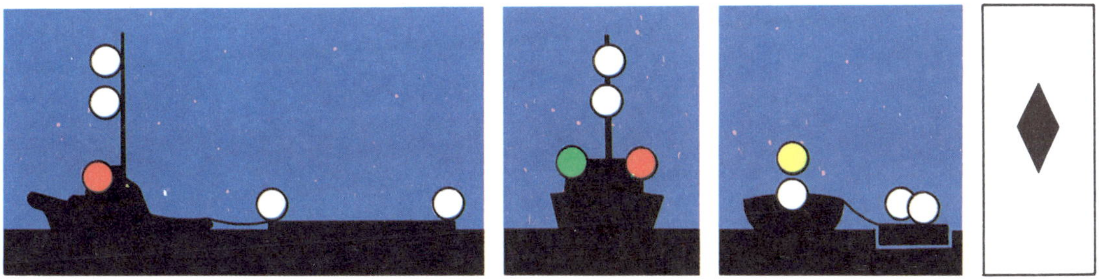

Port side *Ahead* *Astern* *Day signal*

Three masthead lights are shown on the towing vessel if the tow exceeds 200 m.
If the towed object is 25 m or more in breadth, two extra white lights are shown at the extremities of the breadth.
Extra white lights are shown if the towed object is more than 100 m in length.

Shown at the after-most extremity of the tow. An additional diamond is shown at the forward end of the tow if it exceeds 200 m.

A POWER-DRIVEN VESSEL PUSHING AHEAD OR TOWING ALONGSIDE (Rule 24c & f)

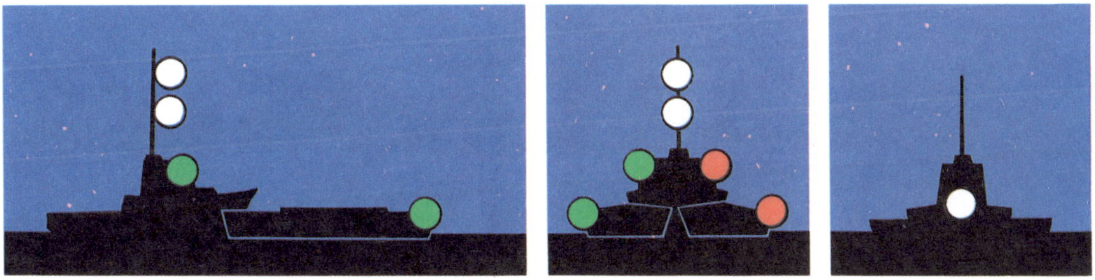

Starboard side *Ahead* *Astern*

The pushing vessel exhibits an aft masthead light if 50 m or more in length.
A group of vessels being pushed ahead is lit as one vessel, with sidelights at the forward end.
A sternlight is exhibited on a vessel only if being towed alongside.

A SAILING VESSEL (Rule 25a)
of any length, underway

Port side *Starboard side* *Ahead* *Astern*

These lights may also be shown by a vessel under oars. Sidelights may be combined if less than 20 m in length.

A SAILING VESSEL (Rule 25b)
of less than 20 m in length, underway

Port side *Starboard side* *Ahead* *Astern*

These lights may also be exhibited on a vessel under oars.

A SAILING VESSEL (Rule 25c)
of any length, underway

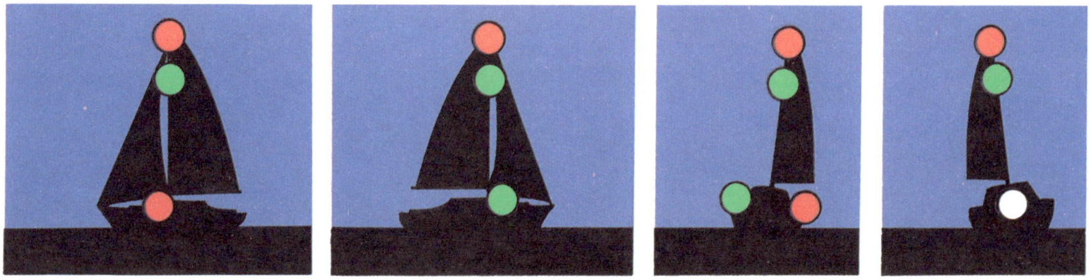

Port side *Starboard side* *Ahead* *Astern*

The red over green all-round lights are optional. Sidelights may be combined if less than 20 m in length.

A SAILING VESSEL
of less than 7 m in length

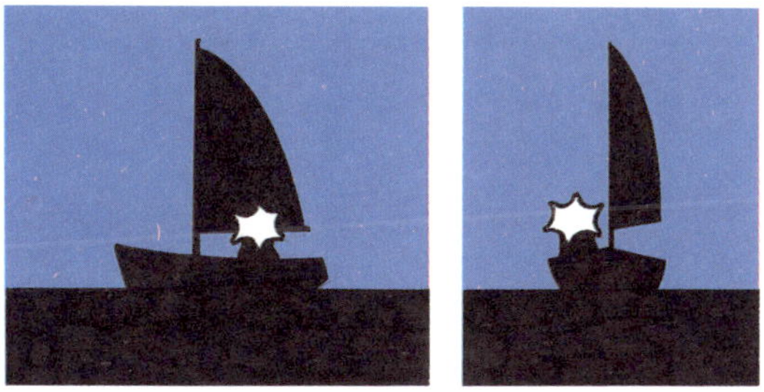

A VESSEL UNDER OARS (Rule 25d)

An electric torch or a lighted lantern, exhibited in sufficient time to prevent collision.

A VESSEL UNDER SAIL AND POWER (Rule 25e)

Starboard side *Ahead* *Astern* *Day signal*

Forward, where it can best be seen.

The appropriate lights for a power-driven vessel of her length.

A VESSEL TRAWLING (Rule 26b)

Port side *Ahead* *Astern* *Day signals*

The basket may be shown if the vessel is less than 20 m in length.

The aft masthead light need not be exhibited if less than 50 m in length.
The sidelights and sternlight are only shown whilst making way through the water.

A VESSEL FISHING
other than trawling (Rule 26c)

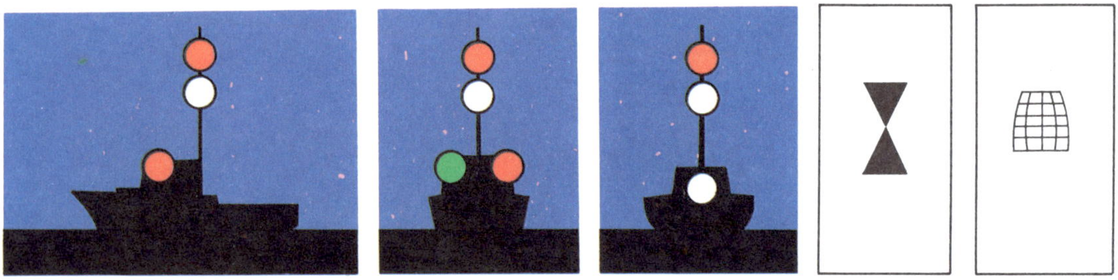

Port side *Ahead* *Astern* *Day signals*

Fishing gear extends less than 150 m horizontally from the vessel.
The sidelights and sternlight are only shown whilst making way through the water.

The basket may be shown if the vessel is less than 20 m in length

A VESSEL FISHING
other than trawling, with gear extending more than 150 m horizontally from the vessel (Rule 26c)

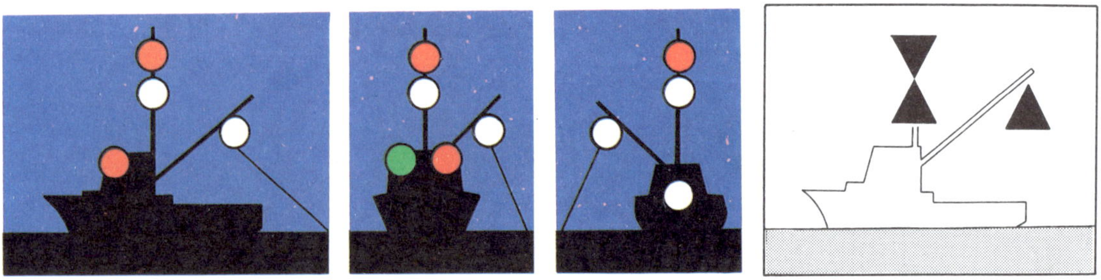

Port side *Ahead* *Astern* *Day signals*

An all-round white light, or single cone, is shown in the direction of the gear.
Sidelights and sternlight are only shown whilst making way through the water.

A basket may be shown instead of the twin cones if the vessel is less than 20 m in length.

OPTIONAL ADDITIONAL SIGNALS FOR FISHING VESSELS
fishing in close proximity to others (Annex II)

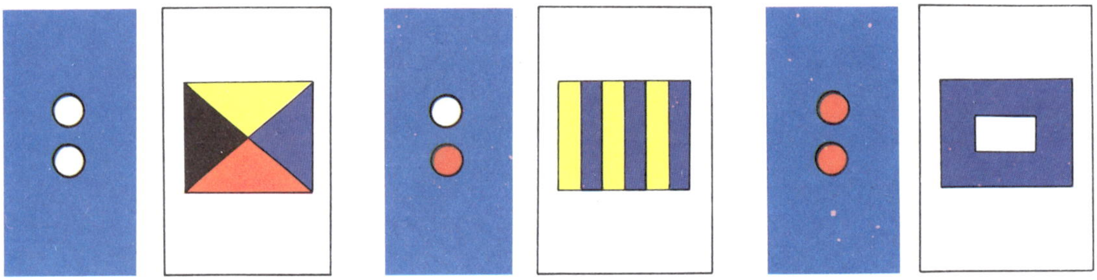

'Shooting nets' *'Hauling nets'* *'Net has come fast upon an obstruction'*

Shown in addition to, but lower than, normal trawling lights.

OPTIONAL ADDITIONAL SIGNALS FOR FISHING VESSELS (Annex II)
fishing in close proximity to others

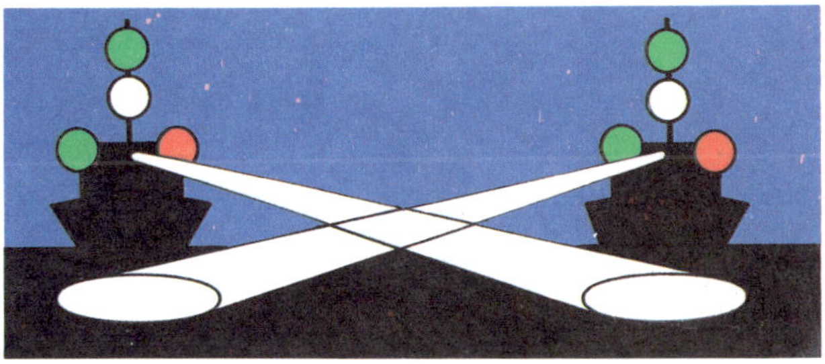

'Engaged in pair trawling'
Crossed searchlight beams

'Fishing with purse seine gear'
Lights flash alternately every second

A VESSEL NOT UNDER COMMAND (Rule 27a)

Starboard side

Ahead

Astern

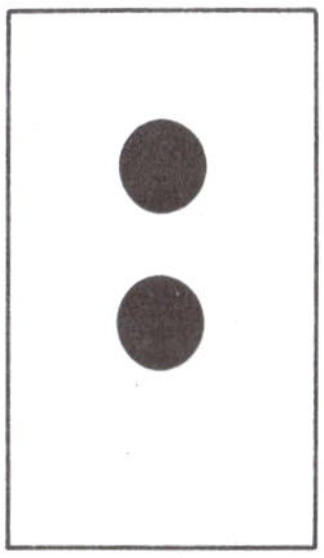

Day signal

Through some exceptional circumstance is unable to manoeuvre or keep out of the way.
Sidelights and sternlight are shown only whilst making way through the water.

A VESSEL RESTRICTED IN HER ABILITY TO MANOEUVRE (Rule 27b)

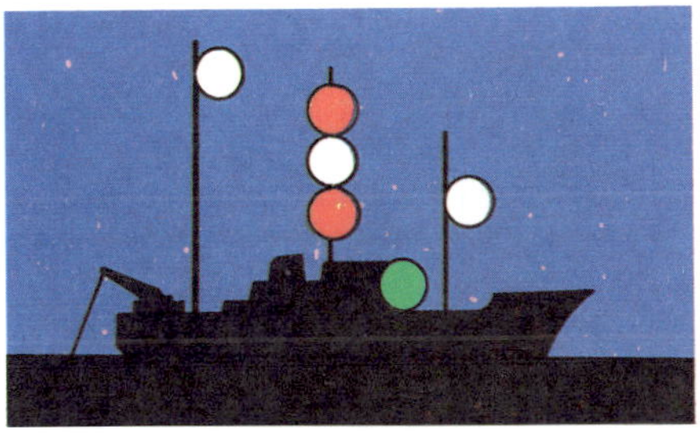

Starboard side

Ahead

Astern

Day signal

Owing to the nature of her work, this vessel is unable to manoeuvre to keep out of the way.
Masthead lights, sidelights and sternlight are only shown whilst making way through the water.
Anchor signals are shown if working whilst at anchor.

A TOWING VESSEL UNABLE TO DEVIATE FROM HER COURSE (Rule 27c)

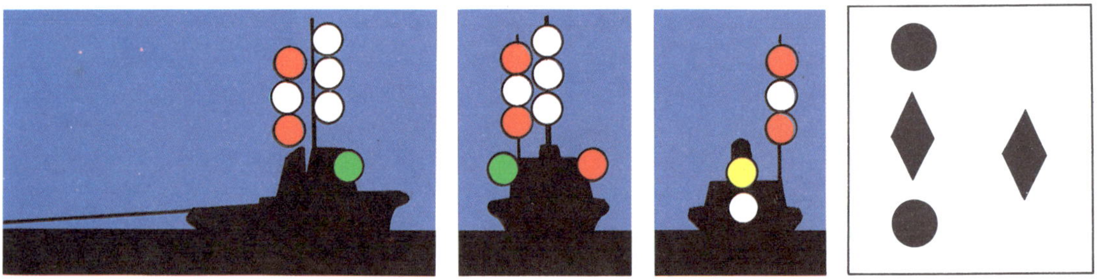

Starboard side *Ahead* *Astern* *Day signals*

The third masthead light and the additional diamond shape are only shown if the tow exceeds 200 m.

A VESSEL DREDGING (Rule 27d)
or carrying out underwater operations, with an obstruction

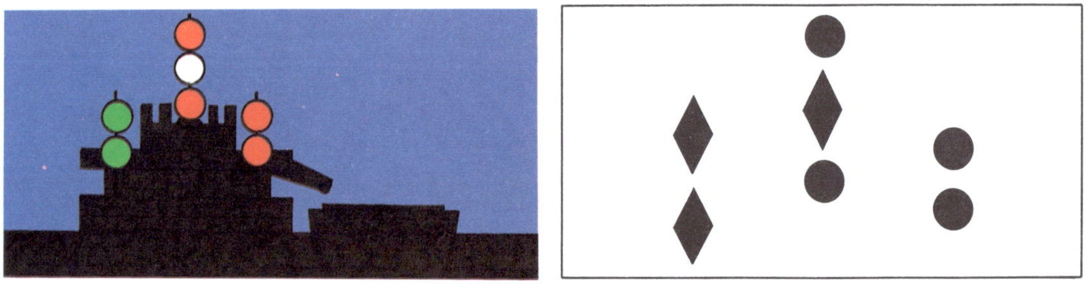

'Side to pass' *'Side of the obstruction'* *'Side to pass'* *'Side of the obstruction'*

Masthead lights, sidelights and sternlight are shown if the vessel is making way through the water.

A VESSEL ENGAGED IN DIVING OPERATIONS (Rule 27e)

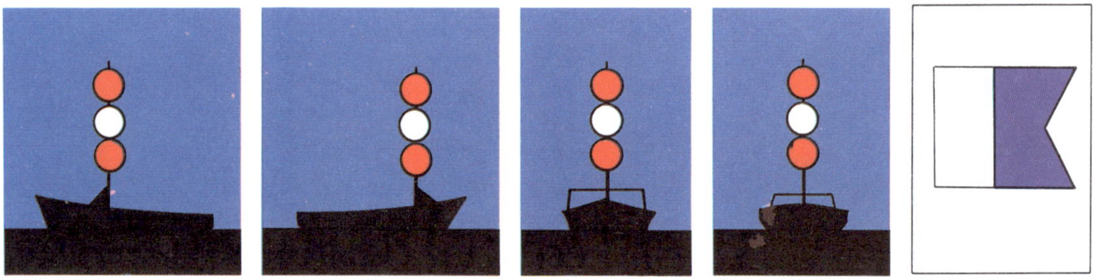

Port side *Starboard side* *Ahead* *Astern* *Day signal*

A rigid replica of the 'A' flag, 1 m in height.

These lights must be shown if it is impracticable to show the full lights for a vessel restricted in ability to manoeuvre.

A VESSEL ENGAGED IN MINECLEARANCE OPERATIONS

(Rule 27f)

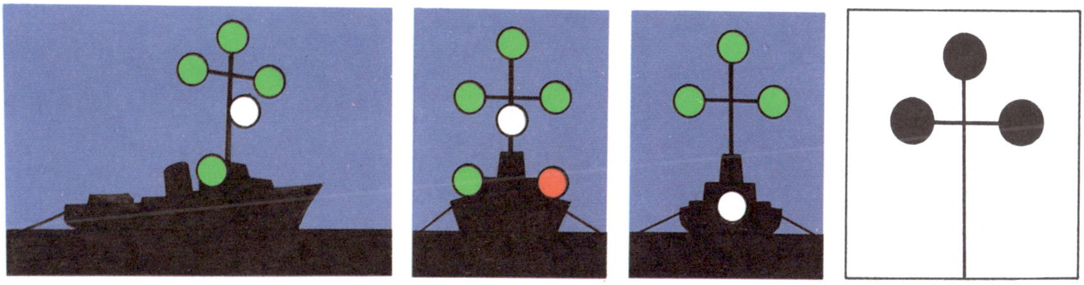

Starboard side *Ahead* *Astern* *Day signal*

An aft masthead light must be shown if more than 50 m in length.
Anchor signals are shown if working whilst at anchor. *It is dangerous to approach within 1000 m of this vessel.*

A VESSEL CONSTRAINED BY HER DRAUGHT

(Rule 28)

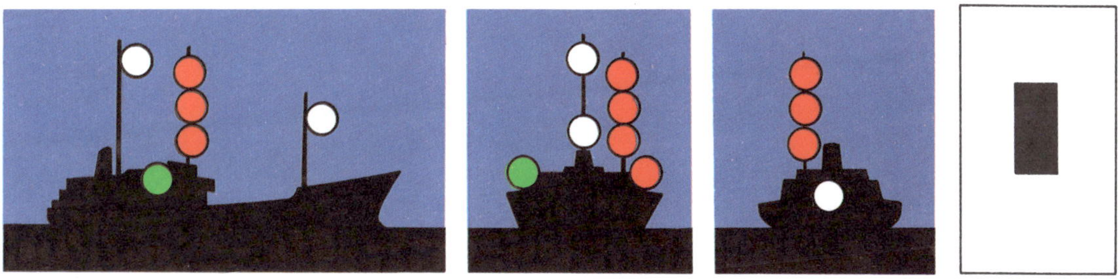

Starboard side *Ahead* *Astern* *Day signal*
A black cylinder

A power-driven vessel which because of her draught in relation to the available depth of water is severely restricted in her ability to deviate from the course she is following.

A VESSEL ON PILOTAGE DUTY
whilst underway

(Rule 29)

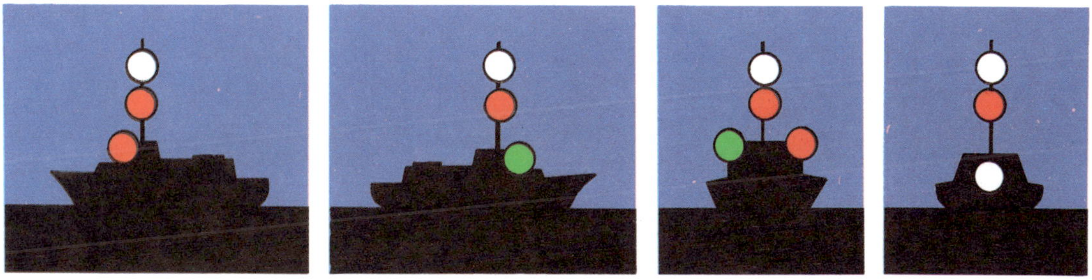

Port side *Starboard side* *Ahead* *Astern*

Anchor signals are shown if at anchor.

A VESSEL AT ANCHOR

(Rule 30)

Starboard side *Ahead* *Astern* *Day signal*

The vessel may, and if 100 m or more in length must, also show deck lights.

Forward, where it can best be seen.

A VESSEL AT ANCHOR
less than 50 m in length

(Rule 30)

Port side *Ahead* *Astern* *Day signal*

Forward, where it can best be seen.

The white all-round light is shown where it can best be seen.

A VESSEL AGROUND

(Rule 30)

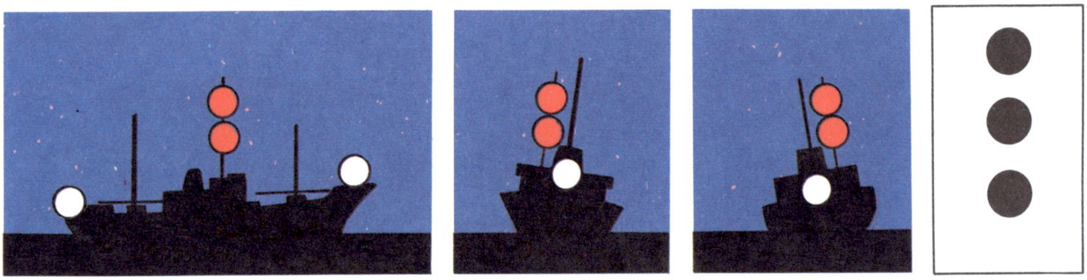

Starboard side *Ahead* *Astern* *Day signal*

Only one of the all-round white lights need be shown, where it can best be seen, if the vessel is less than 50 m in length.

The steering and sailing rules

Risk of collision

On sighting another vessel your first consideration must be 'Are we going to collide?' To determine if another vessel is on a collision course, watch it over your compass. If the compass bearing does not change appreciably over a reasonable period of time, there is risk of collision.

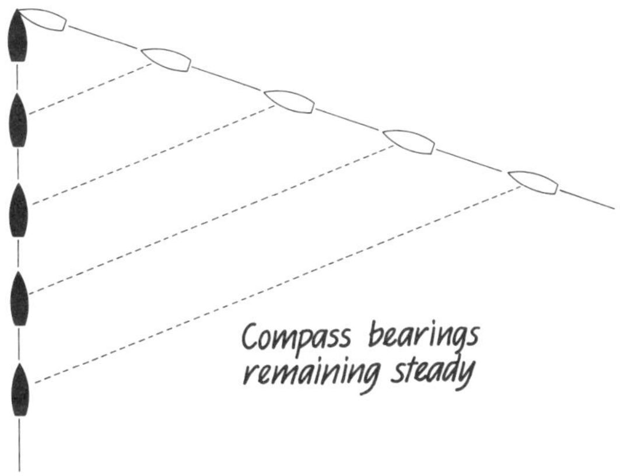

If no compass is available, sight the other vessel across a fitting on your foredeck. If after a short time, while keeping a steady course, it is still in line with this fitting, there is risk of collision. Unless action is taken, the other vessel will hit the fitting on your foredeck!

Lookout

At all times, in all weathers, and in any condition of visibility you must maintain a proper lookout by sight, hearing and any other available means. This is so that you can make a full appraisal of the situation, and of the risk of collision.

Speed

Every vessel must at all times travel at a safe speed; a speed that enables you to take the correct and effective action, including stopping, to avoid collision.

Rule 6 lists 12 factors to take into account when determining a safe speed.

Vessels in sight of one another

The following rules apply only if you can see the other vessel visually.

Overtaking

'Overtaking' is defined as approaching from a direction more than 22.5° abaft the beam; that is, within the arc of visibility of the sternlight.

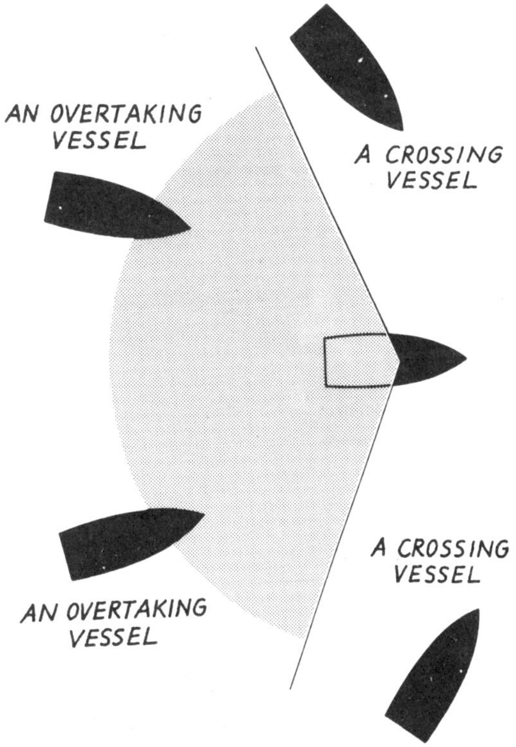

Any vessel overtaking any other shall keep out of the way of the vessel being overtaken.

If both vessels are sailing vessels

When each has the wind on a different side, the vessel that has the wind on the port side shall keep out of the way.

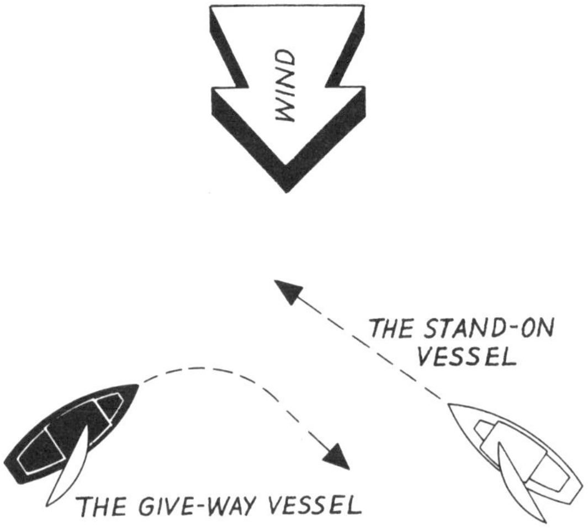

When both have the wind on the same side, the vessel that is to windward shall keep out of the way.

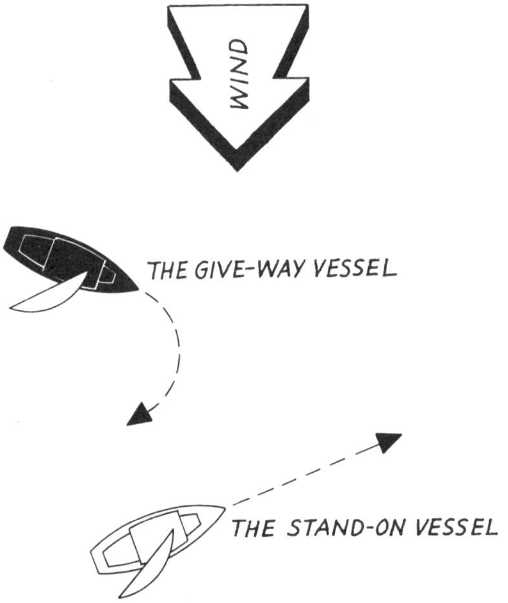

■ The windward side of a sailing vessel is the side opposite to that on which the mainsail is carried.

■ A sailing vessel with the wind on the port side and which is unable to determine the side on which a sailing vessel to windward has the wind should keep out of the way.

If both vessels are power-driven vessels

Head-on situation

When two power-driven vessels are meeting on reciprocal or nearly reciprocal courses so as to involve risk of collision, each shall alter her course to starboard so that each shall pass on the port side of the other.

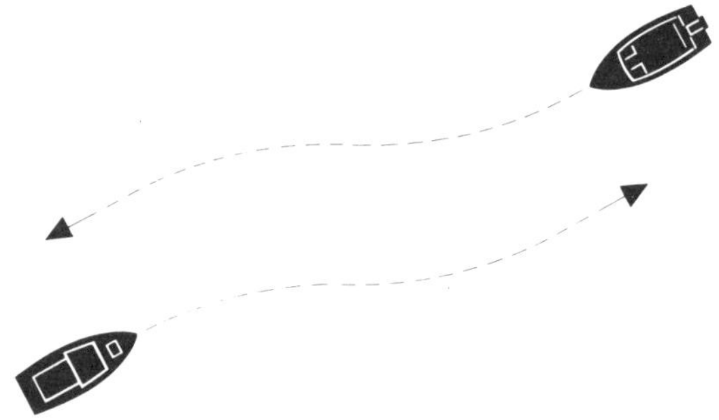

If in doubt whether a head-on situation exists, assume that you are head-on and turn to starboard.

Crossing situation

When two power-driven vessels are crossing so as to involve risk of collision, the vessel that has the other on her own starboard side shall keep out of the way.

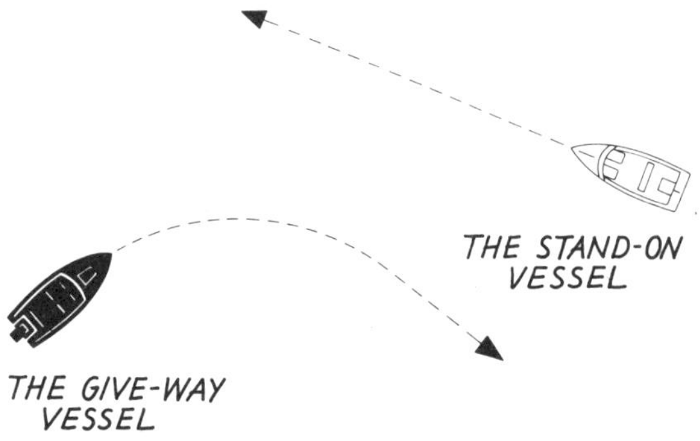

The give-way vessel may slow down or stop to let the other vessel pass ahead. If turning, avoid crossing ahead of the other vessel.

Responsibility between differing vessels

If vessels of different types meet, the onus for keeping clear can be found from this list of descending orders of responsibility:

A power-driven vessel
A sailing vessel
A vessel engaged in fishing
A vessel constrained by its draught
A vessel restricted in its ability to manoeuvre
A vessel not under command

Each vessel, unless overtaking or in a narrow channel, must keep clear of the vessels in a lower position in the table.

The give-way vessel

If it is your duty to keep clear:

■ Take early action. As soon as you realise there is risk of collision, do something. Make a large alteration of course, or a large reduction of speed, so that the other vessel can clearly see what you are doing.

■ It is bad practice to accelerate across another vessel's bows. It is preferable in most cases to pass behind the other vessel, or reduce speed to let the other vessel continue ahead of you.

■ Give the other vessel a wide berth, and, having taken action, keep watching the other vessel in case it takes action that will negate yours.

The stand-on vessel

If it is your duty to stand on, maintain your course and speed to allow the other vessel to take suitable action.

If the other vessel does not appear to be taking avoiding action, a power-driven vessel may indicate doubt and concern by sounding at least five short and rapid blasts on the whistle.

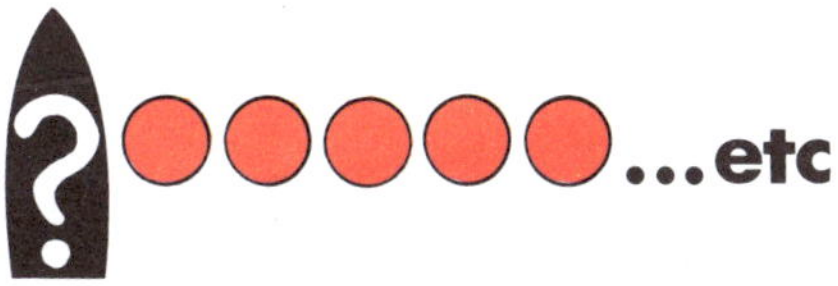

As soon as it becomes apparent the other vessel is not complying with the rules, you may take avoiding action yourself.

You may turn to starboard, away from the offending vessel, or reduce speed or stop; but unless absolutely necessary, do not turn to port if the vessel is on your own port side. That is where he is most likely to turn.

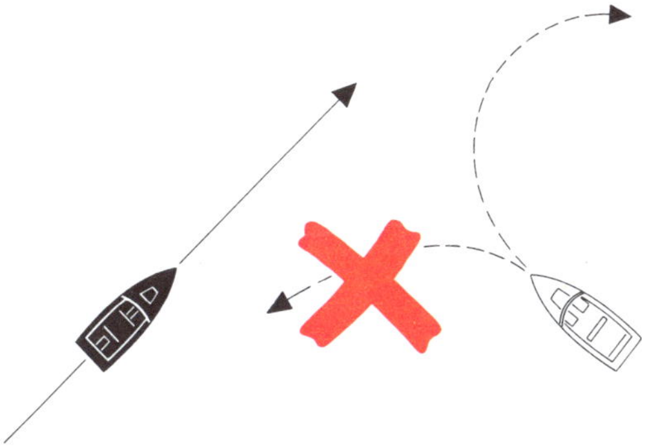

Signalling your manoeuvre

When taking action under the steering and sailing rules, a power-driven vessel should indicate her intended action. The signals are made on the whistle, and consist of one or more short blasts of about one second's duration. The signals must only be sounded if you are in sight of the other vessel.

'I am altering my course to starboard.'

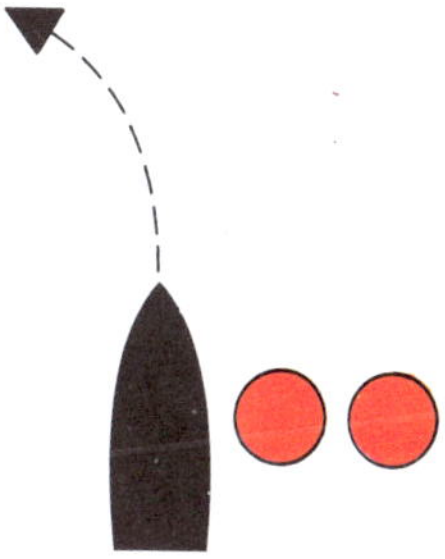

'I am altering my course to port.'

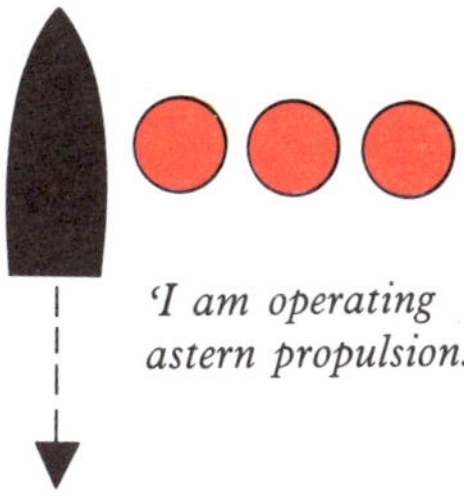

'I am operating astern propulsion.'

Restricted visibility

In restricted visibility you have less time and space in which to take action. Every vessel constitutes a potential hazard, and so all have a duty to keep clear of one another. There are no stand-on vessels.

The following applies only to vessels that are *not* in sight of one another. If subsequently you sight each other, the previously explained steering and sailing rules must then be observed.

■ You must proceed at a safe speed, suitably adapted to the conditions of restricted visibility. If a power-driven vessel, you must have your engine ready for immediate manoeuvre.

■ An extra sharp lookout must be kept, by sight and by hearing. Place an extra lookout outside the shelter of the cockpit, preferably in the bow.

■ Switch on your navigation lights, but no others, whether it is by day or night.

■ If it is fitted, use radar and any other navigational aid to keep track of your position and to make early detection of approaching vessels. Rule 19 specifies how radar should be used to avoid collisions in restricted visibility.

■ You must identify yourself and your position by sounding fog signals at prescribed intervals.

Collision avoidance

If you hear the fog signal of another vessel, apparently forward of your beam:

■ Reduce your speed to the minimum at which you can maintain course-keeping.

■ If necessary, stop altogether.

■ Increase the frequency of your fog signal.

The rules do not prescribe any specific avoidance manoeuvre; you must be guided by your own initiative. Do not sound the manoeuvring signals should you decide to turn or go astern. (These are only to be sounded by vessels in sight of one another.) However, the rules state that you should 'if necessary take all way off and in any event navigate with extreme caution until danger of collision is over.'

Navigation in narrow channels

Much of your navigation will be done in the confined areas of channels, fairways and harbours. These areas seriously affect the manoeuvrability of larger vessels and thus special consideration must be given to these vessels.

A vessel of less than 20 metres in length, or a sailing vessel, must not impede the passage of a larger vessel in a channel. The New Zealand General Harbour Regulations also state that inside harbour limits pleasure craft must not impede the navigation of any vessel of 500 tons gross or more, any hovercraft, or any seaplane in the process of landing or taking off.

Keep to the right

When proceeding along a narrow channel or fairway, you should stay to the starboard side, and keep as far over as safety allows.

Fishing and anchoring

You should not fish in a channel if, by doing so, you restrict the movement of others wishing to use the channel. Similarly, unless unavoidable, do not anchor in a channel.

Crossing a channel

Do not cross a channel if this will impede the passage of a larger vessel that is following the channel and has no room to manoeuvre.

Blind areas

If approaching a blind corner or an area where any approaching vessel could be hidden from view behind an obstruction, particular caution is needed.

On nearing the blind area, sound a long blast on your whistle. This should be answered with a similar blast by any vessel approaching from behind the obstruction. Whether you hear an answering signal or not, proceed with caution.

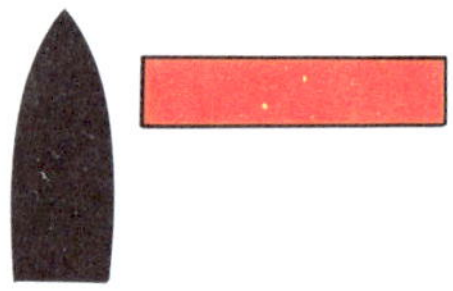

Fog signals

(*Rule 35*)

A POWER-DRIVEN VESSEL underway and making way: 

underway and stopped: 

A VESSEL NOT UNDER COMMAND:
A VESSEL RESTRICTED IN ABILITY TO MANOEUVRE (Underway or at anchor):
A VESSEL CONSTRAINED BY HER DRAUGHT:
A SAILING VESSEL:
A VESSEL FISHING (Underway or at anchor):
A VESSEL TOWING OR PUSHING:

A VESSEL BEING TOWED or if more than one, the last vessel of the tow if manned: 

A VESSEL AT ANCHOR Under 100 m in length: 

100 m or more in length: 

Giving warning of her position: 

A VESSEL AGROUND Under 100 m in length: 

100 m or more in length: 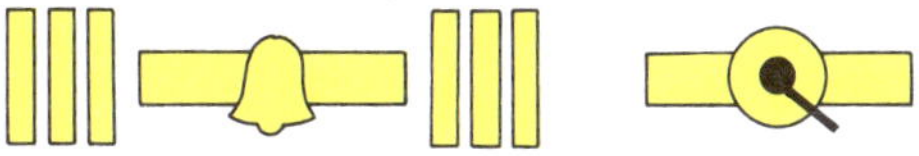

May also sound an appropriate whistle signal

A PILOT VESSEL on pilotage duty:
sounds appropriate signals, as above, plus identity signal: 

A VESSEL LESS THAN 12 METRES IN LENGTH may make the appropriate signals, as above, or make some other efficient sound signal at intervals of not more than two minutes. 

A SHORT WHISTLE BLAST
of about one second's duration. 

A LONG WHISTLE BLAST
of from four to six seconds' duration. 

Whistle signals are sounded at intervals of not more than two minutes.

A RAPID RINGING OF A BELL
for about five seconds' duration. 

A RAPID SOUNDING OF A GONG
for about five seconds' duration. 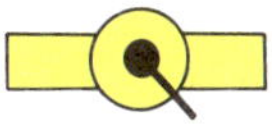

Bell and gong signals are sounded at intervals of not more than one minute.

Overtaking

When overtaking in a narrow channel, as at any other time, it is the overtaking vessel's duty to keep clear. If space is restricted, however, these signals may be used to request the vessel ahead of you to move over and allow you more room to pass.

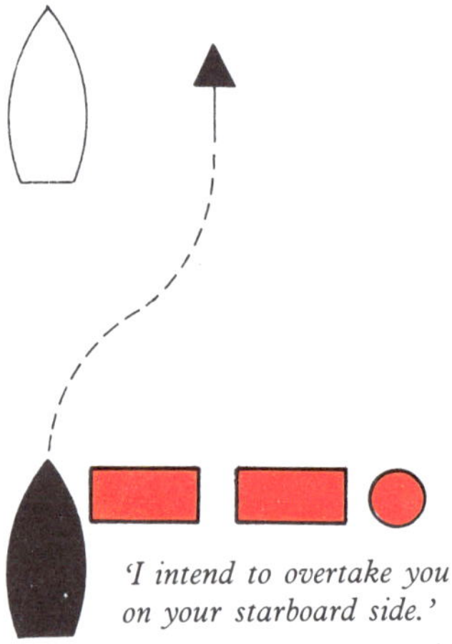

'I intend to overtake you on your starboard side.'

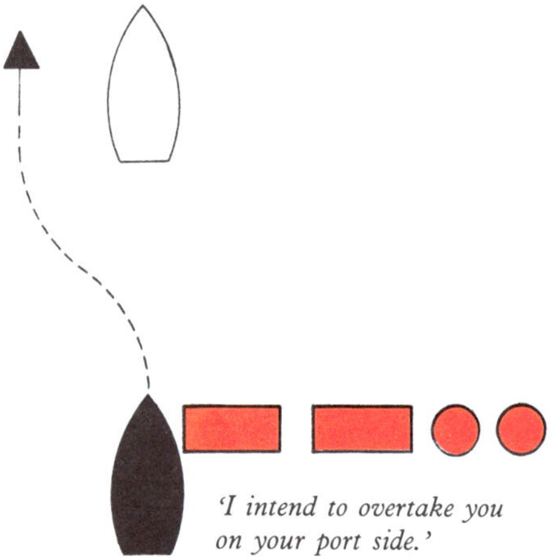

'I intend to overtake you on your port side.'

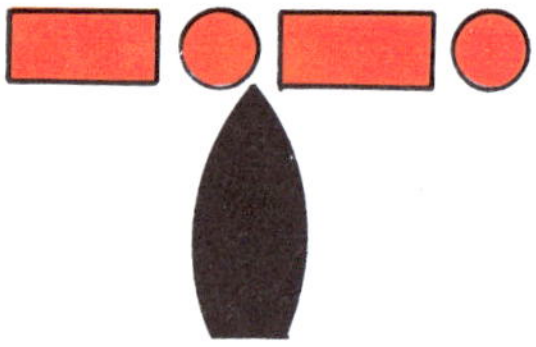

'I agree to take steps to permit safe passing.'

The Water Recreation Regulations

Harbour boards and local authorities who have been given a grant of control of waters under the Harbours Act 1950 have their own bylaws for the waters under their control. The Water Recreation Regulations 1979 apply to all other sea waters and to all navigable lakes and rivers. Many harbour boards have made their bylaws similar to the regulations, to ensure as far as possible that there is uniformity throughout the country. If you contravene any part of these regulations you commit an offence. These are some of the important provisions.

Noise

The exhaust from your boat motor must be discharged through an efficient silencing device.

Speed

You must not travel at a proper speed (speed through the water) greater than five knots:

- When within 200 metres of the shore or any structure.
- When passing within 200 metres of any vessel or raft flying the 'A' flag, indicating there is a diver below.
- When passing within 30 metres of any other vessel, whether underway or moored.
- When within 30 metres of any person bathing.

Water-skiing

A launch towing a water-skier must contain at least two people — the driver, and another to watch the skier and communicate his or her actions and signals to the driver. The same speed restrictions apply to skiers and their tow-boats, but special access lanes may be provided to the shore where the five-knot restriction would not apply. (See page 106 for ski-lane markings.)

Age limit

Any power boat capable of a speed exceeding 10 knots should not be operated by a person under 15 years of age.

Launch wardens

These are appointed by the local harbour authority or by the Maritime Safety Authority. While they act in a voluntary capacity, most are widely experienced and have the authority to police the regulations. They may simply draw attention to a minor lapse, but, in cases of obvious misuse of boats, they will initiate the prosecution of offenders.

They are also appointed to provide assistance in promoting boating safety and to help inform boaties of the recommendations of the Small Boat Safety Committee and the Water Safety Council.

Wardens are identified by a badge and may fly a blue patrol flag with a circular yellow and white symbol. They also carry an official warrant.

You must, on demand of a launch warden:

- Stop.
- Supply your name and address.
- Give any information that may lead to the identification of another offender.
- Move or light your vessel if it is moored or anchored in a dangerous position.

STOP

LAUNCH WARDEN

IF THIS 'STOP' SIGN IS USED TO FLAG DOWN YOUR BOAT, YOU HAVE PROBABLY BROKEN A BOATING LAW

STOP AT ONCE!

13
COMMUNICATIONS

Ships that pass in the night, and speak
each other in passing;
Only a signal shown . . .
— Henry Wadsworth Longfellow

Clear and concise communication is necessary in any field, and there is no exception at sea. We must be able to pass information to others, perhaps to those who do not normally converse in the same language as our own, and our message must be understood without the risk of ambiguity or misunderstanding. We must use a procedure and terminology that is understood by all, whether in distress or emergency situations, or in normal daily exchanges of information.

The language used for communciation at sea, and the channels of communication, must be internationally recognised. English is generally accepted as the language of the sea, but our use of the language, our terminology, and our use of the channels of communication must be to a standard that can be understood by everyone.

The 24-hour clock

To avoid confusion between a.m. and p.m. the 24-hour clock should always be used. Time is expressed as four figures, the first two indicating the hours of the day, from 00 to 23, and the last two indicating the minutes, from 00 to 59. Decimals are not used in timekeeping, and no decimal point should be inserted between the hours and minutes.

For example:

1 a.m. is expressed as 0100
1 p.m. is expressed as 1300
2.15 a.m. is expressed as 0215
7.45 p.m. is expressed as 1945

When communicating time by the spoken word, the four figures are still used, but they may be expressed digitally or in hundreds.

For example:

0100 may be expressed as 'Oh one oh oh' or as 'Oh one hundred'.

1300 may be expressed as 'One three oh oh' or as 'Thirteen hundred'.

0215 may be expressed as 'Oh two one five' or as 'Oh two fifteen'.

1945 may be expressed as 'One nine four five' or as 'Nineteen forty-five'.

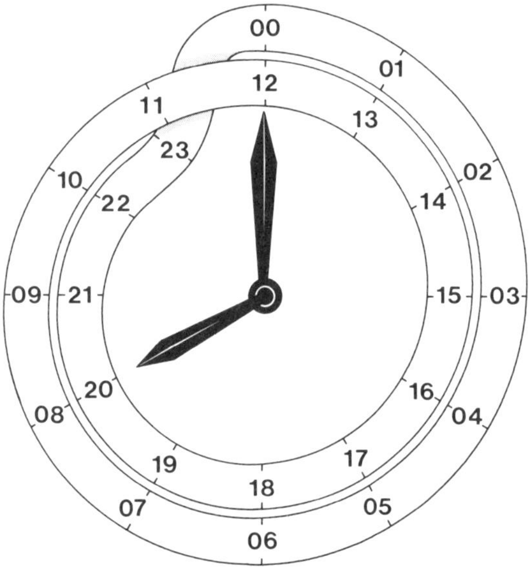

The radiotelephone

The authority controlling the use of radiotelephone in this country is the New Zealand Radio Frequency Service. A radiotelephone installation must be of a type and specification designated by the service, and must be licenced. Except in the case of emergency involving safety of life or property, any person using a radiotelephone on a boat is required to hold a Restricted Radiotelephone Operators Certificate, or an equivalent or higher class certificate.

As with any method of communication, correct control, procedure and terminology must be used. Full details of radiotelephone procedure is contained in the publication *Small Ships Radiotelephone Service, General Instructions*, which must be available at all times on any boat on which a radiotelephone is installed.

Callsigns

On being licensed as a radio station, each boat is allocated a callsign consisting of letters and numbers. This is for identification and must be used for every transmission. Coast radio stations are also identified with a callsign.

Coast radio stations

A complete list of all New Zealand coastal radio stations is included in the latest edition of the *New Zealand Nautical Almanac*. Each station's frequencies and listening times are given, and details of broadcasts relating to navigational and meteorological warnings, reports and forecasts. Details are also given for Sealink, an automated radphone service operated by Telecom Mobile Radio on the marine VHF band.

Frequencies

Certain frequencies are designated for certain purposes. Important among these are:

2182 kHz International distress, safety and calling frequency for radiotelephony

All ships licensed for operation in the authorised marine radiotelephone service frequency bands between 1605 kHz and 2850 kHz must be able to transmit and receive on the frequency of 2182 kHz. Distress, urgency and safety calls should be made on this frequency. It is also the general calling and reply frequency when establishing communication with other stations of the maritime service, and for use by coast stations to announce the transmission on other frequencies of traffic lists. The exchange of other radio communications except distress or urgency traffic should be carried out on a working or intership frequency so as to leave 2182 kHz available for the reception of distress calls. Safety traffic should also be exchanged on a working or intership frequency.

Stations other than those in distress should listen for a reasonable period before transmitting on 2182 kHz to make sure no distress traffic is being sent.

Channel 16 (156.8 MHz) International distress, safety and calling frequency for the maritime mobile VHF radiotelephone service

All ships licensed for operation in the authorised bands between 156 MHz and 174 MHz must be able to transmit and receive on this frequency.

The silence period

To enable any weak distress signal to be heard, silence periods are observed for three minutes commencing on each hour and half-hour. If you are manning your radiotelephone during these periods, listen on 2182 kHz in case any such call is made. But at these times you must not transmit by radiotelephone on frequencies

between 2173.5 and 2190.5 kHz, except for distress, urgent or safety purposes.

There is no provision for silence periods in the VHF service.

Always keep your clock accurate so that you observe the correct three-minute silence periods.

The distress signal

The radiotelephone distress signal consists of the spoken word 'MAYDAY' (from the French *m'aidez*, 'help me'). The use of this signal is absolutely forbidden except in the case of distress. It indicates that the vessel (or aircraft) is threatened by grave and imminent danger, and immediate assistance is required.

A distress call is addressed to anyone who can receive it, and it has absolute priority over any transmission. It indicates that the vessel (or aircraft) is threatened by grave and imminent danger, and immediate assistance is required.

The urgency signal

The radiotelephone urgency signal consists of the spoken words 'PAN PAN'. It indicates that the station sending it has a very urgent message to transmit concerning the safety of a ship, aircraft or person.

The urgency signal has priority over all over communications except distress, and it can be addressed to 'all stations' or to a specific station. The correct procedure for the transmission of an urgency call is shown on page 141.

Important: Distress and urgency calls and messages must be cancelled if it is subsequently found that assistance is not required.

The safety signal

The radiotelephone safety signal consists of the spoken word 'SECURITE' (pronounced *say-cur-etay*). This indicates that the station is about to transmit a message concerning an important navigational or meteorological warning.

Voyage reports (TR)

To enable coast radio stations to maintain information on the whereabouts of vessels, which could prove useful in a search and rescue situation, you should inform the coast station of your position and voyage. Include, for example, your name and call sign, ports of departure and destination, and estimated time of arrival.

The radiotelephone alarm signal

This consists of two audio-frequency tones transmitted alternately at quarter-second intervals over a period of betweeen 30 seconds and 1 minute. The two tones (2200 Hz and 1300 Hz) give a distinctive warbling sound that can be clearly distinguished through any radio interference or speech.

The purpose of the alarm signal is to attract attention prior to an important message or distress call. It can also actuate automatic devices fitted to other vessels to alert those off watch.

Phonetics

For added clarity in any communication by the spoken word, including messages given by radiotelephone, the phonetic alphabet may be used. Each letter of the alphabet has a distinctive word ('Alfa', 'Bravo', 'Charlie', etc.) so that words of a message may be spelt out using individual phonetics. Numerals may also be expressed phonetically by using the figure-spelling phonetics ('Unaone', 'Bissotwo', 'Terrathree', etc.). The phonetic alphabet, and the figure-spelling phonetics, are shown opposite.

The International Code of Signals

This is a method of communication at sea designed to be used in situations involving safety of navigation and persons, particularly where language difficulties arise. The code is listed in the code book *The International Code of Signals*, which is available in nine languages. The code is suitable for all methods of communication — visual, radio or sound. A specific procedure is laid down in the code book for each method of communication. The more important signals of the International Code have each been allocated a single letter only. These are shown opposite.

Flag	Meaning	Flag	Meaning	Flag	Meaning	USED ON ALL OCCASIONS WHEN IT IS REQUIRED TO REPRESENT NUMBERS IN FLAG SIGNALLING
A ALFA 	I HAVE A DIVER DOWN; KEEP WELL CLEAR AT SLOW SPEED.	K KILO 	I WISH TO COMMUNICATE WITH YOU.	U UNIFORM 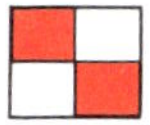	YOU ARE RUNNING INTO DANGER.	ONE 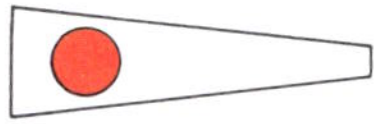 UNAONE
B BRAVO 	I AM TAKING IN, OR DISCHARGING, OR CARRYING DANGEROUS GOODS.	L LIMA 	YOU SHOULD STOP YOUR VESSEL INSTANTLY.	V VICTOR 	I REQUIRE ASSISTANCE.	TWO  BISSOTWO
C CHARLIE 	YES (AFFIRMATIVE OR "THE SIGNIFICANCE OF THE PREVIOUS GROUP SHOULD BE READ IN THE AFFIRMATIVE").	M MIKE 	MY VESSEL IS STOPPED AND MAKING NO WAY THROUGH THE WATER.	W WHISKEY 	I REQUIRE MEDICAL ASSISTANCE.	THREE 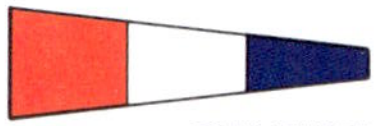 TERRATHREE
D DELTA 	KEEP CLEAR OF ME; I AM MANOEUVRING WITH DIFFICULTY.	N NOVEMBER 	NO (NEGATIVE OR "THE SIGNIFICANCE OF THE PREVIOUS GROUP SHOULD BE READ IN THE NEGATIVE").	X X-RAY 	STOP CARRYING OUT YOUR INTENTIONS AND WATCH FOR MY SIGNALS.	FOUR 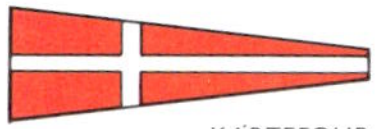 KARTEFOUR
E ECHO 	I AM ALTERING MY COURSE TO STARBOARD.	O OSCAR 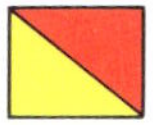	MAN OVERBOARD.	Y YANKEE 	I AM DRAGGING MY ANCHOR.	FIVE 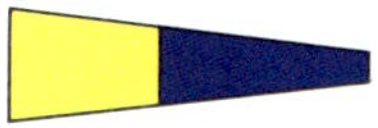 PANTAFIVE
F FOXTROT 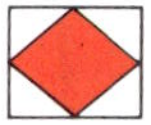	I AM DISABLED; COMMUNICATE WITH ME.	P PAPA 	IN HARBOUR: ALL PERSONS SHOULD REPORT ON BOARD AS THE VESSEL IS ABOUT TO PROCEED TO SEA. AT SEA: IT MAY BE USED BY FISHING VESSELS TO MEAN "MY NETS HAVE COME FAST UPON AN OBSTRUCTION".	Z ZULU 	I REQUIRE A TUG. WHEN MADE BY FISHING VESSELS OPERATING IN CLOSE PROXIMITY ON THE FISHING GROUNDS IT MEANS "I AM SHOOTING NETS".	SIX  SOXISIX
G GOLF 	I REQUIRE A PILOT. WHEN MADE BY FISHING VESSELS OPERATING IN CLOSE PROXIMITY ON THE FISHING GROUNDS IT MEANS "I AM HAULING NETS".	Q QUEBEC 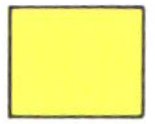	MY VESSEL IS HEALTHY, AND I REQUEST FREE PRATIQUE.	1ST SUBSTITUTE 	USED TO REPEAT THE FIRST FLAG OR PENDANT IN THE SAME HOIST.	SEVEN 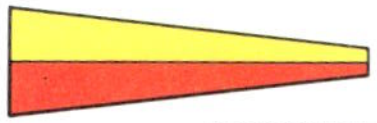 SETTESEVEN
H HOTEL 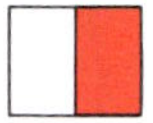	I HAVE A PILOT ON BOARD.	R ROMEO 	—	2ND SUBSTITUTE 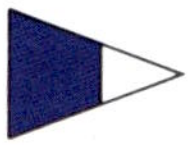	USED TO REPEAT THE SECOND FLAG OR PENDANT IN THE SAME HOIST.	EIGHT 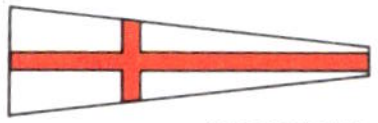 OKTOEIGHT
I INDIA 	I AM ALTERING MY COURSE TO PORT.	S SIERRA 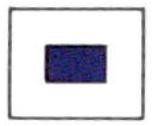	MY ENGINES ARE GOING ASTERN.	3RD SUBSTITUTE 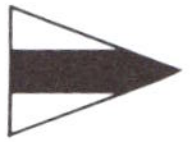	USED TO REPEAT THE THIRD FLAG OR PENDANT IN THE SAME HOIST.	NINE  NOVENINE
J JULIETT 	I AM ON FIRE AND HAVE DANGEROUS CARGO ON BOARD: KEEP WELL CLEAR OF ME.	T TANGO 	KEEP CLEAR OF ME; I AM ENGAGED IN PAIR TRAWLING.	CODE AND ANSWER 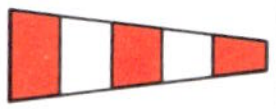	USED TO ACKNOWLEDGE A SIGNAL.	ZERO 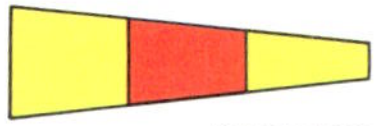 NADAZERO

The need and importance of communication between boats and the shore cannot be over-emphasised. Keeping in touch is not only of benefit to yourself but will also enable assistance to be given quickly and effectively to others who may be less fortunate than yourself. By knowing your whereabouts, a station can ask you to assist in a rescue, or direct others to assist in your own rescue.

Before leaving on any boating trip, large or small, use the ten-minute or two-minute form to let someone know where you are going, when you are leaving, and when you expect to arrive. (See page 141.) If you are delayed or have to divert for any reason while on passage, let this be known.

Remember, although you know that you are safe, others may not!

Landing signals

Day and Night signals	 Vertical motion of a white flag, arms or white light or flare	 or firing of a green star signal	— • — or code letter K given by light or sound signal apparatus.	This is the best place to land.
Day and Night signals	 Horizontal motion of a white flag, or arms extended horizontally - or white light or flare	 or firing of a red star signal	• • • or code letter S given by light or sound signal apparatus.	Landing here highly dangerous.
Day and Night signals	 1 Horizontal motion of a white flag, light or flare followed by 2 the placing of the white flag, light or flare on the ground and 3 by the carrying of another white flag light or flare in the direction to be indicated	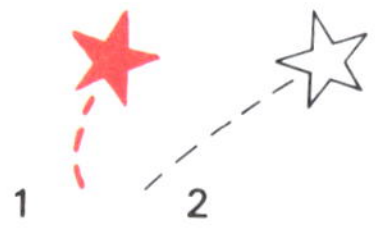 1 or firing of a red star signal vertically and 2 a white star signal in the direction towards the better landing place.	1 or signalling the code letter S (···) followed by the code letter R (·–·) if a better landing place for the craft in distress is located more to the right in the direction of approach, 2 or signalling the code letter S (···) followed by the code letter L (·–··) if a better landing place for the craft in distress is located more to the left in the direction of the approach.	Landing here highly dangerous. A more favourable location for landing is in the direction indicated.

14

HELP!

The ocean has no compassion, no law, no memory. The more a man goes to sea, the greater respect he has for it.

— Joseph Conrad

Good seamanship requires you to keep yourself, your crew and your boat out of trouble. But no matter how well versed you are in the arts of boatmanship and seamanship, and no matter how careful or well prepared you are, trouble may still arise in one form or another. As a good seaman you must have the knowledge and ability to cope with that trouble, and this must include knowing when, and how, to call for help.

There are many methods of summoning help — a hearty shout may be all that is required — but if the nearest boat is several miles away, a more distinctive signal must be used. Waving to a passing boat may bring the required help but is just as likely to invite a friendly returning wave as the boat cruises on past.

A number of distinctive signals have been drawn up that are internationally recognised. They are designed for use on ships, boats or aircraft of all sizes and are annexed to the Collision Regulations.

You must know these signals so that you may use them to summon help. You must also know these signals so that you can recognise a call for help from anyone else.

The distress signals

The following signals, used or exhibited either together or separately, indicate distress and need of assistance.

(a) A gun or other explosive signal fired at intervals of about a minute.

(b) A continuous sounding with any fog-signalling apparatus.

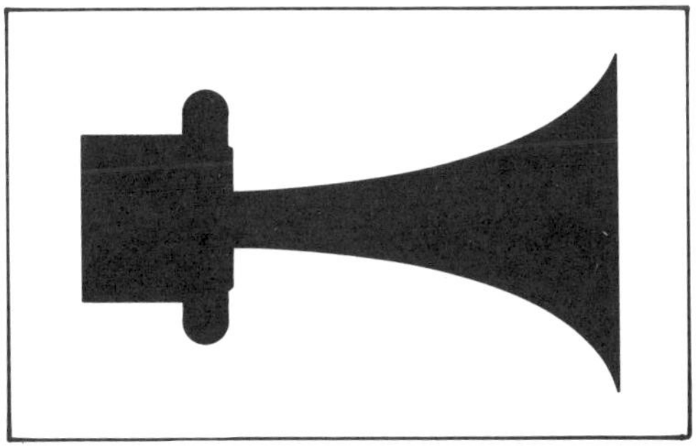

(c) Rockets or shells, throwing red stars, fired one at a time at short intervals.

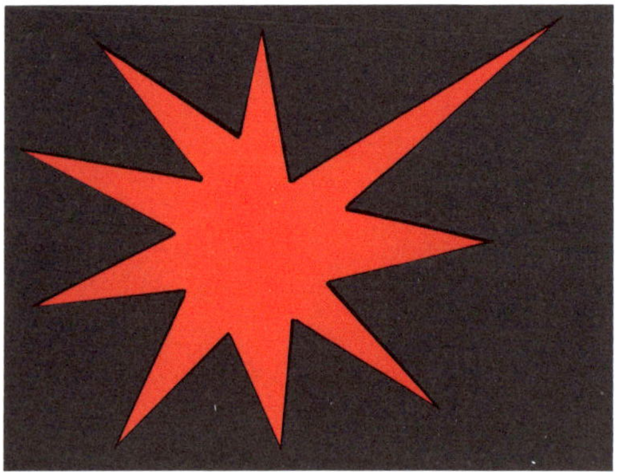

(d) A signal made by radiotelegraphy or by any other signalling method consisting of the group •••▬▬▬••• (SOS) in the Morse Code.

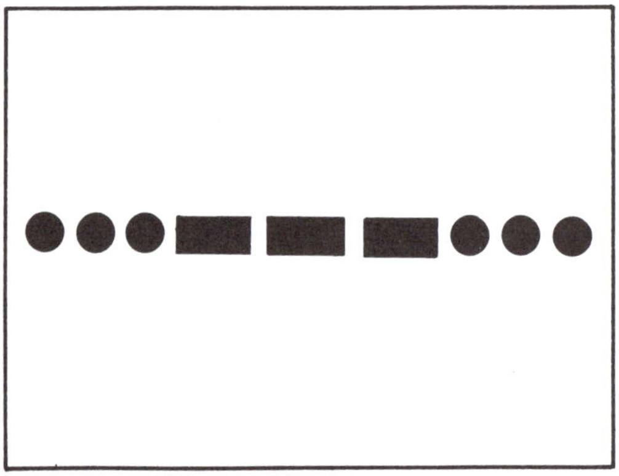

(e) A signal sent by radiotelephony consisting of the spoken word 'MAYDAY' (see page 140).

(f) The International Code Signal of distress indicated by N.C.

(g) A signal consisting of a square flag having above or below it a ball or anything resembling a ball.

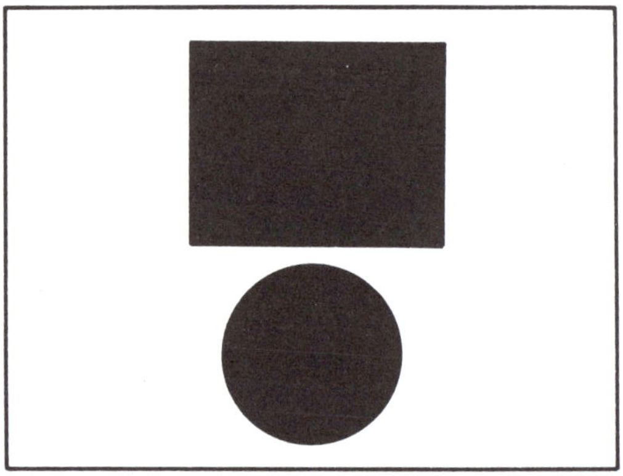

(h) Flames on the vessel (as from a burning tar barrel, oil barrel, etc.).

(i) A rocket parachute flare or a hand flare showing a red light (see page 138).

(j) A smoke signal giving off orange-coloured smoke (see page 139).

(k) Slowly and repeatedly raising and lowering arms outstretched to each side.

(l) The radiotelegraph alarm signal.

(m) The radiotelephone alarm signal (see page 132).

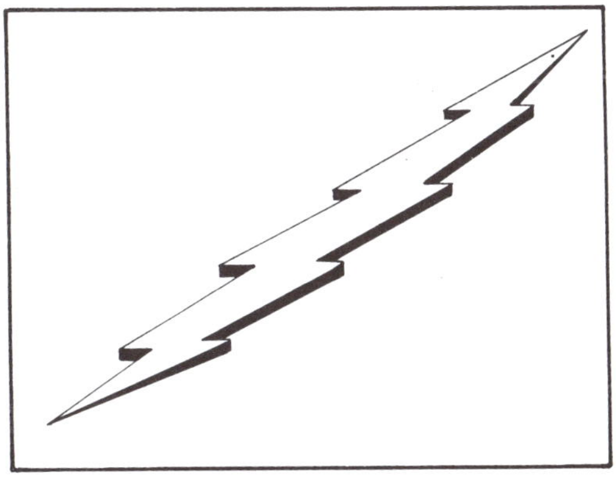

(n) Signals transmitted by emergency position-indicating radio beacons (see page 139).

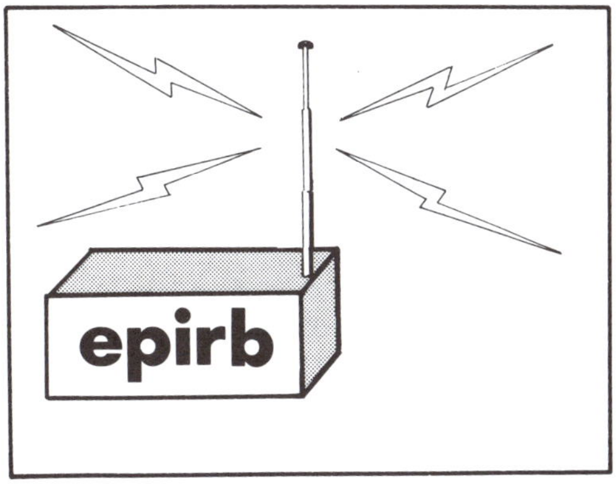

The use or exhibition of any of the foregoing signals, except for the purpose of indicating distress and need of assistance, and the use of other signals that may be confused with any of the above signals is prohibited (see page 139).

Attention is drawn to the relevant sections of the *Merchant Ship Search and Rescue Manual*, and the following signals.

(a) A piece of orange-coloured canvas with either a black square and circle or other appropriate symbol (for identification from the air).

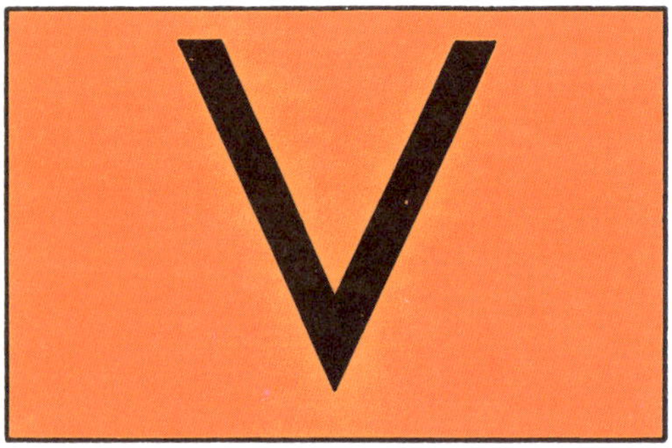

(b) A dye marker.

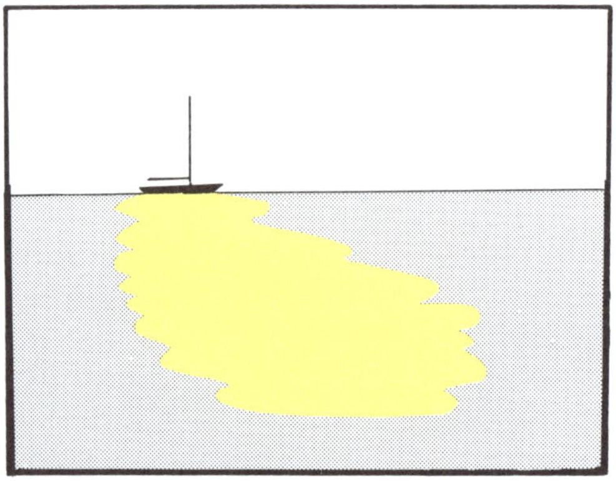

Distress flares

Pyrotechnic signals are the most distinctive of distress signals, but they are also the most short-lived. Do not fire them off unless you know there is someone there to see them.

Flares are available in many colours, including white for illumination purposes. All distress flares are red.

■ Know how to fire all flares. The firing instructions are on the flare, but it may be dark, or you may not have time to read these instructions fully and carefully at the time of the emergency.

■ Keep your flares where they are readily accessible, but protected from rain, spray and damp.

Inspect all pyrotechnic signals frequently for signs of damage or deterioration.

■ All flares have a limited lifespan and are date-stamped. Replace them by their expiry date, or before if they are damaged or suspect — it is not worth the risk of hoping they may work when you need them. Date-expired pyrotechnics are dangerous and must be disposed of.

■ Never dispose of damaged or date-expired flares at sea or into the garbage. They should be handed to the police, the Maritime Safety Authority, or your supplier.

■ If you see a distress flare, take its bearing — it will soon disappear. Use your boat radio to inform the coast station, and then investigate. If ashore, telephone the police.

The rocket parachute flare

Use as an effective long-range alert signal. The rocket ejects a very bright flare at a height of at least 330 metres. The flare then descends slowly by parachute, burning for at least 40 seconds.

Firing instructions are on the signal case. Fire from the downwind side of the boat. Hold firmly. The rocket will turn into the wind, so aim vertically or 15° downwind in stronger winds — never aim into the wind. Squeeze the trigger gently.

The hand flare

Use to summon help from closer range, and to

pinpoint position. It will display a bright red hand-held flare that will burn for one minute.

Firing instructions are on the flare case. Hold the flare firmly, downwind and preferably over the boat's side to prevent burning waste dropping into the boat. Shield your eyes to prevent loss of night vision.

The hand-held orange smoke signal
A daylight-only signal that emits orange smoke for about 40 seconds. Use in lighter winds — a strong wind will disperse the smoke. This is an effective short-range signal, and useful for pinpointing position to boats or aircraft.

Firing instructions are on the signal case. Stand on the downwind side of the boat and allow the smoke to build into a cloud.

The buoyant orange smoke signal
A daylight-only signal that burns for longer than the hand-held signal — usually up to about four minutes.

Firing instructions are on the signal case. After ignition, place in the water on the leeward side of the boat and allow the smoke to build up against the hull.

The radiotelephone

Pay careful attention to the correct procedure for transmitting the call. Give the call in the order described on page 141, and do not stop transmitting until the completed message has been given. On completion, wait a suitable period for acknowledgement before repeating.

Position may be given as a latitude and longitude, but when coasting it should preferably be given as a bearing and distance from a well-known landmark.

It is useful to give searchers a good description of your boat. They need to know what to look for. Indicate also how many persons are aboard, and whether you are using any other distress or distinctive signals.

Give your message as slowly and calmly as possible. Do not allow panic to affect its clarity; your life may depend on it.

Emergency position-indicating radio beacons

An emergency position-indicating radio beacon, or EPIRB, is a small, lightweight radio transmitter that, when activated, will alert rescue services and allow aircraft or vessels to home in to effect a rescue. Until recently, New Zealand detection of EPIRBs has relied upon aircraft to monitor EPIRB frequencies, but with the installation of a Local User Terminal (LUT) at the National Rescue Co-ordination Centre at Lower Hutt, New Zealand is now linked into the Cospas-Sarsat satellite surveillance system.

Most new EPIRBs are 'satellite-coherent', meaning that their signal will be picked up by a passing Cospas-Sarsat satellite and relayed to the LUT. The distress position is automatically targeted at the LUT, and the NRCC will then direct rescue services to the distress site where final location can be made by homing in on the EPIRB.

There are two types of marine EPIRBs available:

121.5/243 MHz. These are small, reasonably priced units that are easily transported into a liferaft or attached to a lifejacket. Most new models are compatible with the Cospas-Sarsat satellite system and will provide an initial alert and distress position in areas covered by the LUT with an accuracy to within 20 kilometres.
Caution: Owners of 121.5/243 MHz EPIRBs manufactured before 1990, or whose EPIRBs do not comply with Standard MS241, should assume that their EPIRB is ***NOT*** *compatible with the Cospas-Sarsat system.*

406 MHz. These are specifically designed for satellite detection and are more bulky and more expensive. They provide an initial alert, a distress position to within 5 kilometres, and can identify the EPIRB through a unique code and international registration system. Cospas-Sarsat satellites can also memorise information from a 406 MHz EPIRB in areas not covered by a LUT and download the information to the next Earth station as it is passed. These EPIRBs also emit a homing signal on 121.5 MHz for search authorities. For offshore and overseas cruising, the 406 MHz is the obvious first choice.

All EPIRBs are fitted with internal batteries that will keep the unit operating for at least 48 hours. The batteries must be replaced and the unit serviced at intervals stated by the manufacturer. There is no licence fee for an EPIRB, but it must be type-approved by the Radio Frequency Service.

■ If an EPIRB is inadvertently activated, you must inform authorities immediately to prevent a Search And Rescue operation being mounted. Failure to do this will result in heavy fines, and the costs of a fruitless search by rescue services.

Giving assistance

You have an obligation, both as a responsible seafarer and under the New Zealand Shipping and Seamen Act, to proceed with all speed to the assistance of those in distress providing it does not place you or your crew in serious danger. If responding to a distress call, always advise someone else of the distress, and of your own actions and intentions.

Improper use of distress signals

Maritime regulations prohibit the use of distress signals (and any signals that could be confused with these signals) except for genuine reasons. Severe penalties may be imposed for improper use, and any offender is also liable for any search and rescue expenses, which may be quite substantial.

Making your boat conspicuous

A small boat is not an easy target for searchers, whether searching at sea level or from the air.

White, blues or greens do not contrast well with the sea; reds, oranges and yellows are extremely distinctive. Even if you do not wish to paint the whole boat in these colours, consider painting some part of the boat in a bright colour to aid detection. As an alternative, or as an extra measure, carry an orange sheet to drape over the boat in an emergency.

Radar is often used in search and rescue operations, and small boats are poor radar targets. Carry the radar reflector described on page 42.

Search and rescue

The New Zealand Search and Rescue Organisation comprises a number of government departments and volunteer groups whose task is to seek out and give assistance to those who are missing or in distress.

Inshore and coastal incidents are dealt with by the police, Maritime Safety Authority, and by coastguard and other local volunteer organisations. Offshore incidents are handled by police, Maritime Safety Authority, Civil Aviation, the Royal New Zealand Navy, and the Royal New Zealand Air Force.

The more information supplied to search and rescue personnel, the faster they are able to give assistance. They must know for whom they are looking, and they must know where to look.

The ten-minute form

For use by skippers intending to go offshore for extended voyages. It is so named because it only takes about ten minutes to complete. The form contains all relevant details of the boat, its crew, and its intended voyage. Spare forms are available from government shipping offices, Customs offices, and from some boat clubs and coastal police stations.

The completed form should be placed in the care of a reliable friend, who will pass it on to the police if you become overdue. Thus, on arrival at your destination, or if for any reason you are delayed or diverted from your original route, you must advise your contact ashore to avoid an unnecessary alert.

The two-minute form

This follows the same principle as the ten-minute form, but is designed for the shorter, localised outing or trip, probably returning to the same point. The form will take about two minutes to complete. Forms may be obtained from the police, coastguard, and from some service stations. Leave the completed form with friends or

MARINE NOTICE

AFFIX THIS NOTICE NEAR YOUR RADIO

DISTRESS & URGENCY INFORMATION

DISTRESS

If in imminent danger and immediate aid is required, use MAYDAY.

1. Switch to 2182 kHz or 156.8 MHz (Chl. 16), International Distress Frequencies (any other frequency may be used if it is known that the nearest station or ship is keeping watch on that frequency).
2. Alarm Signal (where possible), say: "MAYDAY" (3 times).
3. Say: "This is
   *.." (3 times)
4. Say: "MAYDAY *......................................."
5. Give your position.
6. State nature of distress.
7. State nature of help required.
8. Give any other information which may assist rescue.
9. Listen on the same frequency for acknowledgement.
10. If any other ship interrupts, say: "SEELONCE MAYDAY."

URGENCY

If MAYDAY not warranted, but urgency required for safety of ship or person, use—

PAN PAN

1. Switch to 2182 kHz or 156.8 MHz (Chl. 16), International Distress Frequencies (any other frequency may be used if it is known that the nearest station or ship is keeping watch on that frequency).
2. Say: "PAN PAN" (3 times).
3. Give the name of the station required (3 times).
4. Say: "This is
   *.." (3 times)
5. Give urgency message.
6. Listen on the same frequency for acknowledgement.

If you hear SECURITE (SAY-CURE-E-TAY) this indicates that a navigational or meteorological warning is to follow.

CANCELLATION OF DISTRESS OR URGENCY CALLS AND MESSAGES

DISTRESS and URGENCY calls and messages must be cancelled if it is subsequently found that assistance is not required.

Example—MAYDAY:
Say: "MAYDAY (once) All Stations (3 times), this is:
*.. (3 times)
Cancel my earlier MAYDAY, help no longer required—out."

Example—URGENCY:
Say: "All stations (or a particular station) (3 times), this is:
*.. (3 times)
Cancel my earlier URGENCY call, engine now repaired—out."

UNECESSARY TRAFFIC SHOULD BE AVOIDED AT ALL TIMES

*Insert your ship's name and call sign

IF YOU HEAR A DISTRESS MESSAGE

1. LISTEN CAREFULLY. If possible, write down the message and time.
2. LISTEN FOR ACKNOWLEDGEMENT from a coast radio station.
3. If no acknowledgement heard—acknowledge, then re-send the message.
4. Say: "MAYDAY RELAY" (3 times).
5. Say: "This is *............................" (3 times)
6. Give distress message as sent by vessel in distress.
7. Give assistance if possible. Advise coast station of what you are doing.
8. Continue to listen in.
9. If other radio traffic interrupts, say: "SEELONCE DISTRESS
   This is *.."

relatives, and advise them of your schedule and the action they must take if you do not meet your schedule.

Night air search technique

This night-searching technique takes advantage of the excellent range of pyrotechnics, but it also relies upon the co-operation of those being sought.

An aircraft flies at an altitude of 900 to 1500 metres, following a 'creeping line ahead' pattern with track spacings of 10 to 12 miles, depending upon visibility.

Every five to ten minutes (if searching at 120 knots) or every two to five minutes (if searching at 240 knots) the aircraft fires a green flare. When clear of the glare, the aircrew keep a lookout.

If you are in distress, on seeing a green flare:

1. Wait for the aircraft to clear the glare.
2. Fire one red parachute or hand flare.
3. About a minute later, fire a second flare. The aircraft will turn towards the first flare, and check course on the second.
4. Fire a third flare when the aircraft is almost overhead, or if going off course.

The aircraft may drop a marine marker flare to mark your position. This burns with intense heat, do not handle it or tie it to your boat. It may burn for up to two hours.

An Orion aircraft may also release a sonobuoy to use as a homing marker. This must not be removed from the water, but may be held alongside the boat.

Cancellation of distress calls

If assistance has been successfully given, or if a distress situation no longer exists, a distress call must be cancelled to prevent unnecessary searching by those unaware that the emergency is over.

15

SURVIVAL AT SEA

No one is a survivor until rescued.

First-aid kit

Make sure your first-aid kit at least contains the basic items required for dressing wounds, as well as those extra items that apply to your style of boating, your locality and your crew's particular needs.

Include in your kit a checklist of its contents and a comprehensive first-aid manual. Stow the items in a well-marked watertight box or locker. Make sure each item is clearly labelled and individually packed so it cannot move around. Check the contents frequently to see that there is no leakage or deterioration of medicines.

Hypothermia

Hypothermia is a very real danger to anyone who goes to sea. At risk are all those in small boats, who are liable to sudden immersion; those engaged in water sports that involve prolonged exposure to the cold water and weather; and anyone who becomes a man overboard victim. In fact, anyone on, in or under the water is at risk. You should therefore be fully aware of its dangers and have adequate knowledge of its prevention, symptoms, and treatment.

First-aid kit contents

Amethocaine eyedrops*	Adhesive dressings
Antibiotic cream or powder*	Adhesive sutures
Antiseptic detergent	Adhesive tape
Antiseptic wound cream	Bandages (25 mm and 50 mm)
Antihistamine cream	Triangular bandage
Anti-sunburn lotion	Burn dressings
Calamine lotion	Crêpe bandages
Codeine, aspirin or paracetamol tablets	Eye shade
Golden eye ointment	Notebook and pencil
Insect repellant	Safety pins
Seasick pills	Scissors
Stomach tablets or powder	Sterile wound dressings
Zinc ointment	Tweezers

First-aid manual
List of contents

*available on prescription only

How the body reacts to cold

The body must maintain the vital organs in its inner core, the heart, lungs, brain, etc., at a constant temperature of about 37.6°C to enable them to function normally. At normal temperatures the heat generated by the body is carried by the blood to all regions of the body. This blood flow is varied to regulate and control body temperature. Any excess heat is removed by transferring it to the outer layers for dissipation.

As the temperature of the environment falls, the outer layers of the body begin to cool. The body now reduces blood circulation to these outer regions, so that the cooling is not transferred to the important organs in the deeper regions of the body. Hands and feet feel cold because of the reduced blood supply to these areas. Shivering starts, as an involuntary muscular attempt to generate more body heat.

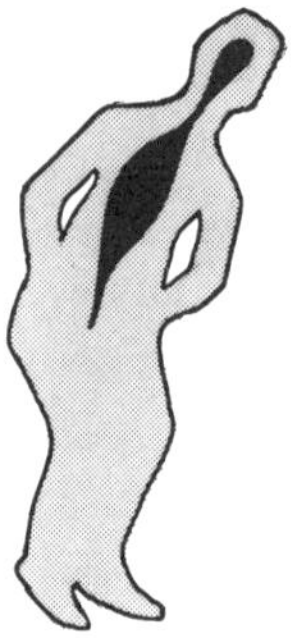

With further cooling, the inner core begins to cool. The blood supply to the body's outer regions is further reduced, as the body now takes drastic measures to maintain the temperature of its vital organs. Shivering may now decrease or stop. The organs in the core are now being affected. As the brain cools, there is reduced control and consciousness is affected. Further cooling of the core will cause the organs here to stop functioning.

Consciousness is lost. Death will follow unless treatment is immediate and correctly given.

What is hypothermia?

Hypothermia means lowered deep-body temperature. In cold air or cold water the skin and external tissues become cooled very rapidly. However, it takes 10 to 15 minutes before the temperature of the heart and brain begins to cool. Intense shivering occurs in a futile attempt to increase the body's heat production and counteract the large heat loss.

Decreased consciousness occurs when the deep-body temperature falls from the normal 37° to 32°C.

Heart failure is the usual cause of death when deep-body temperature cools to below 30°C.

Prevention

In cold, wet or windy conditions be on continual lookout for symptoms of exhaustion or hypothermia. Generally, the more clothes that are worn, the better. It should be remembered, however, that conventional clothing is designed for insulation in normal conditions; not for extreme cold, and not when wet. The more windproof or waterproof the clothing, the more the body will be protected against loss of body heat. Inner clothing should be wool or flannel.

- When going out in your boat, always take extra clothing. Cold weather may occur at any time; man overboard may occur at any time.
- Prevent fatigue.
- Eat or drink frequently. Provide high-energy foods (chocolate, glucose sweets, raisins, etc.) and warm, sweet drinks or hot soup.
- Keep yourself and your crew warm and dry.
- Avoid excessive sweating.
- Pay special attention to the protection of head, hands and neck. Over 40 per cent of body heat loss occurs from the head.
- Do not drink alcohol to keep you warm. Alcohol is a stimulant and will increase blood flow to the outer regions of the body. Heat loss will increase by 20 per cent. You will die happier but sooner.

Ranges of hypothermia symptoms

Note: Most physical symptoms vary with each individual and may be unreliable indicators of core body temperature. Only a low-temperature rectal thermometer gives reliable core temperature (the mouth cools too rapidly). In general, as body temperature falls, symptoms will increase.

MILD CONDITION
(36–34°C)
- Shivering, cold hands and feet.
- Still alert and able to help self.
- Numbness in limbs, loss of dexterity, clumsiness. Pain from cold.

MODERATE CONDITION
(34–32°C)
- Shivering may decrease or stop.

SEVERE CONDITION
(32–28°C)
- Shivering decreases or stops.
- Loss of reasoning and recall, confusion, abnormal behaviour.
- Victim appears drunk, very clumsy, slurs speech, denies problem and may resist help.
- Victim semiconscious to unconscious.
- Muscular rigidity increasing.

CRITICAL CONDITION
(28°C and below)
- Unconscious, may appear dead.
- Little or no apparent breathing.
- Pulse slow and weak, or no pulse found.
- Skin cold, may be bluish-grey colour.
- Eyes may be dilated.
- Very rigid.

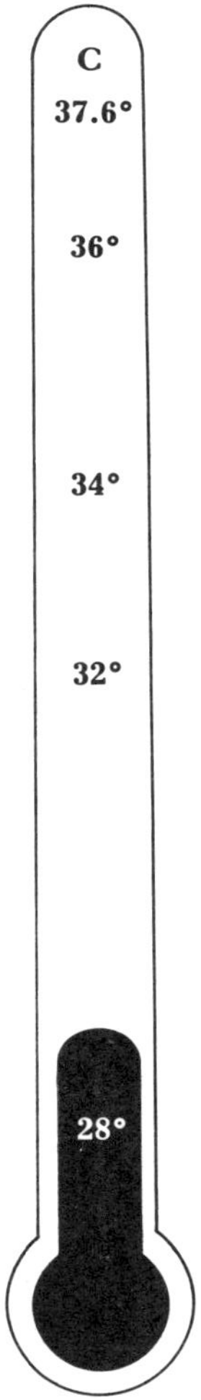

Core body temperature (taken rectally)

Hypothermia first aid

IN ALL CASES
- Move victim to dry shelter and warmth, and handle gently.
- Remove wet clothes and apply mild heat (comfortable to your elbow) to the chest region only. Use hot water bottles, warm moist towels.
- Cover with blankets or sleeping bag; insulate from the cold. Keep head and neck covered.

MILD CASES
- Primary task is to prevent further heat loss and allow body to rewarm itself.
- Give warm, sweet drinks — *no* alcohol.
- Apply gentle heat source to stabilise temperature.
- Exercise to generate heat, and keep victim warm for several hours.

MODERATE CASES
- Same as above but limit exercise and offer sips of warm, sweet liquids only after victim is *fully conscious*, begins to rewarm and is able to swallow.
- Have victim checked by doctor.

SEVERE CASES
- Ignore pleas of 'Leave me alone, I'm okay.' *Victim is in serious trouble* — keep continuous watch over the victim.
- Obtain medical advice as soon as possible.
- Assist victim, but avoid jarring — rough handling may cause a cardiac arrest or other complications.
- No food or drink if there is any sign of unconsciousness.
- Treat as for shock — lay down in bunk, wedge in place, elevate feet, keep immobile.
- Apply external mild heat to chest region — keep temperature from dropping but avoid too rapid a temperature rise.
- Transport to hospital or other medical post as soon and as gently as possible.

CRITICAL CASES
- *Always assume the patient is revivable — don't give up.* Handle with *extreme care.*
- Tilt the head back to open the airway — look, listen, and feel for breathing and pulse.
- If there is any breathing or pulse, no matter how faint or slow, *do not give CPR*, but keep close watch on vital sign changes.
- Stabilise temperature with external heat sources; also use naked chest-to-chest warming (leave legs and arms alone). Use rescuer's warm breath exhaled in victim's face and in unison with his breathing.
- If no breathing or no pulse for one to two minutes, *begin CPR immediately.*
- *Medical help is imperative — hospitalisation is essential.*

Critical heat-loss areas

In addition to the head, certain other body regions have high rates of heat loss while a subject is holding still in cold water. The sides of the chest, where there is little muscle or fat, are a major route for heat loss from the warm chest cavity. The groin region also loses more heat, owing to the large blood and lymph vessels near the surface. To reduce body heat loss, these regions deserve special attention.

Rewarming

The very first consideration in all cases must be to prevent further heat loss. A hypothermia victim may be unable to generate enough body heat to raise the internal temperature of his or her body to normal levels. Warming by applying heat is therefore an important first-aid measure, but in doing so great care must be taken. Improper warming methods may increase blood circulation and allow the blood to flow through the arms and legs; since these may have taken on the temperature at or near that of the cold water, any blood flowing through them will be drastically cooled. When this very cold blood returns to the body's inner core, the temperature of the core may drop to a level where life can no longer be sustained.

Body rewarming methods could include any of the following:

- Body contact. A warm person, or persons, should huddle with the victim.
- Give warm water to drink.
- Apply warm, wet towels and hot water bottles.
- Use electric or chemical warming pads.
- Apply heated blankets. These may be electric, or heated by pouring warm water over them.
- Use hot baths or showers, but keep the arms and legs well clear.
- The inhalation of heated, water-saturated air or oxygen. Use the steam from a kettle, carefully directed under a makeshift hood over the victim's head.

Remember, it is important to heat the core of the body only; the head, neck, and trunk. Leave the arms and legs alone. Do not rub the surface of the body; this will stimulate blood circulation on the cooler outer surfaces. Do not allow the victim to be active; muscular action and increased blood circulation will draw warm blood away from the central body areas.

Warning!

First aid for severe and critical hypothermia is to add heat to stabilise temperature only. Rapid rewarming may be fatal; it will cause shock, and other complications. Allow the body to rewarm itself slowly.

If a person is severely hypothermic, perhaps unconscious, handle the body carefully and avoid jolts that may affect the heart's function.

Body core temperature lags behind skin temperature during rewarming. Keep the victim protected for an extended period after apparent full recovery or medical help arrives. Many hours, even days, are required for a return to normal temperature. Avoid re-exposure to the cold.

Survival in the water

Get out of the water

The body surrenders its heat to the water many times more quickly than to air of the same temperature, and it is often possible to stabilise body temperature once you are out of the water. Therefore, if at all possible, get on top of an overturned boat or any wreckage that is available — even if it feels colder out of the water than in it.

What do I wear?

Do not get undressed to enter the water; put on more clothes. If you stay still in the water, the layers of clothing will trap water between them and thus form layers of insulation. Experiments have shown that a person wearing two layers of woollen clothing in the water will lose less than a quarter as much heat as a person wearing only bathing trunks. So wear as many layers of wool as you can, and cover these with a waterproof garment to trap the warmer layers of water close to the body. On top of this, wear a lifejacket.

Should I swim to keep warm?
No! Although the body produces almost three times as much heat when swimming slowly and steadily, this extra heat, and more, is lost to the cold water, owing to more blood circulation to the arms, legs, and skin. Increased water circulation through the clothing will also destroy those trapped insulated layers. Experiments have shown that the average person swimming in a lifejacket cools 35 per cent faster than when holding still.

HELP (Heat Escape Lessening Posture)
This technique involves holding the inner sides of the arms tight against the chest, to protect this critical heat-loss area. The thighs are pressed together and raised to protect the groin heat-loss region. This posture will result in nearly a 50 per cent increase in predicted survival time.

- Head out of the water, including the back of the head.
- Arms against sides, chest and buoyancy aid.
- Lower legs crossed, knees raised as much as waves and stability permit, but keep the knees together.

It should be noted that a lifejacket, with its buoyancy high on the body and close to the surface of the water, is especially suited for the HELP. Where the buoyancy is more evenly distributed, as in a buoyancy vest, the centre of buoyancy is lower, and the drawing up of the knees can lead to occasional instability in the water.

The huddle position
This position can be used for groups of three or more. The sides of the chests and the lower body areas are pressed together. Apart from reducing the rate of body cooling, there are probably some psychological advantages in being together as a group.

- Heads out of water, including backs of heads.
- Arms hugging each other over buoyancy aids.
- Maximum body contact, especially at chest, to reduce heat loss.
- Legs intertwined as much as possible.
- Talk to maintain morale.

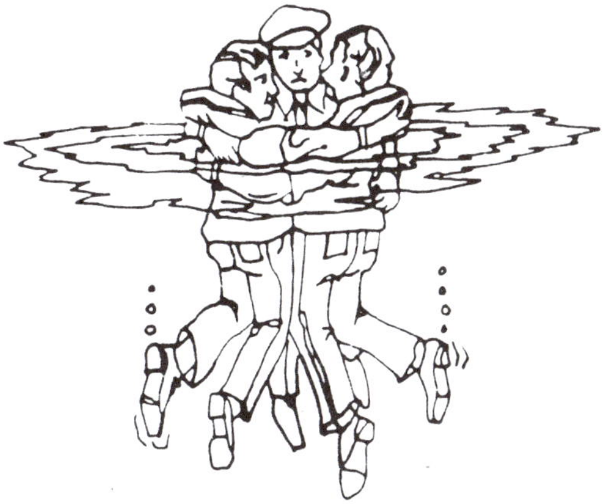

The huddle was developed for adults; however, it can also be used to slow down the rapid rate at which children's bodies cool, by sandwiching them in the middle of the group.

Predicted survival times
The graph on page 148 shows average predicted survival times of normal adults in water of various temperatures. The figures are based on experimental cooling of average men and women who were wearing a standard lifejacket and light clothing, and were holding still in ocean water.

Predicted survival times are increased by extra body fat, and reduced by smaller body size.

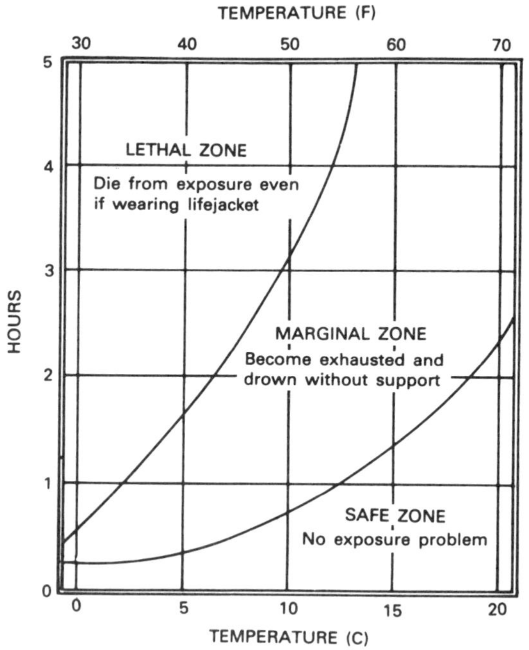

Although women usually possess slightly more fat than men, they often cool faster because of their generally smaller body size. Because of their even smaller body mass and relatively little fat, children cool much faster than adults.

How far can I swim?

The shore may be close enough to reach by swimming, despite the faster cooling rates that may be brought about by swimming. Tests conducted on people swimming in ocean water of 10°C, while wearing a standard lifejacket and light clothing, have shown that the average person could cover a distance of one mile (1.85 km) before being incapacitated by hypothermia.

It is not easy to judge distance, especially under emergency conditions in rough, cold water, but at temperatures of about 10°C the shore should be within about one mile before making the decision to swim. The distance covered will obviously be affected by one's swimming ability, amount of insulation, the tidal flows and the water conditions.

Sudden immersion in cold water

Immersion in cold water, especially if sudden, causes immediate reflex disturbances in circulation and breathing. There are instances of sudden death occurring because of heart attack, brought about by the increase in heart rate and changes in blood pressure that accompany sudden immersion in cold water. Difficulties, or even sudden death, may also be caused by hyperventilation (overbreathing), which everyone experiences in response to the shock of cold water. It is possible that if a person is plunged underwater in a rough sea, hyperventilation could lead to uncontrolled inhalation of water and eventual drowning. Prolonged hyperventilation can lead to unconsciousness, and subsequent drowning.

Because panic can magnify any of the above responses, it is important to remain calm and methodical if faced with a cold-water emergency. If possible, enter the water gradually, allowing the body to adjust to the changing temperature. Consciously control your breathing as much as possible. The more clothing and insulation your body has, the less will be the initial shock on entry into the cold water.

Rescue breathing

Place the victim on his or her back, and begin rescue breathing immediately. Your first blowing efforts will show if the air passages are blocked and, if they are clear, will provide the urgently needed oxygen. If the throat is blocked, clear it quickly with your fingers. Slaps between the shoulder blades should dislodge a stubborn blockage.

In an unconscious person with the head slumped, the tongue blocks the throat and little or no air can get into the lungs. Lift the neck and tilt the head right back — a halfway tilt is not enough — and the victim may start breathing. If they do not, start rescue breathing.

■ Hold the head fully tilted with the chin pulled forward. Open the mouth with your thumb on the chin, but keep the chin pulled forward. Take a deep breath.

■ Seal your lips around the victim's mouth, blocking the nostrils with your cheek, or by pinching them with your fingers, to prevent air leakage. Now blow until you see the chest rise.

■ Remove your mouth and listen to the victim breathing out through mouth and nose, while you take another breath. Inflate the victim's lungs again as soon as they have breathed out.

■ Make the first five to ten breaths deep and rapid, then continue at a rate of about 10 to 15 breaths a minute. When the victim starts trying to breathe, keep your breaths in time with their efforts.

■ Use only puffs from your cheeks for infants. Stop blowing as soon as the chest starts to rise. Repeat at a rate of about 20 breaths a minute.

Don't give up!

Recent cases have shown that persons who are apparently dead from hypothermia or drowning in cold water can often be resuscitated successfully, even after periods as long as 40 minutes without breathing and blood circulation. Cold body tissues, including the brain, require less oxygen than when warm and can sustain life longer. Therefore, don't give up. Maintain rescue breathing until medical assistance is available.

Seasickness

Seasickness is one of the main causes of unseaworthiness in small vessels. It can reduce a victim to such a state of physical weakness, impaired judgement, inattention and disinterest that a situation of considerable danger may exist. Many vessels have had to be searched for, and their crews taken off, because of seasickness.

Prolonged seasickness can lead to dehydration. Mildly seasick cases should be encouraged to drink as much as possible (not alcohol), and should eat a little at frequent intervals.

Several seasickness cures and preventatives are available. If you or your crew are known to be susceptible to seasickness, consult your doctor or chemist. Some medicines have side-effects, such as drowsiness, which it is wise to be aware of beforehand.

16

ASSOCIATED WATER SPORTS

I must go down to the seas again, for the call of the running tide
is a wild call and a clear call, that may not be denied;
and all I ask is a windy day, with the white clouds flying,
and the flung spray and the blown spume, and the seagulls crying.

— John Masefield

New Zealanders enjoy many varied sporting activities on, in and under the water. Many of these sports involve boating, and all share the same environment. They are therefore susceptible to the same dangers.

If you are taking up any water sport as a beginner, or even if you have enjoyed the sport for a while and consider yourself an expert, join a club that specialises in your activity. Here you can enjoy the company of others interested in the same sport as your own, and can exchange experiences and draw upon the experience of others.

Board sailing

This sport has seen rapid growth in recent years. It is also a sport where getting into difficulty is almost as easy as falling into the water, for board sailing carries with it the inevitable risk of falling off, often frequently — and this makes you highly susceptible to hypothermia. If sailing any distance offshore in cold water, wear a wetsuit.

Continually falling off and remounting the board will also sap your strength. The more frequently you fall, the more difficult it will be to remount. Know your own limitations. Do not push yourself beyond your capability to return to the shore.

Remember that as a board sailor you are classed as a sailing vessel, and you must obey the Collision Regulations as such. Also observe the Water Recreation Regulations and General Harbour Regulations, and be fully aware of any local bylaws that may affect your activity.

Be aware of others using the beach and water's edge. They also have a right to enjoy the water, without the need to be constantly aware of board sailers sailing a path amidst them. Serious injury can result from a collision. Carelessness or disregard of others may lead to restrictions being placed on board sailing in certain areas.

- When carrying equipment up and down the beach, keep well clear of the public.
- Be courteous to other beach users when rigging and launching your board.
- Attempt your launching in an area that is clear of swimmers.

As a beginner, remember that manoeuvring a board requires skills that have yet to be learned. You have to learn how to balance, as well as how to sail and steer the board — there is no rudder. Practise and acquire these skills in calm water, with onshore winds, and well away from other water users. Until you become more competent, stay close to the shore and use a small sail.

Safety hints for board sailors

■ An ability to swim is essential for board sailors.

■ Sailing in company with others is desirable; or at least have one person watching from the shore, preferably someone who knows your abilities and intentions and who can rapidly bring help if required. If sailing alone, tell someone where you are going, and when you expect to return.

■ Wear a buoyancy vest. Should anything go wrong and you have to wait to be rescued, you will stay afloat with minimal effort. A wetsuit will give some buoyancy, but is no substitute for a buoyancy vest.

■ The most suitable distress signal, if on the board, is to slowly and repeatedly raise and lower arms outstretched to each side.

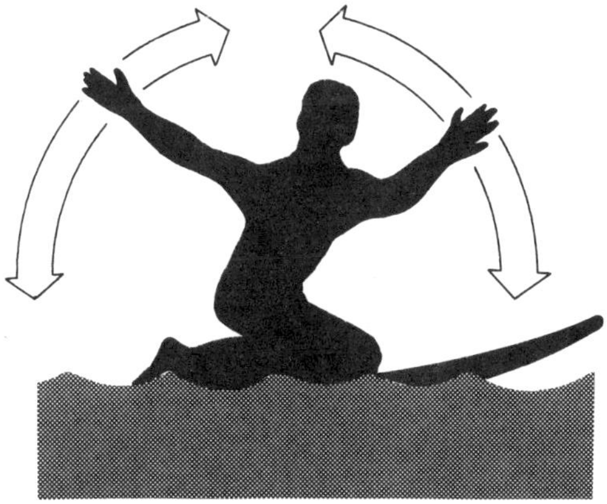

If in the water, the raising and lowering of one arm is the call for assistance.

■ Caution should be exercised in coastal waters when there is an offshore wind. It may take six times as long to return to shore against the wind as it did to sail out.

■ In an emergency never leave your board unless there is no doubt you can reach the shore.

■ Do not sail at night.

■ Obtain a weather forecast and be fully aware of the existing and forecasted winds and conditions.

■ Choose to sail only in weather conditions that will not exceed your own capabilities.

■ Be aware of the tides and currents in your area, and how they are affected by weather conditions.

■ Remember you are required to keep a proper lookout. The sail should contain a window of adequate size for a person of your height.

■ The mast and sail should be attached to the board with a line. When capsized, the sail will prevent the board from drifting away from you.

■ Safety harnesses are available to attach you to the boom. The harness should have a quick-release buckle.

■ An eye in the front of the board is desirable for towing purposes.

■ Take a spare line with you in case you have to be towed. Carry it lashed to the forward part of the boom, where it is readily available, or in your harness.

■ Know how to de-rig and roll up your sail at sea in case you are to be towed or have to paddle back to the shore. In an emergency, a board is easier to paddle without a rig.

■ Always inspect your gear for damage before setting out.

■ Replace any damaged lines or parts before you put to sea.

Surf sailing

Surf sailing requires a greater degree of skill than general board sailing. Pay close attention to the recommendations for board sailors, and

- Always wear a wetsuit and buoyancy vest, whatever the wind conditions.
- Make sure the rig is connected to the board with a safety strap.
- The sail should not be stretched too flat, even in strong winds.
- Make sure the mast foot is held firmly in the step, so that the mast cannot jump out when hitting a wave.
- Take a piece of rope with you for a spare control line.
- The outhaul should be cleated on the boom without a knot tied in its end. Quick release is essential.

The New Zealand Windsurfing Association has been formed to look after the interests of board sailors at all levels. The association is actively involved in training, the promotion of safety standards, monitoring the development and manufacture of boards and their rigs, and the organisation of competitions and national championships. For further information, or to find a club within your area, contact The New Zealand Windsurfing Association, P.O. Box 37-213, Parnell, Auckland.

Water-skiing

Safe water-skiing requires good co-operation and communication between the boat skipper, the observer, and the skier. The skipper of the boat has ultimate command, but the skier must communicate his or her requirements via the observer to the skipper, who in turn carries them out. The skipper may countermand the skier's instructions in the interests of safety — perhaps if he or she sees a danger not visible to the skier; or if asked to contravene a regulatory requirement.

The skipper must know the regulations pertaining to his or her sport, and be aware of any local bylaws that may affect its practice. The skipper must be fully conversant with the Water Recreation Regulations, particularly those governing age restrictions for fast boat operators, speed limits, the carriage of observers, and conduct in access lanes, and must know the Collision Regulations.

As driver of the boat the skipper must always be aware of the skier's speed and position behind the boat. He or she must carry out smooth starts, stops and turns, and be constantly aware of other boats, skiers and obstacles. Both the skipper and the observer must know the hand signals that will be given by the skier.

Water landings are usually preferable because they reduce the chance of hitting the shore at misjudged speeds. Shore landings should only be made onto sandy or grassy beaches. Avoid those beaches with rocks, trees or other visible and invisible obstructions. Never attempt to land near swimming areas.

In the absence of a regulated pattern, the pattern to be skied should be pre-arranged. Any pattern must maintain the required distance from the shore, swimmers and other boats, and maintain a safe distance from rocks and other obstacles. Remember that a skier swinging out parallel to the boat may pass 15 to 25 metres closer to obstacles than does the boat.

The observer must keep the skier under constant observation. A fallen skier is particularly difficult to see, and may not be visible to other boats or skiers. Always return to a fallen skier immediately. When approaching a fallen skier, do so at a reduced speed and heading into the wind or current. Always place the engine in neutral to pass the skier. When manoeuvring, remember you have a person and a towline in the water, and your propeller must be kept well clear of both. Practise placing the towline within easy reach of the fallen skier, and know how to get him or her aboard without capsizing the boat. It is advisable to stop the engine when boarding the skier, but never allow your skier to climb aboard using the engine as a ladder.

Tips for water-skiers

- Learn to swim proficiently before attempting to water-ski.
- All skiers should wear an appropriate skiing buoyancy aid. This should be of jacket design, not a belt.
- If you fall: Raise both hands clenched above your head to signal 'I am okay.' Recover the skiis. They will help to keep you afloat. If in a congested area, raise a ski so that other boats can see you.
- Stay away from docks, sea walls, jetties and other boats. Skiers seldom get hurt hitting the water but have been killed hitting solid objects.
- Be thoughtful of the rights of other water users.
- Do not signal the tow boat to accelerate until your ski tips are up, and the rope is taut.
- A recommended start signal is to yell 'Hit it!' or 'Okay!'. (The words 'Go' and 'No' may be confused by the observer or driver.)
- When landing parallel to the shore, come in slowly and release the tow bar at a safe distance from the shore.
- Do not land in swimming areas.
- Never wrap the tow rope around any part of the body, and never place any part of the body through the bridle.
- Do not ski at night, or in shallow water.

The New Zealand Water-Ski Association protects the interests of water-skiers. It heads four divisions; the Tournament Skiing Division, the Barefoot Water-Ski Division, the Ski Racing Division, and the Disabled Skiers' Division.

It should not be difficult to find a club involved in water-skiing in your area, there are over 30 water-ski and powerboat clubs affiliated to the association. To participate in any national event you must belong to an affiliated club.

'Faster'

'Slower'

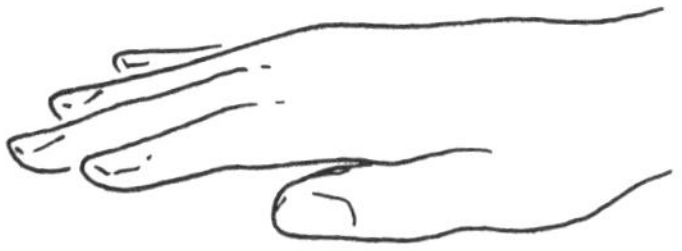

'Same speed'

'Speed okay'

'Back to the dock'

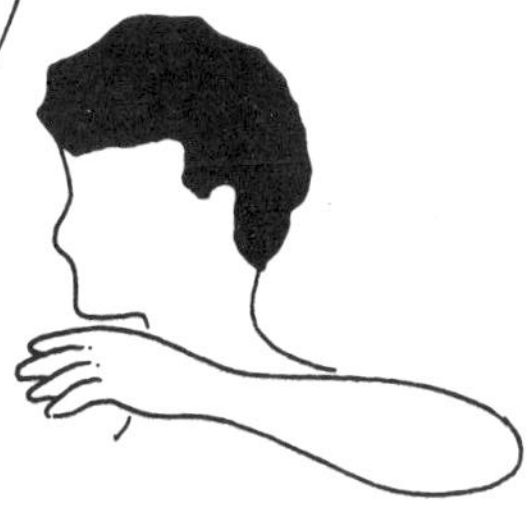

'Stop' or *'Cut the motor'*

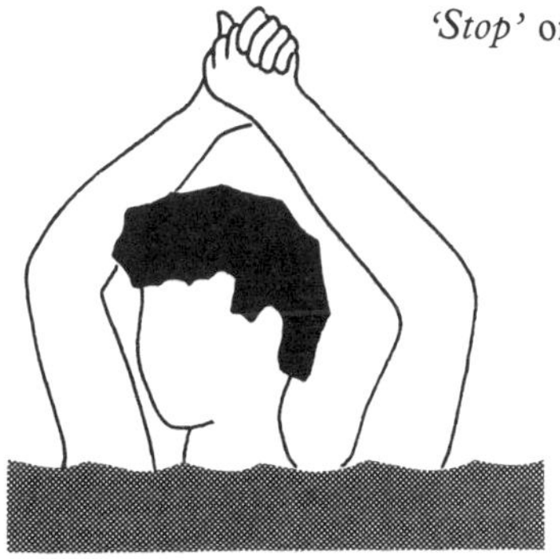

'I'm okay'

'Turn around'

Diving

This information applies to most underwater activities, including snorkelling.

■ Avoid shipping lanes, or any area where there is a large number of surface craft.

■ Display the international code flag 'A' meaning 'I have a diver down; keep well clear at slow speed.' You may use a marker float trail with a small 'A' flag mounted upon it. (Because of its colour, the red and white sport diving flag is visible over long distances; however, it must only be shown in conjunction with the 'A' flag for added recognition, never instead of it.)

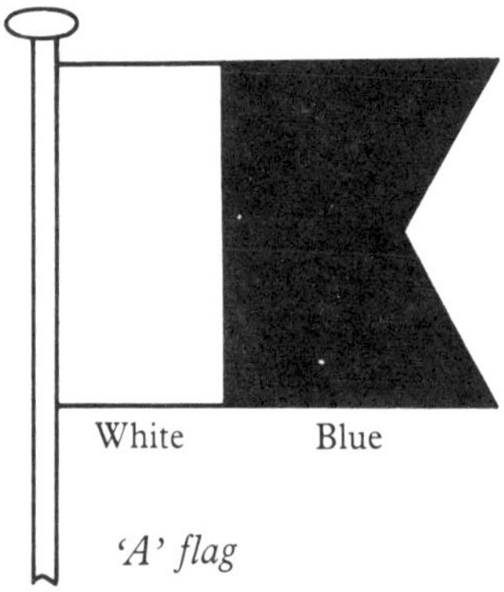

'A' flag

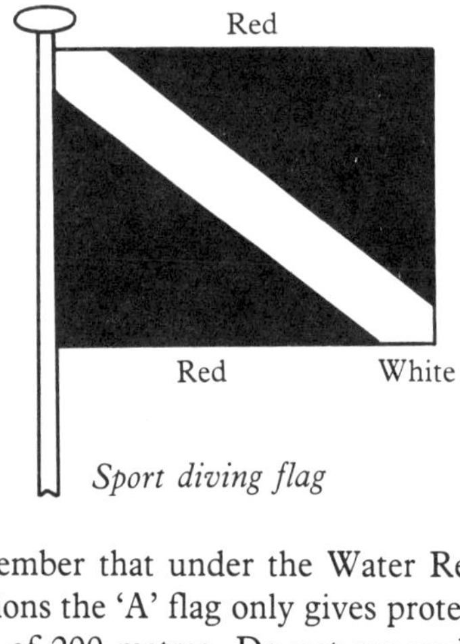

Sport diving flag

■ Remember that under the Water Recreation Regulations the 'A' flag only gives protection for a radius of 200 metres. Do not proceed beyond this distance from the flag.

'I'm okay'

■ It is desirable that an observer remains in the boat whenever a diver is below.

■ Use the buddy system. Dive in pairs.

■ Be familiar with your dive site. If you have not dived there before, obtain advice from a knowledgeable, local source.

■ Agree on a dive plan and adhere to it. Agree on a system of communication, procedures for reuniting in case of separation, and emergency procedures with your buddy and the observer in the boat.

■ If in difficulty on the surface, to indicate that you need assistance repeatedly raise one arm over your head and then lower it to your side.

'I require assistance'

■ If diving conditions are worse than those in which you are experienced, postpone your dive or find an alternative site with better conditions.

■ If a diver is overdue, summon help immediately.

- Take care while surfacing. Helmsmen of other vessels may not know your position, with the risk of running you down as you surface.
- Keep away from fishermen's markers.
- Check with the harbourmaster or other authority about local prohibitions and local fish and game laws.
- Keep clear of water-ski access lanes.

The New Zealand Underwater Association is the recognised national body for all underwater activities in New Zealand. Within the association there is a national sporting committee to cater for all underwater sporting activities and competitions, and a scientific committee to handle all scientific aspects of the recreation. A commercial division and an international college at Auckland have recently been established to serve the needs of professional divers. For information on the NZUA, or affiliated dive clubs, contact the NZUA Administration Office, P.O. Box 875, Auckland.

Diver emergency service

For advice in diving emergencies only, telephone: (09) 445-8454.

This 24-hour emergency telephone response service, installed and funded by the NZUA, is manned by naval personnel, and is linked to volunteer doctors versed in hyperbaric medicine.

Calls may also be made on VHF using the Sealink service.

Canoeing

- Be able to swim.
- Keep away from waterfalls and larger boats.
- Provide internal buoyancy for your canoe, so that in the event of a capsize it will not sink.
- Beginners should not canoe alone. Take an experienced person as a guide.
- Always wear a lifejacket, preferably one that also gives protection to the kidney regions.
- Always wear a canoe helmet when in rapids, shallows or surf. A capsize in rapids or shallows could cause you to be swept against rocks or sustain injury through contact with the bottom; and in surf there is the risk of capsize or collision with other canoes.
- Sea canoeing requires special expertise, and should not be attempted alone. It is best undertaken in a group, under the control of a club or school, and with an accompanying launch.
- Obtain a weather forecast and check the conditions in your area before you take to the water. An increasing onshore wind will build up a larger surf, which may make landing difficult on your return. An increasing offshore wind may make returning to the beach after a tiring trip very difficult.
- If you are going out alone, tell someone where you are going, and at what time you will be back.
- On extended river trips which may take a few days, always allow extra time to your programme in case the river floods and you are forced to wait for water levels to drop. Even the Whanganui River, with its easy rapids, can rise three metres or more in less than a day.

Should you require more information, or details of local canoe clubs in your area, contact the New Zealand Canoeing Association, P.O. Box 3768, Wellington.

Sea angling

This may involve a long trip out to your fishing ground, so as well as your fishing tackle, make sure your boat has the necessary safety equipment. Remember that a return trip is also included, so be aware of the tides throughout your outing. Check the weather before you leave, and constantly monitor the weather situation visually and by radio while you enjoy your fishing. If a deterioration is observed or forecast, return ashore. The fish will still be there when the weather improves.

Whether drifting or at anchor, check your position frequently. Avoid anchoring in shipping lanes or narrow channels. It is better to fish in the company of others likewise occupied.

Practise tidiness. Do not leave gaffs or spare rods lying around the decks, where you could trip over them. Do not allow your decks to become fouled with fish oil or slime and become dangerously slippery. Remember that a fishing line wrapped round a propeller is a common cause of trouble.

The taking of certain species of fish is subject to regulations. If in doubt, consult your local fisheries officer for details. If fishing commercially, you must take out a fishing permit and register your boat. You may also require a certificate or licence to operate the boat. See Chapter 17 for details of certificates, or contact the Maritime Safety Authority.

Offshore voyaging

Skippers of yachts intending to cruise more than 50 miles from the coast, or sailing for ports outside New Zealand, have certain obligations to fulfill before departure. These obligations are set out in Section 246(b) of the Shipping and Seamen Act, 1952.

Briefly, these requirements are as follows:

Offshore cruising

New Zealand yachts going on a cruise that will take them more than 50 miles from the coast must complete a ten-minute form and hand it to the yacht club or nearest harbourmaster or police station. (The ten-minute form may also be completed by skippers going on cruises of less than 50 miles offshore.)

Sailing to foreign ports

New Zealand yachts going to a port outside New Zealand must be inspected by honorary yacht inspectors, who will determine the suitability of the yacht and crew for the proposed voyage, and their ability to navigate. If they are satisfied they will issue a certificate that must be produced to the Collector of Customs in order to obtain customs clearance. The boat must be a New Zealand-registered vessel. The skipper must complete a ten-minute form, which must also be handed to the Collector of Customs before departure.

17

BOATING COURSES

And gladly wolde he lerne, and gladly teche.
— Chaucer

The professional seafarer takes many years to learn his trade. Training schools teach the theory, and practical knowledge is gained from years of apprenticeship at sea. To practise his profession a series of rigid examinations must be passed to obtain a certificate of competence. In New Zealand, the Maritime Safety Authority is the responsible authority for these examinations.

No such requirements exist for pleasure boating. However, considerable time and effort is spent in promoting safe boating by the Royal New Zealand Coastguard Federation and many other voluntary organisations who actively campaign to educate and encourage boat operators to improve their safety standards.

This policy of education rather than legislation has kept much of our pleasure boating free of legislative burden. It does, however, place the onus with the boat owners. It is the boat owners themselves who bear the ultimate responsibility to see that their crafts are seaworthy and that they themselves are prepared to cope with all the sea can throw at them.

Like their professional counterparts, pleasure-boat operators can gain knowledge by going back to school. Some boat clubs offer training schemes that combine theory and practice with a good social atmosphere. Voluntary coastguard organisations, polytechnics, schools and many other establishments throughout New Zealand offer courses in an increasing variety of boating associated subjects.

Pleasure-boat certificates

Pleasure-boat certificates have no commercial value, but as well as encouraging boat safety, they offer an incentive to any boating enthusiast to improve his or her knowledge. There is no compulsion to obtain these certificates, but the prestige and self-satisfaction they offer are compelling enough for any conscientious boatie. It is, of course, not only the certificate that is important, but all that is learnt while preparing for it. If examinations are not your thing, take the course anyway.

The Education Committee of the Royal New Zealand Coastguard Federation offers a carefully structured range of pleasure-boat certificates, from those for the pure novice to those for round-the-world voyagers. Various organisations offer courses leading to these certificates, but the Education Committee continually assesses the standard of the courses and their tutors, and handles the arrangements for examinations and the appointment of examiners.

If you cannot find a course being offered near you, contact your nearest boat club, community education centre, polytechnic; or the Royal New Zealand Coastguard Federation Education Administration Officer, P.O. Box 51-163, Pakuranga, Auckland. Telephone (09) 576-6696.

A summary of courses is given here. Full details of these courses, and their syllabuses and examination requirements, can be obtained from the Education Administration Officer.

Students at school

The Education Committee has designed two courses for use in schools and by youth organisations. The courses are run and assessed by teachers or leaders within the school or organisation. It is intended that the courses will encourage a child's confidence on the water, increasing awareness of boat safety and water safety while instilling the basics of seamanship and rules of the road at sea. The school courses are operated with the support of the Small Boat Safety Committee, the New Zealand Water Safety Council, and the New Zealand Lottery Grants Board.

Junior Safe Boating is for students at the intermediate school level. A Junior Safe Boating Certificate is awarded free of charge to participating students at the conclusion of their course.

Safe Boating is for students from fifth-form level upwards, using a syllabus identical to that for the New Zealand Day Skipper course. On completion of the course a Safe Boating Certificate is awarded free of charge to qualifying students. A Safe Boating Certificate may be upgraded to a New Zealand Day Skipper Certificate by sitting and passing an external examination.

New Zealand Day Skipper

This course is designed to cater for those who go down to the sea relatively occasionally, in small open boats, runabouts, dinghies and trailer sailers. The course is also suitable for the real beginner who has not yet purchased that first small boat, and for those who crew on other people's boats and feel a need to know something about what is going on. No previous experience or time-at-sea is necessary, and the course and certificate have no commercial application.

Syllabus

The syllabus is designed for a course of 12 hours duration, and courses may be offered as six evening lectures or as a weekend seminar.

The course will cover the basic elements of the rules of the road at sea, the Water Recreation Regulations, distress signals, buoys and beacons, navigation, basic boat equipment, boat handling, emergencies, tides, weather, and knots.

Examination

For those who complete the course there is an optional examination at the conclusion of the course, consisting of 40 multichoice questions and some short interpretive questions. On passing this examination a New Zealand Day Skipper Certificate is awarded. The minimum age for obtaining this certificate is 15 years.

Boatmaster

This is New Zealand's premier boating course, intended for anyone who is just entering the world of pleasure boating for the first time, or for those who have enjoyed boating for a while and are ready to admit that they need to know more.

The course is of 30 hours duration, usually offered over 15 weeks of evening classes or as a one-week block course. Correspondence courses are also available. The course and certificate have no commercial application, but the Boatmaster certificate is a prerequisite for the more advanced Yachtmaster Coastal Certificate.

Age

Any person may attend the course, but the minimum age for obtaining a Boatmaster certificate is 15 years.

Examination

A one-hour written examination is taken at the conclusion of the course, the paper having a pass mark of 70 per cent. The written examination is followed about one week later by an oral examination of about 30 minutes duration. During the oral examination the candidate's written paper will be discussed and any errors explained. Full details of the examination procedure will be explained by the tutor during the course. The Boatmaster Certificate is awarded on successful completion of the written and oral examination.

Syllabus

1. INTERNATIONAL REGULATIONS FOR PREVENTING COLLISIONS AT SEA

1.1 A simple knowledge of:
Avoidance of collision by day and night.

Clear weather rules, including sound signals.
Recognition of lights and shapes on the various classes of vessels.
Avoidance of collision in fog.
Fog signals.
Precautions in poor visibility.

2. BUOYS AND BEACONS
2.1 Recognition of the colours, shapes, lights, characteristics and meanings of the New Zealand system of buoyage.

3. LIFESAVING
3.1 Use and care of the equipment appropriate for various types of pleasure craft.

4. FIREFIGHTING
4.1 The causes and prevention of fire and the use of the appropriate equipment to control it.

5. DISTRESS
5.1 Recognition of all the distress signals.
5.2 Recognition of the international code flags A C N V, and their meanings.
5.3 The correct Mayday procedure.
5.4 Knowledge of Pan Pan and Securite R/T procedures.

6. EQUIPMENT
6.1 For example; boat-hook, bucket, first-aid kit, sails, sea anchor, engine spares, tools, flares, warm clothing, etc.

7. CHARTWORK AND PUBLICATIONS
7.1 Latitude, longitude, courses, bearings and distance.
7.2 A simple knowledge of the use of charts, including symbols and abbreviations.
7.3 Information contained in the Marine Notices (Series B) and the *New Zealand Nautical Almanac*.

8. COMPASS
8.1 How it works, care and maintenance, how to steer a course, use of transits and clearing bearings.

9. TIDES
9.1 Finding the times of high and low water at main and secondary ports. Spring and neap tides. Finding the direction and rate at a charted tidal reference point.

10. BOAT HANDLING
10.1 Management in rough seas, surf.
10.2 Securing to a berth or buoy.
10.3 Jet-boat handling (as appropriate).
10.4 Simple stability.
10.5 Anchors and anchoring.

11. REGULATIONS
11.1 The Water Recreation Regulations.
11.2 The General Harbour (Nautical and Miscellaneous) Regulations.

12. WEATHER
12.1 Information available, and its interpretation.

13. ACCIDENTS
13.1 Collision, stranding, man overboard, fire, breakdowns, heaving to, leaks, towing.

14. SEARCH AND RESCUE ORGANISATION
14.1 A knowledge of its operation.

15. ROPES
15.1 Rigging, bends and hitches — e.g., sheet bend, round turn and two half-hitches, bowline and clove hitch.

16. Any other questions relating to the operation of pleasure craft which the examiner may consider it necessary to ask.

Yachtmaster Coastal

The course for Master of a Pleasure Yacht (Coastal) is intended for the more advanced boating enthusiast, providing him or her with the knowledge to be able to travel on longer cruises around the coast. The certificate has no commercial value but is a prerequisite for the more advanced Yachtmaster Ocean Certificate.

Courses usually run for a total of about 20 weeks as evening classes, but may be split into two terms, each covering a different examination paper.

Age
To be eligible for examination you must be not less than 17 years of age.

Prerequisites
You must hold a Boatmaster Certificate, or other approved certificate, and have completed not less than 200 hours qualifying time-at-sea on pleasure craft over a period of not less than 12 months.

Certificate of Coastal Navigation
For students who do not have the time-at-sea requirements or a Boatmaster Certificate, the same course and examination may be taken. Successful candidates will be awarded a Certificate of Coastal Navigation.

Examination
The examination consists of two written papers,

either of which may be taken first. Paper 1 is a chartwork examination of three hours duration, and Paper 2 is a two-hour examination on Compass and Meteorology. The passmark for each paper is 60 per cent. Examination papers are set and marked by examiners appointed by the Royal New Zealand Coastguard Federation Education Committee and candidates are notified individually of their results.

Syllabus

CHARTWORK

The chart; passage planning; courses and bearings; water tracks and ground tracks; fixing and monitoring position; tides.

COMPASS AND METEOROLOGY

The magnetic compass; magnetism; the deviation card; air masses and fronts; pressure systems; the weather associated with the passage of weather systems over or close to New Zealand; surface wind; fog; the effect of topography on wind and weather; sea, waves and swell; the interpretation of weather maps in the New Zealand region; weather forecast information; aids to local forecasting.

Yachtmaster Ocean

Master of a Pleasure Yacht (Ocean) is the highest grade pleasure-boat certificate available in New Zealand and provides you with the knowledge to be able to navigate a pleasure craft world-wide, out of sight of land. The certificate has no commercial value.

Age

To be eligible for examination you must be not less than 18 years of age.

Prerequisites

You must hold a Yachtmaster Coastal certificate, and be able to prove at least 400 hours time-at-sea with 50 hours beyond harbour limits plus at least 72 hours continuous time at least 30 miles offshore. You must also hold a current first-aid qualification and a Restricted Radio Operators Licence.

Astro Navigation Certificate

Students who do not have these prerequisites may sit Paper 1 of the examination only and, if successful, will be awarded a Certificate of Astro Navigation. This certificate is accepted for New Zealand Yachting Federation Category 1 Navigator qualification.

Examination

The examination consists of two written papers, and an oral examination. Paper 1 is on Ocean Navigation, of three hours duration, and Paper 2 is a General Knowledge examination of two hours duration. On successfully completing the written examinations the candidate may then apply for an oral examination before an examiner appointed by the Education Committee.

Syllabus

OCEAN NAVIGATION

Meridian altitude; time; compass error; position lines; star sights; estimated position; magnetic compass; electronic navigation aids.

GENERAL KNOWLEDGE

Legal knowledge; meteorology; yacht stability; yacht construction.

ORAL EXAMINATION

The Collision Regulations; instruments; making an ocean passage; equipment; communications; ship handling; emergencies; responsibilities of a master.

Commercial certificates

Courses for commercial certificates are conducted at the New Zealand Maritime School, and at certain polytechnics approved by the Maritime Safety Authority.

Full details of the examination requirements for these certificates are contained in the Masters and Mates (Coastal, Fishing and Restricted-Limit Ships) Qualification Regulations 1993. The syllabuses for these certificates may be obtained from the Maritime Safety Authority, or from approved polytechnics. A brief summary of those certificates that are available to commercial boat operators is given here.

New Zealand Coastal Master Certificate

The New Zealand Coastal Master Certificate allows the holder to act as:

(a) Skipper of any fishing boat operating within 100 miles of the coast of New Zealand, and

(b) Master of a passenger or other commercial vessel of any length within Extreme Limits, and
(c) Master of a coastal cargo ship under 200 gross tons within 100 miles of the coast of New Zealand (provided that the certificate carries an IMO endorsement).

Commercial Launchmaster Certificate

The Commercial Launchmaster Certificate allows the holder to act as:

(a) Skipper of an inshore fishing boat not more than 15.24 metres in length, within 12 miles of the coast of New Zealand (i.e., the entire Inshore Zone), and
(b) Master of a passenger or other commercial vessel of any length within Extended River Limits, and
(c) Master of a passenger or other commercial vessel not more than 20 metres in length, within Extreme Limits.

Local Launchman's Licence

This licence allows you to take a specific launch within a specific area, the name of the launch and the area being endorsed upon the licence. The launch must be 20 metres or less in length, and the area must be within Extended River Limits. The licence is valid for a period of five years, and is renewable.

Miscellaneous Certificates

There are many and varied courses available for the conscientious boat enthusiast; boat building, boat maintenance, engineering, radar and G.P.S., to name but a few. You will find out about these from your local boat club, polytechnic or coastguard centre. There are also many specialised 'onboard' courses offered for sailing tuition and general boat safety.

The following courses and certificates you will find useful, and in some cases, essential.

First-aid Certificate

The standard first-aid course usually consists of approximately 16 hours of tuition, and may be conducted as evening sessions, or as a two-day seminar. Following the course is a written and practical examination. On successful completion of the course and examination you will be awarded a standard first-aid certificate, which is valid for three years.

Restricted Radiotelephone Operators Certificate

Except in cases of emergency involving the safety of life or property, every person operating a radiotelephone on a boat is required to hold a Restricted Radiotelephone Operators Certificate or a General Radiotelephone Operators Certificate (according to the type of radio installation) or an operator's licence of higher class.

Courses for these certificates are available at many centres. An examination at the conclusion of the course is conducted by officers of the New Zealand Radio Frequency Service.

INDEX

NOTES